YOU AND YOUR MONEY

ALSO BY ALVIN HALL

Winning with Shares:
Investing Wisely and Profitably in the Stock Market

Your Money or Your Life:
A Practical Guide to Solving your Financial Problems and Affording a New Life You'll Love

YOU AND YOUR MONEY

MASTERING THE EMOTIONS BEHIND THE NUMBERS

ALVIN HALL

with Karl Weber

ATRIA BOOKS

NEW YORK LONDON TORONTO SYDNEY

ATRIA BOOKS
A Division of Simon & Schuster, Inc.
1230 Avenue of the Americas
New York, NY 10020

Copyright © 2007 by Alvin Hall

Published by arrangement with Hodder & Stoughton Ltd.
Originally published in Great Britain in 2005 by Hodder & Stoughton Ltd.

All rights reserved, including the right to reproduce
this book or portions thereof in any form whatsoever. For
information address Atria Books Subsidiary Rights Department,
1230 Avenue of the Americas, New York, NY 10020

First Atria Books trade paperback edition February 2008

ATRIA BOOKS and colophon are trademarks of Simon & Schuster, Inc.

The quiz on page 127 is based on a quiz developed by Seton Hall University's National Education Center for Women in Business and was originally published on their student-focused entrepreneurship website: www.e-magnify.com/envision/quiz.asp.

For information about special discounts for bulk purchases,
please contact Simon & Schuster Special Sales at
1-800-456-6798 or business@simonandschuster.com.

Manufactured in the United States of America

1 3 5 7 9 10 8 6 4 2

The Library of Congress has cataloged the hardcover edition as follows:

Hall, Alvin D.
You and your money : it's more than just the numbers / Alvin Hall ; with Karl Weber.
p. cm.
"Originally published in Great Britain in 2005 by Hodder & Stoughton, Ltd."
1. Finance, Personal. I. Weber, Karl. II. Title.
HG179.H233 2007
332.024—dc22 2006048013
ISBN-13: 978-0-7432-7958-1
ISBN-10: 0-7432-7958-1
ISBN-13: 978-0-7432-7959-8 (pbk)
ISBN-10: 0-7432-7959-X (pbk)

To my New York friends who have been supportive,

helpful, and forbearing over the years:

Ed, Mary, Edna, James, Janet, Chris, Fred,

Susan, Rick, Emily, Betsy, Jonathan, Karen,

and Jonathan C. . . . and Oso, too

ACKNOWLEDGMENTS

Three groups of people have been the inspiration for, and in some cases contributors to, this book.

First are the many individuals who have stopped me on the street, in stores, and in restaurants as I've traveled throughout the United States and the United Kingdom and told me the positive and negative experiences they've had with money and how they've handled them successfully and not so successfully. Some of these stories were uplifting and heartwarming; some nearly brought me to tears of joy or sadness; others were unnerving, even haunting. From each of these encounters and the tone in which each story was told to me, I have accumulated many insights into people's feelings about money and its role in their lives.

The purpose of this book is to share this knowledge and wisdom about emotions and psychological issues that people bring to money management, to make these insights available and accessible to those who want and need them so they can better manage themselves and consequently make better use of their financial resources. I hope that as you read this book, you'll find a thought, a story, or some practical advice that will motivate you to:

- Stop ignoring the financial aspects of your life because of fear or the irrational hope that money will somehow magically or miraculously take care of itself;
- Think of smart behavior with money as a way of refocusing yourself from a day-to-day struggle with dollars and cents to longer-term, more thoughtful, and ultimately more profitable uses of your money;
- Gain wisdom from people who have used their money to build success and financial comfort, as well as from people who have made mistakes that should be avoided;
- Begin correcting any bad habits, attitudes, or concepts that may be affecting how you handle your money and your financial life; and
- See in yourself both the possibility of a better financial future and the practical steps you can take to make this future a reality.

In short, I want this book to help you acquire the mind-set, the wisdom, and the practical skills to make your money work in more positive and constructive ways.

Good money management starts in your mind. You have to discover the switch within yourself that will let you alter your ineffective or destructive behaviors, and instead take and *keep* control of your dollars and cents. This book will help you look inside yourself and find that switch.

My second source of inspiration has been Dr. Roger Bakeman of Atlanta and Dr. Emily Stein of New York. They encouraged me to write an in-depth book about the emotional and psychological issues that cause people to handle money well or badly. Both of them gave generously of their time for interviews, phone calls, and follow-up conversations about topics in which they have much experience as psychologists—Dr. Bakeman in child development and Dr. Stein in couples and trauma. By asking me sometimes difficult questions, telling me frankly when I was off the mark, and helping me to clarify my message and my advice, they were invaluable in making this book useful, its insights clear, and its advice practical.

Finally, I owe a special debt of gratitude to a group of publishing professionals who have helped make this book a reality.

The list starts with Judith Curr, publisher of Atria Books. She has followed my television and publishing work in the United Kingdom for years and generously offered me not only this publishing opportunity, but most important the belief that my work could find a receptive market in the United States. With her encouragement, I've incorporated in this book experiences and insights drawn from both countries and cultures.

I believe it is important to surround myself with people who will help me produce the best work I can, and even more important, with people who will always be honest about my writing, even when I may not want to hear it. Karl Weber has served that role in my writing life for over a decade. I am thankful for his unique skill in helping me to find the right tone for my message and put my best writing on paper.

Malaika Adero, my editor at Atria, helped me to keep focused on "the reader over my shoulder" and thoughtfully shared her personal point of view and experiences with money. The entire Atria team—Krishan Trotman, Michael Selleck, Gary Urda, and Christine Saunders—were enthusiastic and optimistic from our first meeting. I could not have asked for a more engaging, enthusiastic, or creative team.

Finally, I want to thank my agents, Vicki McIvor in the United Kingdom and Robert Allen in the United States. Both gave generously of their weekends and evenings, reading the manuscript with a keen eye and insight. Vicki offered ten pages of comments that proved invaluable in helping me to keep the tone open, accessible, and not so "absolutist." ("I sometimes see and hear your Baptist background rising up in your words like a preacher" was her comment that still makes me laugh, because my great-uncle Son always wanted me to be a preacher—but not about money, I am sure.)

While I was writing this book, my mother died. She left no will, despite my many attempts to get her to write one. The resulting situation, although deeply personal and difficult, is instructive for anyone who has avoided thinking about what will happen after they die.

At the same time, a friend who had been struggling with his finances—overspending, ignoring his debts, complaining about earning too little—and resisting any suggestions that I made to him, began to let himself see that his situation was not hopeless, that he could rethink and remake his life financially. And he started to do so. Now he frequently tells me that he didn't know he could feel so unburdened by "just spending a little time with my money every week" to make sure everything is in order.

My own money experiences and those of my friends and acquaintances have played an important role in shaping this book. I hope it will help you to reflect, gain self-insight and wisdom, and create a balanced and responsible financial path to the richness you want in all areas of your unique life.

Alvin Hall
New York City
September 2006

CONTENTS

YOU AND YOUR MONEY

INTRODUCTION
YOUR MONEY CONNECTIONS

The novel *Robinson Crusoe* tells a story like something out of today's reality TV. The hero is the sole survivor of a shipwreck near the shores of a desert island. He must figure out how to stay alive on the island until he is rescued, which may take months or years.

Fortunately, Crusoe is able to salvage a number of useful items from the ship before it sinks to the ocean bottom: some tools, a couple of guns, even a little food and drink. All are important in helping Crusoe survive. But one item that he discovers on the wrecked ship is totally useless to him: a stash of money.

Back in the real world, it's hard to imagine surviving without money. We devote countless hours and enormous energy to earning it, saving it, protecting it, investing it, and spending it. Yet to Robinson Crusoe it is meaningless. Why? Because he is alone, with no way to use it. Without other people to give it value, money is just so much worthless paper. *Only human relationships give meaning to money.*

Think about the many things that money represents in your own life. Here are some examples:

- Money is a reward for the time and energy you devote to work.
- Money offers security—your ability to live without worrying about the future.
- Money brings freedom—the opportunity to enjoy the good things of life.
- Money provides a sense of status and respect in society.
- Money opens doors to education, travel, and new experiences.
- Money helps family members nurture and care for one another.
- Money lets you support worthwhile causes that enrich your life.

All these functions of money—and the list we've offered only scratches the surface—are based on human relationships. Money looms so large in our inner lives because it plays such a powerful role in our relationships. Marriage and other loving partnerships involve shared economic goals and obligations. Parenthood involves a financial commitment to support and protect the younger generation. Your connection with the workplace begins with money. Even your relationships with brothers, sisters, friends, and neighbors have a financial element—as you know if you've ever quarreled over an inheritance or felt embarrassed about the size of your income in a social setting.

As a result, money is deeply intertwined with our emotional lives. When your finances are out of control, it's likely that your personal relationships will suffer, starting with your spouse and your family and spiraling outwards. And when your relationships are deeply flawed—for example, when you can't talk honestly with the people you love about your dreams, hopes, and fears—it's likely that your financial management will suffer as well.

So fixing your personal money problems requires more than a knowledge of basic financial information (such as how to open a checking account or how to choose a mortgage). Those kinds of facts are important. But they only address one of the three major elements in your money personality—*your mind.* Equally important are the other two elements—*your heart* and *your soul.*

Your heart controls your connections to other people. Parents, children, siblings, spouses, lovers, friends, bosses, colleagues, neighbors, rivals—all are connected to you through emotional ties: love, desire, admiration, fear, respect, disdain, approval, hatred, acceptance, and more. Your attitudes toward money and the ways in which you use (and misuse) money influence and are influenced by these connections.

Your soul controls your connection to your deepest self and your most profound aspirations. Perhaps you believe in God or in some higher power that created and rules the world. Perhaps you are not religious but are instead driven by a desire to live an ethical, moral life or to seek a deeper truth that gives meaning to human existence. Or perhaps you simply hope, at the end of your days, to be able to look back with satisfaction and feel you have lived life to the fullest. Your soul rules all these aspects of life. And yes, your relationship to money has a significant impact on this connection as well.

In this book, we'll examine your nine most crucial money connections:

- Your money and yourself.
- Your money and your parents.
- Your money and your siblings.
- Your money and your career.
- Your money and your peers.
- Your money and your partner.
- Your money and your children.
- Your money and your retirement.
- Your money and the end of life.

Each chapter begins with a quiz, titled "Test Yourself," that gives you an opportunity to consider some of the important questions and challenges posed by a particular relationship. You'll find that certain money connections are more problematic for you than others. The quizzes will help you quickly focus on those connections that deserve your greatest attention.

Each chapter ends with a list of "Take-Aways"—bite-size summaries of the most essential lessons taught in that chapter. You'll find these Take-Aways a handy way to review and remind yourself of the best ways to strengthen and improve your own money connections.

Along the way, I'll recount stories of people I've met and worked with over the years—men and women; single and married; young and old; rich, poor, and in-between—through my television programs and in other ways. I call these "True-Life Tales," and each chapter includes several. (The names and personal details of the people described have been altered out of respect for their privacy, though the essential stories and the lessons they teach remain intact. Any resemblance to an actual individual is purely coincidental.)

You're almost certain to find your own circumstances reflected in some of these stories, perhaps in many of them. When one of these True-Life Tales elicits a shiver of recognition—"Oh my goodness! That's *me* he's talking about!"—pay close attention to the lesson it teaches. Chances are good that you can benefit from it personally.

And if a particular tale irritates or troubles you for some unknown reason, pay attention to that one, too. It may well be that the story deals with a theme or an emotion that hits just a little too close to home. Perhaps you recognize yourself in the story, even though you may be too uncomfortable to admit it.

Let me close with a story drawn from my experience in creating my television series *Your Money or Your Life.* During the filming, I met a lovely lady who was far too generous with her children, especially after they'd grown up. Eventually she found herself in serious financial trouble, yet she couldn't talk about her problems with her family. She even borrowed money she couldn't afford to repay so that she could buy Christmas gifts for her children and grandchildren. It was an understandable emotional gesture, though not a rational one.

I spent time with this lady and, through our conversation and mutual storytelling, she came to see the mistakes she was making and how to correct the situation. She was grateful. But when our session was over, she shook my hand and said, with a sly grin, "You know, Alvin, if I ever come into some money again, I'll probably do exactly the same things—and get into the same mess again."

We both laughed. That's human nature, in a nutshell. But does that mean there's no point in trying to shape our behaviors for greater success and happiness in life? I don't believe that. I'm an optimist, one with (almost) infinite faith in the power of human beings to grow, change, and learn. I hope the stories and lessons in these pages will help you develop deeper insight into your own money personality and help you achieve a greater and more lasting degree of financial happiness.

1

MONEY AND YOURSELF

TEST YOURSELF. Is the relationship between yourself and money a healthy one, or is it a potential source of trouble? To find out, answer the questions below—and *be honest!*

Yes	No	
☐	☐	1. Can you describe, with reasonable accuracy, the things you spent money on last month?
☐	☐	2. Can you list all your major sources of income for the last year?
☐	☐	3. Can you name your main spending habits, good and bad?
☐	☐	4. Do you know how much money you will need in order to support yourself comfortably when you retire?
☐	☐	5. Do you know what you would do in response to a major financial setback, such as being laid off or suffering a serious illness?
☐	☐	6. Can you describe your money personality, including the strengths and weaknesses in the way you handle your finances?

Yes	No	
☐	☐	7. Do you have a realistic picture of your current financial situation?
☐	☐	8. Do you have control over the impulses that drive you to spend money?
☐	☐	9. Are you in control of your personal finances rather than relying on someone else to support you and make major money decisions?
☐	☐	10. Are you able to enjoy spending money without overindulging yourself?
☐	☐	11. Are you able to control your fears and anxieties concerning money?
☐	☐	12. Can you state accurately the amount of debt you carry?
☐	☐	13. Can you state accurately the amount of money you have in your savings account?

HOW DO YOU SCORE? There are no passing or failing grades on this quiz (or on any quiz in this book). But every "no" answer indicates an area on which you need to focus to get your financial relationships in order. For helpful advice and guidance, read on.

KNOW YOURSELF

As a TV money educator and the author of several books of money advice, I've learned that everyone needs to develop his or her own style of financial management. My way of earning, saving, spending, and investing money won't necessarily work for you, and vice versa. The first step is being comfortable in your own skin: knowing and accepting who you are, what you want, and what money means to you.

Success with money isn't matter of having a big bank account (although that doesn't hurt). The real key is your attitude toward yourself and toward the money you have. The wisdom of ancient Greece—"Know thyself"—remains as powerful today as ever. It's at the heart of being a smart money manager. And although it sounds simple, even obvious, "knowing thyself" can be surprisingly difficult to achieve.

Getting to Know You

Here are eight specific exercises you can do that will help you get to know your own money habits and tendencies better. You don't necessarily have to perform all eight; instead, you can pick the two or three that seem most relevant to you, and see what they can teach you.

1. Keep a diary of your spending and the emotions that go with it. Buy a little notebook especially for the purpose, and carry it with you everywhere you go for a month. During that time, write down everything you buy, no matter how big or how small. List each purchase and its price. Include items for which you pay cash (like your morning coffee and newspaper) and items you buy with a check or a credit/debit card (like a new CD or a piece of furniture).

At the end of the day, take a moment to add a brief note describing how you feel about that day's spending. Do you feel joy? Guilt? Regret? Disappointment? Contentment? What you write will vary from day to day, of course. One day you might write, "I'm so excited about the new shoes I bought today. They'll go perfectly with the outfit I'm wearing tomorrow. I can't wait to see what my friends in the office say!" Another day you might write,

"I feel bad about spending so much money on snacks and drinks today. I really meant to save that cash for the weekend. Hope I can do better tomorrow."

There will be times when keeping the diary feels like a total bore or a nuisance. You'll be tempted to quit. Don't! A full month's worth of notes will tell you a lot about your money habits, good and bad, and help you understand the ways in which your money habits bring you happiness and grief.

2. Examine your sources of income. On a sheet of paper, list everyone who provided you with any money during the past year, along with the amounts you received. A few of these sources will be obvious: the salary paid by your employer or the income from your own business, for example. Others may be easy to overlook. Did you receive any payments from the federal, state, or local government? Did your parents or other family members give or lend you money? Did you receive money from a romantic partner, an ex-spouse, or a friend? Did you do any part-time work for which you received a formal or informal payment? Did you get dividend or interest payments from stocks, bonds, or mutual funds that you own, or money from a trust account? Did you win money from a lottery, a contest, or gambling? Did you receive money as a result of a lawsuit or an insurance claim? List everything.

Once you've created the list, consider what it tells you about your present and future sources of income. How secure are the past year's sources of income? Which sources are likely to increase in the future—and which are likely to shrink or disappear? What *new* sources of income can you develop? An honest evaluation of this list can help you figure out whether your future prospects are bright, or you have been living on borrowed time.

3. Analyze one credit card bill from the past year. Identify each item you bought (if you can) and measure how much pleasure it gave you. Do you remember the item? Do you remember why you bought it? Do you still have it? If so, do you still use it? In retrospect, was it worth buying? Count up the number of items you bought that were smart, satisfying purchases, and compare this to the number of items you now wish you hadn't bought. What patterns do you notice? What types of purchases do you consistently regret? Are there particular kinds of items you tend to waste money on? Which kinds of purchases consistently bring you lasting pleasure? When do you stop or cut back using the credit card, and what causes this change?

4. Count the number of purchases you made last year. A relatively easy way to do this is to request the year-end summary of your spending that most credit card companies will provide. Also review your checkbook register or checking account statements, and try to list most or all of the items you bought using cash. How many purchases did you make altogether? How does the number compare to the number of days in the year? Did you buy something every day, every two days, every three days? Is it hard for you to go through a day without spending money? If so, do you know why?

5. Examine your unconscious forms of spending. On a piece of paper, list all the automatic purchases on your credit card: gym memberships, magazine subscriptions, or any other automatic deductions. If you use an automatic banking service that provides for direct debits for regular monthly expenses, list these as well. Automatically deducted expenditures can be an inadvertent trap that can help make it easy for you to spend money without thinking about it. How many of these can you reduce or eliminate?

6. List the things you *hate* to spend money on. Some of these may be needless expenses you can eliminate by making a change in your life. For example, if you hate paying the costs of driving to work, perhaps you can set your alarm clock for half an hour earlier, making it possible for you to walk (if your job is close by), use public transportation, or carpool. Not only will you save money, but you might meet some interesting new people who could change your life or career.

In other cases, avoiding particular expenses may be shortsighted. I have a friend who hates to buy food in restaurants because he dislikes leaving a tip for the waiter. It's a problematic attitude, because sometimes you have to pay to get good service—and a person who refuses ever to visit a restaurant misses out on the fun of eating out with friends. My coauthor, Karl, hates to spend money to get things fixed around the house because, as he puts it, "There's no fun in it." But if you put off patching the roof or servicing the furnace, you may end up having to make a more costly repair or replacement in the long run.

Listing your own pet hates when it comes to spending can show where your emotions may overrule your reason, leading to short-term and self-defeating thinking.

7. List your best and worst expenditures. Make a list of the five things you did with money last year that enhanced your life the most. Then make a separate list of your five worst mistakes—money decisions that were a setback or damaged your life. What were the reasons behind each of these decisions, good or bad? What lessons can you derive from them?

There's no single right or wrong way to compile these two lists. One person's brilliant choice may be another person's disaster. For Susan, spending $3,000 on a week's holiday in the Caribbean may have been just the break she needed to clear her head after a tough year at the office, energizing her to start looking for a better job upon her return to work. For Cynthia, the same holiday may have maxed out her credit card, speeding up a dangerous spiral into excessive debt that ruined any pleasure she might have taken from her days in the sun. Only you can define your best and worst uses of money.

8. Test your money self-discipline. You can also learn more about your money psychology by experimenting with short-term behavior changes. I am testing my own self-discipline right now through a simple but surprisingly tough challenge: for one year, I am forbidding myself to buy shirts. (I have sixty shirts of all kinds and I love to get new ones.) In the past, I have tried other, similar experiments; for example, I once locked away my credit cards for a month, forcing myself to pay for everything in cash. I found that this act of self-discipline made me more aware of my own cash flow and forced me to reevaluate what I spend.

Among other benefits, such limited acts of self-denial help you to appreciate more the good things you have and increase your self-confidence by demonstrating and strengthening your ability to determine what's needless and do without it. Most important, they help you know yourself more intimately. What kinds of money behavior have the greatest hold over you? Which money habits are easy to change? Which changes really hurt? Above all, who is in control: you or your money?

THE BOTTOM LINE

Most people have only a vague awareness of how they relate to money. They spend little time reflecting on how they get money, how they use it, and what sort of emotional impact money has on their lives. Devoting time to becoming more conscious of your money decisions is a crucial first step toward improving your relationship to money.

The goal of all eight exercises is the same: to help you better understand the role of money in your life. How does money bring you happiness? How does it cause you regret, anxiety, or disappointment? Which of your money habits would you like to change? Which ones would you like to strengthen? Answering these questions is a vital first step toward defining the kind of relationship you'd like to have with your money—and taking the steps necessary to achieve it.

What's Your Price?

When I was growing up in a little town in the Florida panhandle, my wise old grandmother had a saying that I've never forgotten. "Always know your price, Alvin. Have a number in mind. Because some day, someone may offer it to you."

What did she mean by "your price"? I've thought a lot about it. I think she was referring to whatever it would take to make me truly satisfied, to meet all my basic physical requirements as well as my emotional and spiritual needs.

"Your price" may be literally a number—a figure in dollars and cents that represents what you need to feel independent. (Hollywood moviemakers refer to the size of the nest egg they need to be able to walk away from any job using a vulgar phrase:

" 'f--- you' money.") It may be the amount of money you would have to have in the bank to support you for a year, or the amount of invested money you would need to generate an annual income you could live on.

Everyone defines their price in their own unique way. For some people whose lifestyles and aspirations are modest, it could be a relatively small sum. For those with grandiose desires, it could be very large. That's up to you.

"Your price" may not even be a number. It could be something else that spells happiness and satisfaction to you. It could be your dream job, the position that will tell you and the world that you've really "made it" in your career. It could be the opportunity to live in a particular place, whether that's a country home on a lake, an apartment with a view in the center of a city, or a condo near a golf course. It could be a trip around the world, a chance to meet the person you most admire, or a lifetime box at the opera.

My coauthor, Karl, worked for many years as an editor and executive at some of the big New York publishing houses. His dream then was independence—the opportunity to work for himself, writing and editing books on interesting and important topics with people he liked and admired. That was Karl's price. Eight years ago, he achieved that goal: he went freelance and has supported himself and his family ever since, working on projects (like collaborating on this book) from his home in the New York suburbs and traveling around the country and the world to research them.

Like Karl, I'm a freelancer. Each year, I put together a combination of jobs and projects that I use to support myself. As a result, I think about my price at the start of every year. I set it at two levels. First, I calculate my living expenses for the year—mortgage payments on my apartment, insurance, food, clothing, retirement contribution, my annual vacation with my friends in the south of France, and so on—and determine the amount I need to earn to cover those costs. Next, I list the special things I'd like to have but don't strictly need—things like a special holiday trip, art I'd like to add to my collection, changes I'd like to make in my apartment. I now have two figures—my Need number and my Want number—against which I can measure how successful my career will be this year.

As the year begins, I do all I can to reach my Need number as quickly as possible. The sooner I can line up jobs or other sources of income that will add up to my Need number (calculated on an after-tax basis), the sooner I can begin achieving some of my Wants. In some years, when the economy is sluggish and my business is challenging, it's all I can do to reach my Need number by December. In boom years, I can meet my Need number by August or September, giving me several months of income with which to indulge myself.

Having these two numbers in mind helps me make the right decisions about earning, spending, and saving money. For example, there have been times when I was offered a work assignment that I didn't much relish: teaching a particular set of training classes that I knew would be very hard work and not *really* interesting. But when I looked at my list of projects for the year and the expected income from each, I could see that these classes would be enough to make me hit my Need number for the year. I accepted the job offer. It wouldn't be much fun, I knew, but it would enable me to move from Needs to Wants, so that all my additional income for the year could be spent on things that brought extra pleasure to my life. The satisfaction of knowing that fact made it easy to take on a less-than-ideal assignment.

The same kind of thinking may apply to you, even if you work at a regular job rather than freelancing. You may be faced with a decision such as a new job offer, a special assignment from the company you work for, or the chance to compete for a promotion. Should you take the plunge, even if you are uncertain as to whether the new situation will be a comfortable one? The answer may depend on your price. Sometimes, taking on a difficult or even unpleasant job for a year or two may be the right decision—if it means achieving your price, and a possible lifetime of future satisfaction.

THE BOTTOM LINE

Know your price and keep it always in the back of your mind. Only if you know your price can you be working toward achieving it and measuring every important decision against the question: What choice will help me get closer to my price? It's an important part of knowing yourself, in terms of your deepest personal desires and the financial implications they have.

Three Money Fantasies

So far, you've examined your relationship to money by looking at real-life situations. Now it's time to take a different approach: to use a bit of fantasy to gain further insights into what money means to you.

Imagine yourself in each of the following three scenarios. These are "thought experiments" (in the phrase made famous by scientist Albert Einstein) that can help you better understand your approach to money. Devote fifteen minutes to each experiment. Read the description below, then jot down on a piece of paper all the thoughts, ideas, and fantasies that fill your mind as a result. I predict you'll find them very revealing.

1. The Windfall. Imagine suddenly receiving a gift of half a million dollars. What would you spend it on? Would you devote some of the money to helping family, friends, or charity? Would you use it to start a business, or to invest? Would you go on a shopping spree or book a dream vacation? Would you pay off your credit card bills or the mortgage on your home? Don't just fantasize vaguely: draw up a list of your expenditures, including your best estimate of the number of dollars involved for each.

Also think about how you would change your life if a lot of money fell into your lap. How much of the windfall would you try to preserve? How long would it take you to run through it? How soon would you have to go back to work? Would you consider moving to another part of the country or the world? Would you make any changes in your family relationships (such as getting married—or divorced)?

The results of this thought experiment will expose some of your deep-rooted dreams, desires, and ambitions. Your answers may include aspirations that you think about every day and others that you rarely allow yourself even to imagine.

What's the point? Well, you may not really be in line for a half-million-dollar windfall, but maybe you should consider reorienting your life so that you can pursue some of the fantasies this experiment has brought to the surface. You probably won't achieve them overnight. But maybe over the next five or ten years you can make some of those dreams come true.

2. The Setback. Imagine if you lost your job (or your other main source of income) due to being laid off, the sudden and unexpected absence of a spouse, or the elimination of a government support program. What would you do? How would you search for a new job? How long do you think it would take to find a new source of income? How much money do you have in the bank or in investments to tide you over? Where and how would you cut back on your lifestyle to make that money last as long as possible? How much of your spending could you cut back on and still be happy? How long would your savings last? How would your relationships with your family and friends be affected? How quickly would you begin to panic?

This thought experiment is likely to make you feel a bit anxious. That's all right—remember, it's only an experiment. But the kind and degree of anxiety you feel is important. Does the very idea of a setback make you feel extremely frightened? Do you fear you'd run out of options in just a few weeks or days? Or, conversely, do you feel relatively confident that you would find a new source of income quickly? The answers may lead you to rethink your saving strategy, your career plans, and your other assumptions about how you support yourself.

Also consider how you react to the idea of trimming your expenses. Does the thought of having to live on 75 percent of your current income unnerve you? How about 50 percent? Do you feel a sense of shame or anger when you imagine having to talk to family and friends about your setback? Again, the answers may be revealing. If having a wad of cash in your pocket or purse is your main source of a sense of self-worth, you need to reconsider your emotional dependency on spending.

3. The Disaster. Imagine if you had to start your life all over again tomorrow. Imagine if your job, your savings, your possessions, and all your relationships were taken away and you were left with nothing but your education, your natural gifts, and a (paid) hotel room in a strange city for a month. How would you rebuild your life? What kind of job could you find? What kind of job could you tolerate? What kind of home would you seek? How would you look for new relationships, new activities, new interests? Would you be bitter over what you'd lost? Or would you find it a stimulating challenge to create a new life starting from scratch?

This experiment is designed to measure your sense of personal resilience. How much confidence do you have in your inner resources—your strength of will, your emotional stamina, your self-confidence, your intelligence? How dependent are you on external props such as your job, your home, your bank account, your friends, and your family?

Of course, it's not likely that this disaster scenario will happen to you; most people are never tested to this extreme (although it does happen—just ask the thousands of New Orleanians who lost everything when Hurricane Katrina struck). But it's a bracing mental exercise to imagine how you would tackle such a challenge.

THE BOTTOM LINE

Engaging in thought experiments like these can be fun and revealing. And each of these scenarios actually happens to people in real life—perhaps more often than you might think. Speculating about them can be a useful preparation for dealing with the ups and downs that life is apt to throw your way. Even more important, taking your money fantasies seriously will teach you more about the relationship between you, yourself, and your money . . . a connection that's crucial for you to understand if you want to get your financial house in order.

MONEY PERSONALITIES: BALANCED AND UNBALANCED

In my years of talking to people about personal finances and listening to stories about how they think about and handle money, I've discovered several distinct patterns of behavior in relation to money—characteristic ways of dealing with money that recur again and again in people's lives. I think of these patterns as *money personalities.* Based on the exercises I've recommended, you may find that a portrait of your own money personality is beginning to emerge.

In the pages that follow, I describe some of the most common money personalities I encounter in my work. Does one of these portraits sound familiar?

The Entitled

How many times have you justified an impulse purchase by saying to yourself, "I deserve it"? And how often have you said to a friend who is trying to decide whether or not to hand over the plastic, "Oh, go on—you deserve it"? If you use this language frequently, your money personality is what I call the *Entitled.*

Don't misunderstand. I'm not saying that you are *not* a perfectly lovely and deserving person—of course you are! But the underlying sense of entitlement can be very dangerous. In fact, when I ask the subjects on my television show about what the phrase "I deserve it" really means, they frequently look at me blankly, as if they've never thought about it at all.

If you find yourself using "I deserve it" to justify purchases you know you shouldn't make, ask yourself the following four questions. I even suggest that you memorize and recite them, like a mantra, every time you find yourself about to indulge your sense of entitlement.

1. What exactly have I done to "deserve" this treat? If you've shown up to work on time, gotten the kids off to school, and handled routine emergencies or crises, then you have simply met the requirements of daily living. And as any employer will tell you, "meeting requirements" does not earn you a bonus!

2. How long will it be before I "deserve" another treat? Next month? Next week? Tomorrow? Be honest! If you are treating yourself to special indulgencies more often than you should, put the brakes on. You are moving from feeling you "deserve" to spend money to making shopping and spending the source of your identity: "I shop, therefore I am." And that is a pretty shallow identity to have.

3. What percentage of my monthly mortgage payment am I spending on impulse buying? Suppose your mortgage payment is $800, and the total amount of your monthly impulse purchases at the mall or in shops in your town is $200. Then you've spent 25 percent of the money you could have set aside to reduce your mortgage burden. If you keep your impulse buys to less than 10 percent of your mortgage payment, your overall debt is much more likely to remain under control.

4. How long will it take me to earn this purchase, given my after-tax hourly wage? Think about how long it will take you to earn the cost of that nonessential treat from your current after-tax wages. Is the momentary pleasure worth all the hours or days at your desk, on your feet, or on the phone that it will take you to earn the money to pay for the item? You may be enslaving yourself to your own sense of entitlement.

"I deserve it"? Maybe so. But even more, don't you deserve—and want—a life free from the anxiety caused by uncontrolled spending and debt?

THE BOTTOM LINE

People with an entitlement personality fail to think through and act upon what matters most to them in life–that is, the values they care about most deeply. Instead, they are thinking and behaving as if they care more about the short-term pleasure from buying something than about a lifetime of security, enjoyment, and happiness. The spiraling descent into debt that too many people experience comes not so much from stupidity or lack of willpower as from a disconnection between their *real* values and their behavior.

The Dreamer

For me—and, I think, for most people—financial happiness means, above all, a sense of security. But some people act as though happiness comes from spending more than they can afford—to impress others, to feel important and powerful, and to enjoy the thrill of consumption. Unfortunately, this pleasure is usually short-lived, a dream of happiness rather than the real thing. People who fall into this trap have the money personality I call the *Dreamer.*

TRUE-LIFE TALE: LIVING THE DREAM

I once worked with a young man I'll call Ron who felt he was living an entrepreneurial dream come true. Ron, who had formerly worked as an assistant record producer, had developed an imaginative and unique business concept: he rented a fully-equipped recording studio, hired (at daily rates) a backup band of competent musicians, and, for a fee of around $5,000, would help an amateur singer create a professional-quality CD with two songs and even a short music video. Obviously, only well-heeled would-be rock stars could afford such an indulgence, but there were enough potential customers around to make Ron's business quite successful and lucrative, netting him some $100,000 a year—what he called his "six-figure dream."

So far, this is a success story. But Ron promptly set about undermining his own future prospects by refusing to invest in the future growth of the business. For example, he might have considered buying a studio rather than renting one at a costly markup. He might have opened a second and a third location in nearby cities. He might have explored the business possibilities of other, similar concepts: in addition to "rock star for a day," what about "fashion model for a day" or "soap star for a day"? One or more of these ideas might have set Ron on the path of being a truly successful entrepreneur with long-term prospects for financial security and a chance at "seven figure" wealth.

Instead, driven by his Dreamer personality, Ron took all the profits out of his budding business and spent them on personal treats: a flashy sports car, a handsomely equipped McMansion, vacations at fancy resorts in the Caribbean and Mexico. Not only did he spend all of his business income, but he ran up significant credit card debt, putting his finances in real jeopardy.

When I pointed out these lurking dangers to Ron, he actually agreed with me. He commented, "Funny, isn't it, how a showy car and nice vacations get to seem like necessities? The income I'm making now would have seemed like all the money in the world a couple of years ago. Now it's not quite enough."

Ron realized, at least in his head, that there was no guarantee that the good times would continue. But he imagined that, if his current business ever suffered a decline, he would quickly come up with a second concept and a third. He didn't understand the reality that most businesspeople eventually come to recognize: that the world's greatest entrepreneurs consider themselves lucky to come up with one or two great ideas in a lifetime, let alone a steady stream of them. The ease with which Ron had parlayed his project into a profitable business made him feel as if the realities of business competition had been suspended for his benefit.

Ron's pleasant dream of life as the next Richard Branson came to its inevitable end. When an economic downturn hit in 2001, the number of people willing and able to spend big bucks to fulfill their rock star dreams declined dramatically. Compounding the problem, two of Ron's most important employees (a keyboard player and a drummer) formed their own band and moved to Europe, and he struggled to find adequate replacements for them. Today Ron's income is less than half of what it was a few years ago, and he has moved back in with his mother. The next big entrepreneurial idea? He is still searching for it.

THE BOTTOM LINE

Don't fall into the trap of believing your most fantastic dreams. Strive to view your life, your accomplishments, and your challenges in an objective, realistic light, based on knowledge,

research, and feedback from people you trust. Then develop your plans, goals, and actions in accordance with who you *really* are—not who you'd like to imagine yourself being.

The Risk-Taker

Like the Dreamer, another money personality that involves a flight from reality is that of the *Risk-Taker.* Of course, anyone who starts a business is taking on some degree of risk, and the prudent entrepreneur does what he or she can to minimize that risk. But the Risk-Taker loves risk for its own sake. Uncertainty creates an adrenaline rush that many people find addictive. Some Risk-Takers express their love of danger in physical ways: they become fighter jet pilots, NASCAR drivers, or mountain climbers. But others prefer financial risks. They launch businesses that have almost no chance of succeeding, invest in highly speculative ventures, or devote their energies to the classic form of financial risk-taking—gambling.

TRUE-LIFE TALE: LIVING FOR THE RISK-TAKER'S HIGH

One young man I met, whom I'll call Peter, had gone seriously into debt because of his reckless gambling on horses, dogs, cards—anything one could possibly bet on. The debts were very real—over $40,000, equivalent to a year's after-tax salary. But somehow they didn't seem real to Peter. He frankly told me, "Money is just numbers to me. It means nothing."

What *was* real to Peter was the excitement he got from his betting—at least, when he won. Peter even compared the ecstasy of a winning bet to sexual orgasm. The momentary release of energy was so thrilling that Peter was willing to gamble away his future in pursuit of it.

Peter's gambling addiction divorced him from reality in other ways, too. When I met him, he had no idea about the seriousness of his debt problem. He blithely told me, "I can get a mortgage or a car loan any time I want. And I can pay off my debts with no problem." Both statements were false. I discovered the first untruth by making a few phone calls to lenders, who reviewed Peter's financial status and quickly replied, "There's no way we can lend money to this guy." The second untruth became apparent when Peter decided to try paying off his debts—only to creep back to the dog track and the casino, and end up in worse shape than when he started.

THE BOTTOM LINE

Some forms of risk-taking can become addictive. If your Risk-Taker's personality has begun to interfere with your ability to face real life and manage it constructively, you have a problem. Don't let it slide; work on turning the problem around before it's too late. The financial guidance offered throughout this book will help.

The Shopping Addict

Shopping Addicts are people for whom shopping is a major pastime, maybe even their chief occupation in life. They wander around malls, looking at store windows hoping to stumble across something that will bring them a thrill they equate with happiness. They leaf through magazines and mail-order catalogs, hoping to be enticed by some treasure they never heard of but which, once they've discovered it, they now can't live without. They spend hours clicking through pages on eBay and other Internet shopping sites, titillated by the fact that the loot of the world is available to them at the click of a button.

I think people become Shopping Addicts not because they are preoccupied with the things they want, but because they don't think *enough* about the things they want. Because they rush into purchases without thinking, they end up buying things that really don't serve any purpose for them or meet any deep-rooted need. Disappointed, they start window shopping again, like alcoholics who keep returning to the bottle even though the pleasure of drinking has long since faded.

I understand the problem because I used to be a Shopping Addict myself. It took me years of learning and painful experience to overcome the syndrome. Today, I have my addiction under control. And one way I keep it under control is by the painstaking way in which I approach the experience of shopping.

Back when I was a Shopping Addict, I used to buy things constantly. (No wonder I often ended up buying things I didn't really want or need.) Today, I think a lot about the things I want *before* I buy them. Between the time I first develop a yen for an item and the time I buy it, months or even years may elapse. During that time, I read about the item, examine it in stores, study comparative products, try out the item in a friend's home, and get price quotes from a variety of sources. By the time I feel ready to buy, I know exactly which item I want, what color and size I want, where it will go in my home, and how much money I'm prepared to pay.

Thus, when the long-planned purchase finally arrives, there are rarely any unpleasant surprises. Instead, the experience feels like the fulfillment of a dream—it's very satisfying and makes me feel good for years to come.

This is the story behind one of my personal treasures, my Bang & Olufsen stereo. For years I'd heard about the exceptional quality of this brand of audio equipment, and I'd admired its good looks. But I hesitated to spend what a B&O stereo system cost. So I saved my pennies, read stereo magazines and guides, and seized every opportunity I could to listen to music on B&O equipment. (I'm sure the salespeople got tired of seeing my face in the B&O showroom in New York and thought I was never going to buy anything.) Finally, as my thirty-fifth birthday approached, I decided the time was right. I'd saved enough money, and I felt I knew enough about my tastes in music and my home decorating preferences to pick a style of stereo that would fit my lifestyle.

I've loved my stereo ever since the day I brought it home. It has brought me pleasure for over ten years, and I haven't thought of replacing it once, which actually has made it a bargain. And I'm sure that if I'd rushed into buying it the minute I heard of it, without waiting for it and knowing exactly why I wanted it, I wouldn't have enjoyed it nearly as much, or as long.

THE BOTTOM LINE

If you are a Shopping Addict, you need to break the cycle of unsatisfied spending. Slow down! Take the time to really think about the things you want, and buy them only when you are ready, both financially and psychologically. As a result, you'll buy fewer things, but enjoy them much, much more.

The Defiant Ones

Those I call the *Defiant Ones* are angry at the world. They express this anger through an aggressive attitude toward money. They spend in accordance with the philosophy of "Live fast, die young," letting money run through their fingers as if there's no tomorrow.

What makes the Defiant Ones so angry? When I talk with them, they describe a deep-rooted belief that life is unfair. They talk about how (unnamed) others have gotten the best jobs, the nicest houses, the fanciest cars, and so on, without deserving them. They're convinced that the social and economic systems are rigged through nepotism, favoritism, and political preference. That's what prevents the truly worthy people—like themselves—from getting their just desserts.

Some of the Defiant Ones have an even broader sense of resentment, blaming not just society for their suffering but the universe at large. They talk about the cruel tricks of fate they've observed around them: "My old man retired when he turned sixty-five. He planned to move to Longboat Key in Florida. Bang! He had a heart attack two days later and dropped dead. Never had a chance to spend a dime of his retirement money. I won't let that happen to me."

Driven by anger and bitterness, the Defiant Ones take a willful pleasure in squandering their resources. Paychecks vanish in a few days at the bar, club, or racetrack. Inheritances, even large ones, get spent within months. The Defiant Ones laugh at the idea of saving for the future; after all, with their fatalistic outlook on life, they don't really believe there will *be* a future.

What happens when a Defiant One, against all expectations, manages to survive past the age of self-sufficiency? You might expect him to be chastened and to wish he'd done a better job of planning for old age. Not a bit. Instead, the Defiant One sees longevity as an act of revenge against the society that has so cruelly neglected him: "Let the government take care of me. Why shouldn't they? I got screwed all along the way. I deserve a little handout in the end."

Unfortunately, fate has one last disappointment in store for the Defiant Ones. The comfortable retirement package they think should be provided by the government never materializes. Too late, the Defiant Ones realize that *they* were responsible for their own future. In the regretful words of baseball legend Mickey Mantle, whose youthful carousing wasted millions and even damaged his health, "If I'd known I was going to live this long, I might have taken better care of myself!"

THE BOTTOM LINE

Living life to the fullest is an admirable goal. But it should be driven by enjoyment and delight, not by anger and bitterness. If your spending on today's pleasures has reached the point where it is endangering tomorrow's necessities, stop and reconsider. In the end, the Defiant Ones are the real losers.

The Parasite and the Fixer

The *Parasite* is continually looking for someone else to solve his or her money problems, someone who will take over the finances, providing a steady stream of money and a calm, adult hand to manage it. Surprisingly often, the Parasite actually succeeds in finding such a provider. I call this person the *Fixer,* someone who feels driven to solve the problems of the world, starting with the financial problems of a loved one.

A classic example of the Parasite-Fixer couple are Tony and

Sheila. Tony is good-looking, charming, smart, but terrible with money. He uses his charm to overcome his financial weakness by persuading his girlfriend (Sheila is the latest) to take on the money responsibilities: "You know my credit rating isn't very good. How about signing off on that loan I need?"

It's not hard to see what motivates the Parasite; after all, he or she gets a free ride on someone else's hard work and responsibility. But what turns someone into a Fixer? I think the Fixer likes the sense of importance, maturity, and virtue that comes with the role. Sheila likes to say, "Poor Tony would be helpless without me," and although she sometimes complains about having to bail him out, she secretly relishes the fact that being his Fixer makes her the center of Tony's universe.

That's why people with the Fixer personality seem to gravitate to Parasites—or even encourage otherwise normal friends and lovers to *become* Parasites. As the poet W. H. Auden put it: "The friends of the born nurse / Are always getting worse."

Of course, I'm not speaking here about couples or families where one partner has an unavoidable or temporary dependence on the other—for example, a stay-at-home mom with small children to care for, who relies on her husband's income to support the family. I'm describing healthy, otherwise self-sufficient adults who simply refuse to take financial responsibility for themselves, and their partners who willingly take on that responsibility for them. It's ultimately a destructive connection for *both* parties: the Parasite becomes increasingly dependent and helpless, while the Fixer's resources are increasingly drained for the benefit of another person.

THE BOTTOM LINE

Are you involved in a relationship of unnecessary or excessive financial dependence? If you find yourself repeatedly stuck in the role of either the Parasite or the Fixer, the first step toward freeing yourself is to recognize the problem.

The Hoarder

As I've discussed, one of the powerful emotional meanings of money is security. Money in the bank means freedom from fear about tomorrow, and the sense of inner peace that comes with it. I'm a great advocate of financial self-discipline and saving, because these are keys to achieving the security we all crave in life.

The *Hoarder* takes this wisdom to an extreme. Having tasted the natural and genuine pleasure that comes from watching a bank account or an investment portfolio grow, he falls in love with it to the point that it's the *only* pleasure money brings him. The Hoarder stops enjoying going out for dinner or a show, buying a present for a friend, picking out a new suit of clothes, or fixing up his apartment. Whenever he is forced to spend a little money, the image of winged dollars flitting away from his bank vault drains away any enjoyment from the new things he is buying.

Eventually, the Hoarder develops a twisted sense of economic reality. In this, he resembles a person with an eating disorder. Just as a young woman with anorexia may be convinced she is grossly fat even though her weight is *below* normal, the Hoarder feels poor even when his bank account is very healthy. The average person, unfortunately, underestimates how much money he or she will need for retirement; the Hoarder *overestimates* it, and refuses to feel secure no matter how big his retirement account becomes. When this happens, the Hoarder may become a miser.

THE BOTTOM LINE

Saving is a good thing, but it's not the *only* good thing to do with money. If your desire to save has grown to the point where you find it impossible to take any other pleasure from your money, you may be turning into a Hoarder. Lighten up! Take a little of your hard-earned cash and splurge on a new flat-screen television, a holiday trip, or a night out with friends. Money, like life, is meant to be enjoyed.

The Ostrich

Avoidance is the central component of the *Ostrich* money personality. An Ostrich doesn't like to know the specific details of his financial situation, and so he avoids knowing them. His philosophy might be summed up as, "See no evil, hear no evil, speak no evil—and my money problems will just take care of themselves."

As a result, the Ostrich ignores, hide from, or denies the full reality of his financial status. He has no budget and never looks at the monthly bank statements, overdraft notices, or credit card bills. As for balancing his checkbook, he'd rather face a root canal without novocaine.

The Ostrich has usually mastered a host of excuses and rationales for his avoidance habit: "It's all too complicated and too much to deal with." "I just don't have the time." "It's so boring." "I just can't seem to remember when my bills are due." Some Ostriches actually talk as if ignoring the realities of money is a more refined, spiritual, morally high-toned way of life—as if they shouldn't have to clutter their beautiful minds with money issues.

And so they *will not* do so. But the Ostrich forgets which part of his body is high in the air while his head is buried in the sand.

Of course, the excuses offered by an Ostrich are empty and dishonest. In reality, he buries his head to get away from a combination of feeling inadequate, annoyed, and anxious.

THE BOTTOM LINE

The Ostrich needs to manage the emotions that cause him to flee from reality. One way he can begin the process is by choosing a time of day or week when his emotional tolerance is highest and then tackling a single small financial task—for example, sitting down with the checkbook and paying off one or two bills. Repeat this step every day for a month, and the situation will have greatly improved, bringing with it a marked reduction in the fear that drives Ostrich-like behavior. The key is to find ways to lift your head out of the sand, if only periodically, until you get your financial house in order.

The Overwhelmed

Some of the smartest people I know exhibit this money personality. The *Overwhelmed* are people who are accustomed to mastering challenging topics and developing impressive skills for dealing with them, but who find personal finance simply too intimidating.

TRUE-LIFE TALE: SEEING THE FOREST BUT NOT THE TREES

Daniela is a bright and talented young woman with two college degrees and a mantel full of prizes for her work as a magazine editor. When we met and Daniela heard about my role in financial education and training, she literally shuddered: "Ooh! I can't bear to think about money. Just the idea makes me feel out of control." And she quickly tried to change the subject to fashion, music, history, politics—anything but personal finances.

Later, when I got to know Daniela better, we talked a bit about why she dreads the topic of money. There are many reasons: the emotional baggage she attaches to money issues; her curious view that you need to understand *everything* about money before you can do anything with it; the inability of Daniela's parents to talk about money with their children; and the complexity of modern global economics. In combination, these factors make money matters seem impossibly difficult to Daniela. And rather than allow herself to feel "dumb," she chooses to flee to the safety of topics she is comfortable with.

Unfortunately, sliding into the ranks of the Overwhelmed can trigger a vicious cycle. This is what happened to Daniela. Being anxious about money matters led her to ignore her checking account statements—she simply stuffed them into a beautiful handmade wicker basket rather than look at them. She also avoided thinking about her spending patterns and about her gradually growing pile of credit card debt. But Daniela is not a stupid woman; deep inside, she realized she was getting into financial trouble, even though she chose to ignore it. So denial led to anxiety, which led to further denial and a deepening sense of failure.

In time, Daniela's unfounded belief that money is "too complicated" for her to cope with became a self-fulfilling prophecy, as small financial problems mushroomed into enormous ones.

Fortunately, there's a simple solution for people like Daniela. It comes with realizing that money is no more complex than child-rearing, gourmet cooking, house repair, or many other topics. The key is to *break it down* into manageable, bite-size pieces—the same way we learn about everything else in life.

Don't try to master everything related to personal finance, from budgeting and saving to stock analysis and asset allocation, within a few days or even weeks. Instead, start small, learning what is most important to you at that time, whether it's mortgages, credit cards, 401(k) plans, or mutual funds. Spend some time every month over a period of a few years learning the basics of money management as and when you need to understand them. Each step along the way will bring immediate rewards, and at the end of the process you'll have developed a comfort level with money and other financial information that will enable you to develop a suitable personal financial plan that lets you create your own happy economic future.

THE BOTTOM LINE

If you're among the Overwhelmed, don't despair! The rest of this book will help you master the complexities of personal finance in manageable, easy-to-digest chunks.

The Balanced Personality

All the money personalities we've sketched so far reflect a *lack of financial balance.* Some, like the Risk-Taker and the Shopping Addict, overemphasize the excitement to be gained from spending money with few or no controls; others, like the Hoarder, overemphasize the sense of security to be gained from having a growing savings account; and still others, like the Overwhelmed, have allowed themselves to be paralyzed by a single, natural emotion (anxiety about their lack of financial expertise) to the point where they can't confront their money issues at all.

The ideal, of course, is a money personality that has achieved a degree of balance, one where no single impulse, desire, or need has taken control of your attitudes and behavior. Instead, *you* are in command, able to recognize the good and the bad in each of your money habits, and able to choose which of your instincts to obey in any given situation.

Here are some of the other characteristics of the *Balanced Personality:*

- When it's appropriate to say "no" to a particular temptation, you can do that with only a minimal amount of regret; when it's appropriate to say "yes," you can do that with complete enjoyment (and only a minimal amount of guilt).
- You're able to allocate some of your income for immediate spending, some to save for longer-term projects, and some to invest for your retirement.
- You can talk about financial matters openly with your spouse, partner, and children, and you don't have any inordinate difficulty in saying things like "We can't afford that," "I'm not comfortable with that decision," or "It's really important to me that we take this step."
- You can make financial decisions that differ from those made by your friends and family without feeling pressured, guilty, insecure, or otherwise diminished.
- You think about the long-term consequences of your current financial decisions, and you make money choices

based not on extreme emotions (greed, resentment, jealousy), but on what will bring you the greatest satisfaction in the long run.

- You are not afraid to make financial mistakes, recognize them, and learn from them without beating yourself up over them.

Does this way of life sound appealing to you? If it does, then you're ready to tackle the rest of this book, where my mission will be to help you achieve the Balanced Personality.

FACING UP TO REALITY

The first step in achieving the Balanced Personality is to recognize the reality of your current money situation. Everything you've read so far has been designed to help you with that recognition, beginning with a deeper understanding of your current money personality. Now it's time to begin facing the realities of your present financial position—something millions of people find extremely difficult to do.

Are you one of the many people (like Daniela) who shy away from even thinking about their personal finances? Have you started stashing your unopened bills and bank statements in a drawer and ignoring them? And each time you open that drawer, does the threatening pile of papers seem to have increased, as if the bills are secretly procreating in the darkness? If this applies to you, you may be afraid to face your financial problems. And you are hoping that the old "out of sight, out of mind" trick will give you some relief.

If you are one of the many people who has allowed a gulf to open up between the reality of your life and the money decisions you make, don't despair. There are specific, concrete, practical steps you can take to close that dangerous gap. Here are some ways to get a better grip on financial reality.

Break your financial problems down into manageable pieces. First, you have to open that drawer or remove the cover from your handmade wicker basket, take those bills and overdue notices out, and make yourself start doing things that will alleviate the stress of the situation. Sit down and calmly divide the big problem into a series of smaller, more easily achieved objectives. For example, if you are in arrears on your high-priority debts—things like mortgage payments, rent, taxes, condo or coop fees, phone, utilities—place the worst one at the top of the list. If credit cards are your problem, organize them according to their interest rates, starting with the highest rate.

Tackle your problems one step at a time. Second, each day you must work on resolving one problem or achieving one step toward the resolution of a part of your financial difficulty, regardless of how painful or dispiriting it might be. For example, one such step might be to call your credit card company, explain the difficulties you are having in paying your bills, and ask for help in developing a repayment plan. Another step might be to give up a bad habit, like smoking or gambling, and reallocate the money you would have spent on the habit toward a debt-reduction fund. Still another might be to ask your boss about overtime work so that you can increase your income.

Each day of your life, take at least one step, no matter how small. Write the action you are going to take to solve the problem on a card and carry it with you until it's completed. Better still, tackle the task first thing in the morning. Don't put it off. The longer you do, the harder it will be to motivate yourself.

Pat yourself on the back. When you have accomplished your assigned task for the day, cross it off your card using a celebratory color. Place the card somewhere you will see it many times each day. Let it be a reminder to you that you can solve your problems by breaking them into smaller steps and achieving each step one day at a time. Enjoy the feeling of accomplishment—and then prepare the next day's card.

Imagine how satisfied you will feel if, at the end of every day, you have removed one more straw from the proverbial camel's back—your back. It may not be easy at first, but eventually you will hit your stride and be able to solve two or three problems every day.

Ignoring your financial problems is more dangerous than most people think. If you do so, you are blindly letting the situation get worse, slowly but surely giving your creditors control of the money you earn today and tomorrow, as well as control of your stress levels, your day-to-day happiness, and ultimately your future financial security.

TRUE-LIFE TALE: BAD NEWS, GO AWAY!

Like most people, you've probably thought, "If only I could earn a few more dollars, all my problems would be solved." But there are some people who can't seem to get out of debt no matter how much income they have.

I once counseled a couple I'll call Fred and Mary Stevenson. The Stevensons were nice people, but hopelessly addicted to spending—and unwilling to face the reality of what debt was doing to them and their family.

When I first met the Stevensons, Fred was a marketing manager with an Internet-based company. Mary's job centered on caring for their three kids, aged four, six, and nine—and shopping. Mary was a demon shopper. She regularly prowled the stores looking for clothes, toys, gadgets, appliances, food, furniture—almost anything and everything that you can imagine. In Mary's life, shopping occupied the place held for other people by work, school, hobbies, or even religion.

When I visited their home, the evidence of Mary's overshopping was everywhere. The kids' closets contained many cute outfits with the tags still on them; they had never been worn and now were already on the verge of having been outgrown. The shelves in the family room were overflowing with CDs and DVDs no one had ever listened to or watched. The refrigerator was stocked with food no one would ever eat; Mary admitted that she often ended up throwing away up to one-third of the food she bought every week.

Fred wasn't much better. I spotted two brand-new kayaks in their backyard. When I asked about them, Fred explained that he'd just bought them (for some $350 each on sale) because the family was planning a lakeside vacation and they thought they might like to try a new sport.

This kind of uncontrolled spending would merely be unfortunate if the family were highly affluent. But the Stevensons were not. In fact, just three years before they'd lost their home when Fred was laid off.

"Don't you worry that something similar might happen

again?" I asked them. "After all, many Internet companies like the one Fred works for have gone out of business in recent years."

Mary just waved her hands. "Oh, I don't like to think about things like that," she declared. "I'm an optimist. I assume things will always work out."

Hearing about Mary's willful, deliberate refusal to face reality gave me a chill. I sensed that bad things were in store for this family. Sure enough, while I was in the midst of my counseling sessions with the Stevensons, Fred got word that his company was cutting back drastically—and he was being laid off. Unless he could quickly find a new job, they'd be unable to pay their mortgage, and within a few months they'd lose their home again.

This bad news seemed to shock Fred and Mary into a belated recognition of reality. When dunning letters demanding payment started to arrive from credit card companies and banks, Mary began to realize the depth of the problems they'd created for themselves. When I asked her how she felt, she replied, "I feel frightened—like a five-year-old kid with an angry dad." Her comparison was a significant one. A small child expects her parents to mediate between her and the harsh realities of life. Mary had been living as if she were still a child. Now that the facts of debt were hitting home, it was as if the cocoon of parental protection were gone. It was time to grow up.

I worked with Fred and Mary to develop a plan for saving their home and their family. While Fred searched for a new job, we developed a spending budget and a savings plan that would rein in their terrible money habits. Within a few months, the Stevensons had at least a toehold on financial security, though a precarious one. It will take them several more years of struggle to overcome the damage they've done to their future by their years of recklessness.

THE BOTTOM LINE

You can run from financial reality, but you can't hide. The sooner you face the facts about your money situation, the sooner you can begin transforming a dangerous problem into a manageable one and ultimately into a state of happiness and security.

The Fear Factor

When I talk about budgeting with people on my television show, they often react in the same way people do when they hear the word "diet." They think, "If I start a diet, I'll never be able to eat pizza again. I'll never be able to have dessert. I'm going to starve to death." And as a result, they never start dieting, despite the health risks and unhappiness caused by carrying around those twenty extra pounds.

Sometimes people have a similar feeling about money. Perhaps they believe they're inept about money. Perhaps they believe they can't ever earn enough to live in the style to which they aspire. So they just figure, "Why start budgeting? It's hopeless and overwhelming." Instead, they just keep spending, leaning on credit cards, unsecured loans, cash advances, or loans from family and friends—the financial equivalent of uncontrolled eating.

Dr. Emily Stein, a New York–based psychologist who has provided therapy to thousands of individuals and families with a wide range of emotional problems—many of them related to personal finance—believes that this kind of reality-avoidance is often a result of fear: fear of being unworthy, of being unable to do what's required. She comments, "Imagine feeling that you could never earn the money needed to let your family dress like others in the neighborhood, to have a house as nice as the neighbors', or to take a vacation as pleasant as the ones your friends take. For some people, facing these facts may be too frightening. They prefer to deceive themselves. We call this an avoidance/avoidance complex, but in lay terms you might think of it as choosing the lesser of two evils. In effect, the person who flees in reality is saying, 'I'd rather overspend than face the terror of not being able to earn enough money.' "

Such fear is human and understandable. But it's a serious mistake to allow it to control your life. If you are feeling paralyzed by fear of financial reality, how can you master it? Here are a few suggestions.

Share the problem. Almost any problem seems more manageable when it is shared. Rather than trying to face down your financial demons alone, let family and friends offer the help they probably are eager to give. If you are afraid to talk about the money bind you are in because you think your spouse, lover, siblings, parents, or friends will be angry or reject you, think again. Most people are more understanding and supportive than our fears suggest. And the chances are good that the people close to you already sense that a problem exists—and are waiting for an opportunity to talk with you about it.

Separate the problem from your underlying fears. Many people, even those who have achieved success in school, on the job, or in their personal relationships, have deep-seated feelings of inadequacy. Perhaps due to childhood hurts or rejections, you may have an inner voice that tells you, "You are bad, you are unlovable, you are unworthy." This negative inner voice intensifies our financial fears by mingling the real problems with a worry that, if the truth comes out, we will be utterly rejected and alone in the world. Such feelings of inadequacy are commonplace. But they don't change the reality of your financial problems. Try to put your money issues into realistic perspective; don't make them worse by imagining that they will determine your ultimate value as a human being.

Talk to a psychological counselor. If your anxiety, fear, or shame is overwhelming, find an expert who can help you control those emotions. Such counseling need not be prohibitively expensive. In many communities there are clinics or mental health centers where a friendly, supportive counselor may be consulted for a modest charge. And some members of the clergy are trained in psychological counseling as well.

Seek professional financial help. You may also benefit from working with a financial professional on your problems with debt, overspending, or other money management issues. Putting your money woes into a realistic perspective with the help of a professional can help you overcome the paralysis that exaggerated fears may cause.

THE BOTTOM LINE

Don't let fear paralyze your efforts at getting your financial house in order. There are many ways to reduce your money anxieties to a manageable level. Take advantage of them.

TAKE-AWAYS

1. **Know yourself.** Only a person with a clear understanding of his or her own needs, desires, fears, strengths, and weaknesses as they relate to money can develop a realistic financial plan that will lead to a truly satisfying life.
2. **Test and develop your self-discipline.** Use financial exercises to enhance your ability to control your spending behaviors.
3. **Face reality.** Avoid the pitfall of believing a fantasy image of yourself and your life.
4. **Beware the power of emotionally addictive behaviors.** Gambling, drugs and drinking, and other forms of risk-taking can destroy your life both financially and psychologically.
5. **Recognize how fears may paralyze your efforts at financial self-improvement.** If necessary, get financial help to overcome those fears.

2

MONEY AND YOUR PARENTS

TEST YOURSELF. Have you developed a healthy, adult relationship with your parents and money, or are you still struggling to outgrow the confusions and misunderstandings of childhood? To find out, answer the questions below—and *be honest!*

Yes	No	
☐	☐	1. Can you describe the type of money personality each of your parents had?
☐	☐	2. Can you explain how your parents influenced your attitudes toward money?
☐	☐	3. When you were growing up, was money discussed at home in an open and informative way?
☐	☐	4. Do you feel that you inherited a balanced, mature attitude toward money from your parents?
☐	☐	5. As an adult, have you been consistently able to make independent financial decisions rather than reacting to parental influences?

Yes	No	
☐	☐	6. Have you outgrown the need to make money decisions partly to "get back at" or "send a message to" your parents?
☐	☐	7. Have you reflected on the ways in which money was managed in your childhood home, and developed your own, better ways of managing it?
☐	☐	8. Have you come to grips with the impact of your parents' financial choices on your life, and learned to move beyond it?
☐	☐	9. As an adult, have you been able to discuss money matters with your parents in a mutually respectful fashion?
☐	☐	10. Are you comfortable with the fact that you and your parents may have significant differences of opinion when it comes to money?
☐	☐	11. Are you planning your own financial future without reference to any inheritance you may someday receive from your parents?

HOW DO YOU SCORE? Every "no" answer indicates an area on which you need to focus to get your financial relationships in order. For helpful advice and guidance, read on.

PARENTS AND CHILDREN: ACTION AND REACTION

Parents are so important, having literally life-and-death power over their children, that it's not surprising that we are deeply influenced by the beliefs, attitudes, and behavior of our parents for many years after we are grown up. In fact, it's only a slight exaggeration to say that every significant parental action produces some kind of reaction on the part of the child.

History tells the story of a roaming peddler of homemade

medical remedies who lived in upstate New York in the late 1800s. Seemingly consumed with a desire for money, this eccentric character would abandon his family, leaving them to fend for themselves for months at a time, while he traveled the roads selling his fake cures. Then, with no advance notice, he would return in triumph carrying a suitcase full of cash. He would pay off the family bills, treat everyone in town to drinks and meals at the local restaurant, and buy lavish gifts.

During these almost magical appearances, the peddler would impress people by flashing tightly rolled bundles of greenbacks, often with a hundred-dollar bill stuck on the outside. Distrusting banks, he even kept a dresser drawer filled with stacks of money, which he would greedily count and recount for the sheer pleasure of seeing it. Then, when the money ran out, he would take to the road, leaving his family behind, desperately awaiting his reappearance and the return of good times. He was a classic example of a Dreamer, one of the money personalities we described in chapter one.

Imagine the effect of this Dreamer's strange behavior on his family, including his young son John. In the boy's eyes, money itself seemed magical, symbolizing power, happiness, security—and the love of an often-absent father.

Who was that boy? His name was John D. Rockefeller, and he grew up to found the Standard Oil Company and become one of the richest men in the history of the world. He would be praised as a generous philanthropist and reviled as a grasping, greedy mogul. Combined with his great intellect and driving ambition, Rockefeller's strange boyhood surely influenced the unusual relationship he was to have with money throughout his long life. Action and reaction—with a vengeance.

Of course, the *ways* in which we react to our parents may

vary widely. (None of John D. Rockefeller's brothers or sisters became successful businesspeople—except for his brother William, who succeeded mainly through John's help and ended up in a lifelong feud with his brother!) In fact, our personalities are largely determined by the ways in which we choose to react to parental influences—either by *acting out* the same behavior or by *reacting* against it.

Here are some examples of how the action/reaction syndrome may work, using three of the money personalities we described in chapter one:

The Parent	Action	Reaction
The *Entitled Parent* is careless with money, fails to pay bills, doesn't save, and runs up debts, always feeling as though he or she "deserves" the latest treat.	The *Acting-Out Child* behaves in the same way, wasting money and running up debts, as if to reenact (and thereby justify) the parent's failings.	The *Reacting Child* goes to the opposite extreme: burdened with a sense of unworthiness, the child can never feel deserving of any good thing and lives a life of self-deprivation and sadness.
The *Hoarder Parent* is stingy with money, hoarding it and refusing to spend even on worthwhile, important things like education.	The *Acting-Out Child* imitates the parent's stinginess, and may inherit the attitudes of fear or insecurity that helped to prompt the behavior.	The *Reacting Child* becomes a spendthrift, giving away lavish gifts and eagerly saying yes to any opportunity to spend.
The *Risk-Taker Parent* is excited by the thrill of dangerous money ventures and continually risks his or her finances by gambling or investing in dubious ventures.	The *Acting-Out Child* shares the parent's love of financial danger and is eager to follow him or her to the racetrack, the betting parlor, or the casino.	The *Reacting Child* handles money with extreme conservatism and may be afraid to take even prudent risks—for example, by investing retirement savings in a mutual fund.

The choice between action and reaction may be completely conscious. Growing up, some young people admire their parents and strive to imitate them, while others dislike their parents and vow "When I'm an adult, I'll never make the same mistakes as Mom or Dad!" In other cases, the choice may be unconscious: you may imitate or rebel against your parents' example without fully recognizing what you are doing. Sometimes your behavior choices may be obvious to everyone *except* you. If you copy your parents' actions, people call you "a chip off the old block" or comment "The acorn doesn't fall far from the tree." If you react against them, people are more likely to say "Who would believe she's *their* daughter?"

Most people start out in life in one of the two camps: either action or reaction. Which is better? Neither one! Whether you imitate or rebel against your parents' example, you are living a life pattern that has been set by someone else, not you. You reach an important milestone in the process of growing up when you learn to make decisions that are truly independent, based on your own values and goals, rather than simply reflecting your parents' influence. Achieving this independence is a necessary step on the path to developing a Balanced Personality.

How have *you* been influenced by your parents' money attitudes? Do you find yourself mirroring the beliefs and behaviors of your parents (action), or do you tend to behave in the opposite way (reaction)?

If you're not sure about the answer to this question, try the following exercise. It involves exploring the answers to three simple questions.

1. List three money memories related to each of your parents. Take out a piece of paper and spend a few minutes thinking back to childhood memories—good and bad, happy and sad. Jot down the very first memories about your parents that involve money in some fashion. For example, you might recall having your parents buy you a special gift, being told that you couldn't afford a toy or an outing you dearly desired, or watching your parents celebrate a big raise in salary or an unexpected windfall. Write down three memories related to each of your parents. (Of course, if you were raised by an aunt or uncle, adoptive parents, or other relations, think of them in the place of "parents" in this exercise and throughout this chapter.) A memory involving *both* parents should be listed with the parent you feel was most prominent in that event.

2. Identify your parents' money personalities. With your childhood money memories in mind, turn back to chapter one and reread the descriptions of the money personalities. Which one seems closest to your father? Which one resembles your mother? Be honest! And if none of the money personalities described in the chapter appears *precisely* accurate, don't worry—just pick the ones that make the closest match to your parents. Don't be surprised if your mother and father fall into very different categories. It's quite common for people to choose mates whose money personalities differ greatly from their own. (Much more on this in chapter 6, "Money and Your Partner.")

3. Compare your parents' money personalities to your own. Now think back to the money personality that best describes *you,* as discussed in chapter one. How does this compare to your parents' personalities? Do you closely match one or both of your parents? Or have you developed a money personality that is nearly *opposite* to that of your mom or dad? If your parents were quite different from each other, perhaps you've gravitated toward one and away from the other.

As you work your way through this exercise, you may find yourself making new discoveries about your own motivations and behavior. Suppose you've been stuck in a lifelong struggle to get out of debt. Looking back at your parents' behavior may help you realize that you've been imitating a pattern of overspending that you learned from your Shopping Addict father; or, conversely, that you've been unconsciously rebelling against your mother, who was an extreme Hoarder and never learned to enjoy even moderate spending.

For some people, simply *recognizing* these influences can be an important step in breaking away from them and moving toward an independent, Balanced Personality. When working with people on my television show, I've often heard comments like, "It's the funniest thing—ever since we talked about how my parents affected my money attitudes, I find it's a lot easier for me to think clearly about my choices."

TRUE-LIFE TALE: STRIKING BACK AT MOM AND DAD

A classic case of a young person whose ability to deal constructively with money was damaged by her relationship with her parents involves a young woman I'll call Colleen McFarrell.

When I met her, Colleen was a bright young woman of twenty-two who'd been out of her parents' home for four years. She'd moved out shortly after a traumatic family event: her mother had come home one evening and confessed to her father that she'd been having an affair with a man in her office. Colleen's parents had separated; her mother had moved to a distant town where her own parents lived, while her father had remained in the family house.

Colleen, meanwhile, had got a job at a local store and moved into a small apartment with a girlfriend. Colleen and Debra had fun living on their own—maybe too much fun. They got into the habit of going out drinking and partying every weekend. That cost money. So did the stylish clothes they "needed" for their barhopping adventures, along with the cute little car they bought for drives in the country with their boyfriends.

Colleen soon found herself living beyond her means. She maxed out three credit cards and began "borrowing" money from both of her parents (especially her mother) in order to pay her rent and other bills. I put quotes around "borrowing" because Colleen somehow never managed to pay back any of the funds she took from Mom and Dad. In fact, by the time I met Colleen, she had accepted over $20,000 in help from her parents, as well as having over $15,000 dollars in outstanding credit card debt.

When I first met Colleen, I really didn't understand her behavior. Colleen wasn't silly or stupid; she'd earned good marks in school, had played sports and been a leader in clubs, and always talked about wanting to go on to college. Her mature attitude toward life had seemingly evaporated around the time she moved out of her parents' home, which just happened to coincide with their separation.

This coincidence proved to be the clue to Colleen's behavior. One day when Colleen and I were strolling in the park, talking about her financial woes, it occurred to me to ask her, "Colleen, did your moving out have something to do with your parents' breaking up?"

"Oh, sure," she replied. "I just couldn't stand being at home with the two of them fighting constantly. And I hated what my mom had done to my dad. The way she betrayed him just destroyed me. Until then, I'd always thought we had a happy home."

Everything was quickly becoming clear. "Colleen," I asked, "are you living and spending recklessly as a way of striking back at your parents?"

She stared at me for a moment, then burst into tears. Unable to reply, she simply nodded.

After Colleen had had a good cry, we talked through what it all meant. For four years, ever since her parents' breakup, Colleen had been living with a confused tangle of emotions: hurt, anger, grief, disappointment, resentment. As a result, she'd basically given up on her dreams of a productive, happy life and was living for short-term fulfillment—drinking, dancing, partying. And if she overspent and hurt her parents in the process, so much the better. After all, wasn't it *their* fault that she now felt she had nothing to live for?

The good news is that Colleen's seeming inability to control her own behavior changed dramatically once she understood what had motivated her. She still liked going out to parties, but she began moderating her spending. Rather than dancing and drinking all through the weekend, she restricted herself to one night of fun. Colleen began working extra shifts occasionally to make extra money, which she used to pay off her credit card debts. She drew up a budget and (mostly) stuck to it. She even began repaying her mom and dad the money she'd taken from them.

A year later, Colleen was much happier. She'd become a manager at the store where she worked and was looking into taking college courses in business. And the resentment against her parents that had been gnawing away at her had greatly diminished. Now she was living for her own happiness, not just to strike back at her family.

As Colleen's story shows, there's a secondary benefit to outgrowing financial dependence on your family. Standing on your own two feet can allow you to develop a more positive, open, adult relationship with your parents, freed from the burdens of anger, guilt, and need that have distorted the relationship in the past. Who knows? You and your parents may even discover for the first time that you actually like each other!

THE BOTTOM LINE

It's important to recognize how you've responded to the examples set by your parents, whether those examples were good, bad, or (as in most cases) a little of both. This recognition can help you free yourself from excessive parental influence and choose your own path, based solely on what is right for you and driven by neither the need to imitate nor the need to rebel against your family.

What Did Money Mean in Your Family?

Here's another way to think about your parents' influence on you in regard to money. Every family has its own way of dealing with and talking about money—a pattern of behavior and communication that sends a powerful message about the meaning of money to the children who grow up in that family.

Of course, just as there are many kinds of families, there are many ways of dealing with money. But there are also some common patterns that many families share. Each has a different typical influence on the attitudes and behaviors of children, an influence that can last well into adulthood. Which of these is closest to the world of *your* childhood?

1. The Traditional Family: Money as Mystery. In the traditional family, father works while mother stays home. In this kind of family, money is something one person earns. Father is primarily the breadwinner (and may be rather distant from the children as a result), while mother is responsible for raising and imparting wisdom to the children. Mother also runs the day-to-day household finances, often from an allowance provided by father, while father is in charge of the future, through retirement planning and investing.

Strongly traditional parents are often conservative in their beliefs and values, whether consciously or unconsciously. (If their conservatism is unconscious, it may take the form of vague "feelings": "I don't know why I feel this way, I just do!") As a result they tend to believe in specific, even rigid roles for men and women, and they tend to feel that power and knowledge ought to be concentrated in one place—usually in the hands of the father.

As a result, in the traditional family, money is usually not explained in reasonable terms to children. Instead, it remains a rather mysterious substance that clearly has an enormous impact on life yet is rarely talked about in other than hushed terms. When children ask questions about money—as all children do, since they are naturally curious—they may be shushed or even scolded, as if talking about money is slightly "improper": "How much money does Dad make? Why on earth would you ask us that?! Go out to play and stop prying into things that are none of your business!"

If you grew up in a traditional family, you may find that you feel vaguely uneasy about money, and maybe even guilty about your interest in it. (In today's world of sexual freedom, some say money is the last real taboo—and that's certainly true in the traditional family.) Youngsters raised in a traditional family often assume that, when they reach adulthood, they will magically and mysteriously learn all the facts about money that were hidden from them as children. Unfortunately, this doesn't happen; there's no secret "Money Handbook" handed out at age eighteen or twenty-one. Instead, you must learn the realities of money rather painfully on your own—a process for which a traditional upbringing may not do much to prepare you.

2. The Contemporary Family: Money as Time. In the contemporary family, both parents work. (Such families have been around for a long time, although we think of this as the "modern" pattern.) There are some common behavioral patterns that I've observed in this kind of family. In many cases, both parents are overstressed, overworked, and overly busy. Household chores, shopping, and family activities are squeezed in to the week as best as possible, in between long hours at one or two jobs. As a result, many parents feel guilty about the fact that they don't have enough time to spend with their children. This often provokes a financial reaction: the parents may overspend on clothes, toys, gifts, and other treats for the kids as a substitute for the time they wish they had.

Money may be used as a substitute for time in other ways. Too tired to cook? Spend a little extra on a take-out meal or order in a special pizza. Too busy to repair a torn pair of trousers or to take a worn-out pair of shoes to be reheeled? Toss them and buy new ones. Too rushed to take the time to pick out a personal gift for Grandma, or perhaps to make her something special by hand? Pick up a gift certificate at the mall. In the contemporary family, money often expresses the love and concern we'd like to show through actions—if only we weren't so busy.

By contrast with the traditional family, the contemporary family discusses money much more openly; not necessarily because the parents believe in openness, but simply because they have no time to talk except at the dinner or breakfast table or in the family car, when the kids are around. In some contemporary families, the parents still want to keep their children "innocent" of money concerns, even though this may not be possible. In other cases, contemporary parents who would be willing to discuss money with their children fail to do so simply because they haven't the time, or because they've never taken time to learn about wise saving, spending, and investing themselves.

If you were raised in a contemporary family, you may feel a bit confused when you think about money. It's clear that your parents recognized the value of money: after all, they worked night and day to earn it. Yet they were so busy that they scarcely had time to enjoy their money, let alone to communicate its positive value to their children. What's worse, the sense of frantic activity that filled their lives led them to squander money on trivial goodies—the take-out meals, the new outfits, the toys and games—in a search for the life satisfaction that seemed all too elusive.

Your quest as an adult may be to discover a more balanced approach to money that will ultimately be more satisfying than the endless treadmill on which too many contemporary families live.

3. The Single-Parent Family: Money as Magic. A large and growing number of families are headed by a single parent (mother or father) who is living on child support or government benefits. (This happened to be my situation when I was a child in rural Florida.) In most single-parent families, economic struggle is the watchword, and lack of money is nearly always a problem. The child in such a family hears incessant talk about the need for money—naturally enough, since a single parent, lacking adult companionship, often makes the child his or her confidant, sharing the problems of life. As a result, the child grows up with an inflated notion of the importance of money and may even come to believe that *enough* money will solve *all* problems.

Not every child in a single-parent family responds the same way. One of my sisters and I participated in the same kinds of money talk at home. As a rule, we talked about money only on special occasions (like someone's birthday) or when we faced an emergency because we had no money. But my sister and I absorbed these conversations in different ways and came out with very different approaches to the world of money. I developed a feeling that money was above all something to be conquered and controlled. I enjoyed mastering mathematics in school because I recognized that numbers were a tool I could use to tame the money problems I saw plaguing my mom and my siblings. For my sister, money was simply an object of yearning. She loved to daydream about the life she could live if she had money—not that she ever expected these daydreams to come true.

In the relatively rare case where a single parent is affluent (perhaps because of earnings, a large divorce settlement, or inheritance), guilt is often a significant money theme. Feeling guilty because the child has been deprived of a parent by divorce or other circumstances, the single parent may try to fill the absence with things. As a result, the child may grow up to associate money and the things it can buy with love. Of course, that's a dangerous association to make.

If you grew up in a single-parent home, you may find that money is linked in your mind with wish-fulfillment. When you think about money, it's in the form of fantasies about enormous wealth gained through no effort of your own, like the magical ring, sword, or other token in a fairy tale that brings eternal happiness to the deserving hero or heroine.

Does one of these three family patterns resemble the family in which you grew up? Or did your family exhibit a different pattern of behavior when it comes to money, one that fits into some other pattern, one we've not described? If you're not certain, consider the following four questions:

1. Where did the money come from in your childhood home? Did your family contain one or two breadwinners? What kind of work did they do to earn their money? Was working for a living associated with pain and suffering, or was it presented as interesting and fulfilling? Did your family have significant income from sources other than salaries? For example, did you have any inherited wealth? What about government assistance, alimony or child support payments, or charity? Were you raised to feel that money "falls from the sky" in an unpredictable fashion, or that money is the natural result of hard work and self-discipline?

2. Who handled the money? Who controlled it? In many families, the father or some other male authority makes all the significant financial decisions. In others, the mother or the eldest female plays this role—sometimes even taking the paychecks right out of the hands of the men and giving out allowances for spending money. In still others, financial decisions are made jointly by both parents or divided between them according to specific roles. Finally, in some very chaotic households, "decisions" in the true sense are *never* made. Instead, the family drifts along until an emergency strikes (the phone is shut off, a bill collector turns up at the front door) and action is forced upon them. Which of these patterns existed in your family?

3. How was money talked about in your family? Was money a well-guarded secret, as in the traditional family? Was it talked about in hurried snatches amid a frenzy of other activities, as in the contemporary family? Or was in dreamed about and fretted about, as in the single-parent family? Did your parent ever sit you down for a formal discussion about money? Were money concerns talked about in front of the children? Did you ever have the opportunity to participate in financial decisions—for example, to offer ideas about how to economize when times were hard?

4. How was money used in your family? Was money a source of fun and pleasure, or merely a source of anxiety? Did your parents spend money to express their love, to celebrate good news, to help them forget their troubles, or to show off their status to friends and neighbors? Did your parents think long and hard before making any major money decisions (such as buying a new car), or did they leap impulsively?

Take time to think about the answers to these questions. The chances are that the money attitudes you absorbed as a child—consciously or unconsciously—continue to influence your relationship with money today. For example, if you grew up in a household where one parent had an iron grip on every financial decision, you may find it vaguely uncomfortable to share money issues equally with your spouse or partner, perhaps without fully knowing why.

Sometimes a mismatch between inherited parental values and changing economic conditions can cause disappointment, frustration, and anger. In the postwar decades of the 1950s, 1960s, and 1970s, many families in the United States (and elsewhere) were supported by a single breadwinner, usually the father. The nuclear family anchored by a stay-at-home mom and a working dad came to seem "normal," as if God himself had ordained it. Today, however, the world has changed. With more women attending college and developing career plans, with families' economic aspirations rising, and with many working people feeling squeezed financially, more and more families rely on two breadwinners to make ends meet. So today, Mom and Dad are both out in the workforce.

In itself, this isn't a problem. What may be a problem is the unspoken attitudes that Mom and Dad inherited from their parents. Based on many small influences, today's adults may have unconsciously adopted their parents' deep-rooted belief that the one-breadwinner family is the *proper,* kind of family, that a *real* man is able to support his family without help from his wife, and that any family in which "the wife" has to work reflects a moral failure on the part of the "husband." These kinds of assumptions, working quietly behind the scenes, can create resentment that may erupt in anger if they are not recognized and openly discussed.

In some cases—as in the True-Life Tale below—unrecognized parental influences can have a warping effect on an individual's financial attitudes for years into adulthood.

TRUE-LIFE TALE: LIVING IN DAD'S SHADOW

I'm very fond of Mark and Kate Frazer, a couple I met, as I meet so many people, at a time of financial crisis.

Mark and Kate had enjoyed a seemingly successful marriage for twenty-two years. Money was a little scarce, which restricted the activities they could enjoy; for example, they'd never had a real vacation, only short two- or three-day stays in inexpensive seaside motels. Still, they were a happy couple.

Then one day Mark lost his job. Finding a new one proved harder than he expected. Despite the many résumés Mark circulated and the interviews he had, days turned into weeks, then months. The family savings were depleted, and the credit cards were run up to the max. Mark and Kate were nearing their wits' end.

When I met the couple, they were feeling overwhelmed by the mountain of debt they'd accumulated. Yet curiously enough, the Frazers' financial situation wasn't nearly as bad as it might appear at first glance. When I questioned them about their assets, they revealed that they had some $60,000 worth of stock in an investment account. "Why not sell some of the stock to pay off your debt?" I asked. "Then, when your income gets back up to par, you can gradually build up your investment account again."

Mark just shook his head. "I won't touch that money," he insisted.

"Why not?" I asked. "After all, the interest you're paying on your credit card debt every month is more than the dividends and growth you're making from the stock. As long as you hold on to the stock and continue to carry forward your large outstanding debt balance, you are losing money every month."

Mark shook his head again. "You don't understand," he said.

"That's all that's left of the money I inherited from my dad. He died suddenly and left me $120,000. I used half of it to fix up our house, and I invested the rest. That money is not for spending. Not ever."

I began to suspect that Mark's relationship with his dad was crucial to understanding what was happening here. So I spent some time exploring with Mark what kind of man his father had been, and how he had raised Mark to think about money. The account Mark gave of his father made it clear what was going on. Mark's dad had been a famously tightfisted fellow. He'd never taken the family on a vacation, never sprung for a nice meal at a restaurant, never bought a new sofa or table for the house. He could have afforded these things, but he chose not to, whether out of fear or simply an intense desire to maintain tight control over his money.

Ironically, the only time Mark's father allowed himself to relax his iron discipline over money, it indirectly caused his death. At age sixty-six, a recent widower, Mark's father decided to treat himself to his first proper vacation, a golfing trip to California's Pebble Beach. His first day on the links, he'd keeled over on the seventh hole, a heart attack victim. He never regained consciousness.

Mark was haunted by his father's sad life and strange death. He'd inherited his father's extreme anxiety about spending money, which was only intensified by the manner of his death, almost as if the gods had chosen to punish the man for daring to enjoy a bit of self-indulgence. Hence the tenacity with which Mark clung to the remaining inheritance, insisting it not be touched.

At the same time, Mark was the kind of old-fashioned man who regards his role as breadwinner to be sacred. In his view, a man's worth can be measured by his ability to provide for his family, and any failure to do so is a mortal disgrace.

Once these truths were on the table, the Frazers could begin putting the pieces of their lives back together. At my urging, they sold off a portion of their stock and used the proceeds to pay off their credit card debt. Simply having this mounting load of debt off their backs gave both Mark and Kate enormous psychological relief. They worked together to develop a spending budget that reflected the reality of their current hard times. And with his newfound peace of mind, Mark was better able to focus on an effective search for a new job.

Within three months, Mark found a job that paid almost the same as his previous position. He and Kate are gradually building up their investment portfolio again; it will be the centerpiece of their retirement nest egg. And because they both understand the profound psychological meaning that money has for Mark—a legacy of his father's tormented life—they are able for the first time to talk freely together about how to manage their joint finances.

THE BOTTOM LINE

If you find yourself handling money in a way that hurts rather than hinders your happiness, consider your past. Is your relationship with a parent influencing your attitudes toward money in a harmful way? If so, think about how you can move beyond your childhood thinking into a fully adult, responsible mode of reacting and behaving.

You're All Grown Up, Now What?

Naturally, our relationships with our parents change as we get older. Financial, intellectual, and psychological independence should all come together. And as we become less dependent on our parents, we should (ideally) discover the additional benefit of being able to relate to them almost as peers, as adults who appreciate each other.

Unfortunately, in some families, the independence that should go with adulthood appears late, or not at all.

TRUE-LIFE TALE: MOM THE ENABLER

Let's consider the story of a young man I'll call Stephen Hershey. Like Colleen, Stephen succumbed to the temptation to go wild with spending when he first began to earn significant income. But the hidden ingredient in his story—one that took some time to discover—was Stephen's mom, who was making his uncontrolled lifestyle possible.

Stephen was a twenty-four-year-old who worked as an editor at a men's magazine. He had a reasonable income (about $60,000 per year) and good prospects for the future. The trouble was that Stephen wasn't willing to wait. He was spending money like someone with double the income, buying expensive suits and shoes from Italian designers, footing the bill for fancy lunches and dinners with his buddies and a series of girlfriends, and escaping for frequent holidays in places like South Beach, Cancún, and Las Vegas.

Where did all the cash come from? Of course, Stephen spent to the limit on his credit cards. And when that source had been exhausted (which can happen shockingly fast when the taps are turned fully open), he began to borrow from his mother.

Stephen's mom was a widow who'd done admirably well for herself. After her husband's death ten years earlier, she'd opened a store that sold children's clothes. The business had done well, expanding twice, and Mrs. Hershey had put away almost $200,000 in savings for an eventual retirement.

When I met Stephen and his mom, however, only $50,000 was left in her nest egg. Stephen had borrowed all the rest to subsidize his high-speed lifestyle. Why had she let it happen? When I spoke with her alone, the reasons became clear. Stephen's three older brothers and sisters had all moved far away: two to the East Coast, one to Australia. Only Stephen, her "baby," remained nearby. His weekly visits for lunch (and to borrow more cash) were the highlight of Mrs. Hershey's life. She dreaded losing Stephen and being completely alone, which is what she feared would happen if she cut off his funding.

It was terribly sad to realize that this poor lady was sacrificing herself out of a misguided form of love for her son. Even worse was the irresponsibility and selfishness of Stephen, who was taking advantage of his mother's loneliness and vulnerability to prey on her financially.

It's interesting to speculate about what was wrong in Stephen's head. Was he simply a selfish and unrealistic person—a classic Dreamer—who exploited his mother just because she was handy? Maybe so. But maybe something more was going on. I suspect that people like Stephen (sad to say, they are not rare) have a deep-seated fear of adulthood and the responsibilities that go with it. I think Stephen *liked* living off the generosity (and vulnerability) of his mother because it enabled him to avoid facing the fact that he was all grown up, that it was time for him to take care of himself.

Your Future Inheritance: A Mixed Blessing

There's another, more subtle way in which many adults remain financially dependent on their parents. Many people see their parents as a source of financial salvation in the form of a future inheritance. It's common to find young people who are struggling to establish careers in a highly competitive business world looking enviously at their aging parents, who have built up a tidy nest egg after years of hard work. Under the circumstances, it's probably natural that these young people should occasionally think, "If only I could get my hands on a little of the money Mom and Dad have tucked away, all my problems would be solved!" Soon they find themselves wondering about the terms of their parents' will and perhaps counting the years until they inherit all those assets.

This is an unhealthy and even dangerous attitude, for several reasons. First, families where people live in hopes of a future inheritance have less incentive to work hard and save. The notion of a miraculous windfall a few years down the line weakens the sense of urgency that drives most young people to advance their careers and to control their spending and saving. You may feel tempted to run up credit card debt or make unwise financial commitments, assuming, perhaps unconsciously, that money from heaven will bail you out in the end. More often than not, however, the day of financial reckoning comes too soon for any inheritance to help, especially in this era of medical miracles and longer life spans. Better plan on paying your own bills—after all, Mom and Dad may live to be a hundred years old!

Second, the inheritance, if and when it comes, often proves to be smaller than anticipated (sometimes in part because of inheritance tax), producing enormous disappointment, resentment, and regret. Those same longer life spans are also depleting the savings of many older people, leaving little or nothing for the next generation. As far as I'm concerned, that's fine; retirees who worked hard for years should feel no qualms about spending their money to enjoy their twilight time. The problem lies with children who may foolishly assume that a large pot of gold will be waiting for them when their parents die, only to discover that the money has been spent on travel, charitable gifts, health care, and other worthwhile purposes.

Most important, living in expectation of an inheritance has a way of spoiling family life. I don't mean that you'll be actually wishing for your parents' demise; few children are as mercenary and heartless as that. But there are families in which the children, consciously or unconsciously, feel the need to flatter or sweet-talk their parents in order to "stay on their good side" so as to protect their share of the proceeds from the will. The evil consequences include a feeling of competition among the siblings; anger and suspicion directed toward other possible heirs, such as the new wife of an elderly father; and a gradually growing sense of resentment toward the parents themselves. In the worst cases, the children find themselves exploding in frustration: "I wish they'd finally die, so we could all stop jumping through hoops to keep them happy!"

Don't put yourself in this position. Manage your finances without consideration for any possible future inheritance. You'll enjoy the sense of independence this brings you, as well as the ability to relate to your parents and siblings without the intrusion of money anxieties.

THE BOTTOM LINE

Being an adult means much more than just being old enough to have your own place to live and a credit card or two. It means taking responsibility for your own life, including the way you handle money and the long-term consequences of your financial and life decisions.

As Parents Age: Money, Control, and Independence

A curious thing sometimes happens to those of us whose parents are fortunate enough to live to a ripe old age. We find ourselves gradually taking on a caretaking role toward our parents—as if the tables are turned, and Mom and Dad have become our children. It's an odd situation, and anyone with an aging parent must find his or her own way of coping with it comfortably.

In some cases, of course, it's essential for adult children to make provisions for the care of their parents. Elderly people who succumb to Alzheimer's disease or other conditions that severely impair their ability to make independent decisions must ultimately rely on help from children or other loved ones. This can be expensive, time-consuming, and emotionally draining. Ideally, the burden can be shared among two or more children rather than concentrated on a single person, but that's not always possible.

In other cases, where aging parents are still capable of basic self-care, it's more difficult to define the helping role of a child. Let me share my own story as an example.

I was one of seven children raised by my mom, who was a single parent. Life for us was hard. Mom worked as a day maid, cleaning other people's homes, with the kind of small, unreliable income that implies. Every time she got hold of any money, it would always vanish—quickly. So for us children, money was something that would appear unexpectedly, as if by magic, and then go away just as quickly, leaving our lives essentially unchanged.

Although my mother's financial situation has improved over the years, her attitudes have not. To the day she died, Mom was inclined to let money run through her fingers. A little while back, she told me she was having trouble with her toilet. So I sent her some money with a note telling her to call a plumber and have it fixed. What happened? One of my sisters called to say that Mom was still pouring water down her toilet to flush it. Where did the money go? I didn't even ask. I know from past experience that the answer will be incomprehensible.

Naturally, this kind of behavior was frustrating for those of us who loved Mom. It made it very hard for us to give her nice things. We've tried tactics like calling and paying the plumber ourselves. But then Mom would miss the appointment. When Mom needed a new piece of furniture or an appliance, she insisted on paying for it herself, buying on credit and paying (with interest) about 50 percent more than the item was worth. Once when I called her and left a message offering to buy her a new stove and refrigerator, she never called me back.

What's the explanation for my mother's behavior? I've concluded that it was all about control. Mom may not have been financially savvy, but she always wanted things done *her* way. Being independent—financially, psychologically, and especially emotionally—was the most important thing to her.

Reflecting on my mother's life, I can see that this attitude makes perfect sense. For decades, Mom experienced firsthand the disappointments and frustrations of near-poverty. If one of the ladies whose houses she cleaned failed to pay her one week, that meant she had to hold back on paying the electric bill. If one of the children fell and tore a hole in the knee of his trousers, there was no question of buying a new pair; the youngster would have to live with a patched pair of pants till next season's shopping trip. It's no wonder that, over time, my mom learned not to trust in anything or anyone she couldn't control.

And I must admit that Mom was happy living the way she did. So who am I to find fault with her? I learned to accept her just the way she was, and not try to change her.

What's more, when I reflect on how my mother's money attitudes have shaped my own, I realize that we have more in common than I care to admit. Both Mom and I have a strong independent streak. Neither of us can abide the notion of having to rely on someone else for our support. And rather than being grateful when others try to help us—even those who are nearest and dearest to us—we can resist it, because we fear it means loss of control over our own lives, which is the fate we most deeply dread.

The main difference between Mom and me is that I have learned a little more about the realities of earning, saving, and investing money than she has. (It helps to have a career as a trainer on Wall Street, the financial capital of the world!) So I think—I *hope*—that my money choices are more sophisticated and more effective than those of my mother. Yet under the skin, the two of us are really very similar. And, in my heart, I am comfortable with that.

I only hope that, when I'm old, I'll live in a home with a toilet that works!

THE BOTTOM LINE

It can be difficult for an adult child to accept the changing relationship with an aging parent. At times, you may be tempted to switch roles, taking over the job of "parenting" a mother or father whose judgment or thinking seems flawed. Think twice about this. In many cases, it's best to allow your parent to make his or her own choices, even if these are different from the ones you might make. Remember, we all want to be in control of our own lives, no matter how old we might be.

TAKE-AWAYS

1. **Reflect on the ways your parents dealt with money.** How have you reacted to the examples they set and the attitudes they expressed? Do your own behaviors in relation to money tend to mirror or diverge from those of your father and your mother?

2. **Recognize that real independence requires acknowledging the inevitable scars of the parent-child relationship.** Then move beyond them to find your own fulfilling path in life.

3. **Stand on your own two feet.** Be responsible for your own financial needs rather than relying on parental help or fantasies about a future inheritance to support your lifestyle choices.

4. **Examine your own money foibles in the light of your family history.** Recognize the ways in which your handling of money causes you grief or anxiety rather than satisfaction. Do these patterns reflect deep-seated fears, yearnings, or impulses that can be traced back to childhood? Being aware of these motivations is the first step to freeing yourself from their control.

5. **Learn to accept your parents for who they are.** Were your parents perfect? Probably not. But neither are you. Learning to accept your parents, flaws and all, and even developing an open relationship with them as they grow old can be one of the unexpected joys of adulthood.

3

MONEY AND YOUR SIBLINGS

TEST YOURSELF. Do you have a healthy relationship with your siblings and money, or is it a potential source of trouble? To find out, answer the questions below—and *be honest!*

Yes	No	
☐	☐	1. Do your siblings ever use family memories as a way of hurting, embarrassing, or controlling you—or do you do the same to them?
☐	☐	2. Did your parents express a clear preference for one sibling over the others?
☐	☐	3. Is it difficult or painful for you to discuss the topic of parental favoritism with your brothers and sisters?
☐	☐	4. Are you still unsure as to why your parents might have preferred one child over another?
☐	☐	5. Do you ever feel guilt toward a sibling over the privileges you enjoyed as a child, or resentment over your lack of such privileges?
☐	☐	6. Are there great differences in the degree of financial success enjoyed by different siblings in your family?

Yes	No	
☐	☐	7. Do differences in economic circumstances ever cause feelings of awkwardness, embarrassment, or unhappiness among you and your siblings?
☐	☐	8. Have loans or gifts among siblings ever led to hard feelings in your family?
☐	☐	9. In your family, has one child taken on parentlike responsibility for the financial well-being of another?
☐	☐	10. Do you ever find yourself reverting to childhood ways of feeling, thinking, and acting when you are around your siblings?
☐	☐	11. Have issues related to a parent's estate ever caused friction among the siblings in your family?

HOW DO YOU SCORE? For this quiz, every "yes" answer indicates an area on which you need to focus to get your financial relationships in order. For helpful advice and guidance, read on.

A LIFELONG BOND

Perhaps no one is closer than two siblings—a brother and sister, two brothers, or two sisters—who are born and raised in the same household. Shaped by similar, sometimes nearly identical genetic inheritances and environmental influences, siblings often understand each other more profoundly than any other pairs of people, even best friends or spouses. Many people feel their brothers or sisters remain their closest friends for life.

Of course, this exceptional degree of closeness is a double-edged sword. Sometimes, sadly, siblings develop antagonisms that are deep and painful. One of the things your sibling knows more about than anyone else is how to push your emotional buttons. They were there through many of the formative events of your life: the childhood triumphs, traumas, joys, and disappointments that make you who you are. No one understands better than your sister just how devastating it was when the boy of your dreams asked someone else to that special dance when you were fourteen years old. No one except your brother can really fathom how embarrassed you were that time the football game was held up for twenty minutes while you searched the field for a lost contact lens.

If your relationship is a healthy one, this intimacy can produce an extraordinary degree of empathy. Your sister will be the first to defend you when you act strangely sensitive over some trivial slight that reminds you of that twenty-year-old rejection; your brother will tactfully change the subject when someone mentions football. But if the relationship has soured, your sibling may use that special knowledge against you. At a family gathering, your sister may crow, "Oh, pay no attention to Karen, she still hasn't gotten over Eddie Sanchez back in eighth grade!" or your brother may retell the story of the lost contact lens at the first party attended by your prospective in-laws.

The childhood memories we share with our siblings also exert a rather peculiar effect: we tend to think of them as children, no matter how old they (and we) may get. So when we get together with them, especially in the company of our parents, we tend to revert to childlike attitudes and behaviors. Feelings like dependency, jealousy, competitiveness, insecurity, and shame may well up, and we behave in ways more appropriate to an eight- or ten-year-old than an adult.

This tendency is made worse by the fact that family gatherings often happen at times of stress—weddings, funerals, births, graduations, and other times of transition, when emotions are running high and the family members are all wondering (at least unconsciously) about how their relationships will be changed by the latest event. Even celebratory events, like family reunions and holiday parties, can be stressful times that bring out the worst rather than the best in people.

And, of course, when money is involved—that talisman symbolizing power, acceptance, freedom, and love—all the intense feelings of family life become even stronger.

Our relationships with our siblings can be fraught with anxiety, stress, and sometimes hostility—even when, at bottom, we love one another. The first step toward improving those relationships is to recognize this reality and refuse to feel guilty or angry about it.

THE BOTTOM LINE

Mixed feelings about your siblings aren't a sign that you are immature, selfish, or mean; they're simply a natural part of the human condition. Still, the sooner you learn to deal with them in a grown-up fashion, the better, especially where money matters are concerned.

Dealing with the Lingering Effects of Childhood Rivalry

Perhaps the challenge of our relationships with our siblings grows fundamentally from the fact that we are both the same and not the same. We are the same as our siblings in that we are all children of the same parents and therefore occupy the same rank and role in the family—at least in theory. Yet inevitably we are not the same—in our temperaments, talents, needs, and wishes or in our relationships with our parents. Therefore, the equality that seems natural and fair between siblings almost inevitably gives way to an uneasy mixture of equality and inequality in which fairness is hard to find.

The truth is that there is no way all the children in a family can be treated exactly the same, nor should they be. Some parents try to be fair by buying similar clothes, toys, and other things for all their children. Paradoxically, the result is usually *unfair,* since the same plaything that one child loves will bore another.

A possible solution is for the parents to buy different things for their children but spend the same amounts (or as close to this as possible). Again, this seemingly easy solution is often impractical. What if only one child develops a powerful interest in a pastime that is expensive, such as horseback riding or skiing? Assuming that the parents can afford to support this interest, should they be forced to find something equally expensive for the other children to do? Or should the horse lover have to forgo her interest in the name of fairness to her siblings? Neither solution makes much sense.

Similar conflicts can arise throughout the family's life span. It may seem fairest to send all the children to college, but what if only one is really suited to advanced education? Or what if one wins a scholarship while another must pay full tuition? How can the family's investment in all the children be equalized under these circumstances?

In the end, it's impossible for all the siblings in a family to be treated exactly the same. The challenge for parents and siblings alike is to find ways of balancing the inequality so that all the children feel loved and supported by the family, though the specifics of how they are treated are different.

Complicating this challenge is the fact that parents are flawed human beings for whom it may be difficult to find the path of fairness—or even truly to desire it. Much as they may want to love all their children equally, many parents find it hard not to have favorites in their heart of hearts. A mother may love best the child who resembles her most closely, the one who reminds her of a beloved relative, the one who seems to need her most, or (depending on her own personality) the one who needs her *least*—and the same is true of fathers, of course. As a result, many parents may, often unwittingly, give extra attention, support, and material help to one child or another. Or, if they are aware of their tendency to favor one child, they may actually shortchange that child because they bend over backward to avoid favoritism. This may cause tension among the siblings.

Many people carry hurts and resentments from childhood around inside them, sometimes without honestly examining their causes. Now that you're grown up, it's time you worked on putting those bad feelings to rest. Ask yourself the following questions, which can help you start on the process.

1. When you were growing up, was there a "pecking order" among the children in your family? Or did your parents go out of their way to claim that all the children were treated the same? In some families, the parents say that all the children are (or should be) equal. In a few cases, they openly admit that some children are favored over others. Which was usually the case in your family?

2. Regardless of what your parents said, did you perceive a difference in status among the children in terms of being loved, respected, or well-treated? If so, how did the children

rank? Where did you stand on the totem pole? In some families, despite claims by the parents that all the children are loved and treated equally, it seems clear that one or another child is favored and petted. Was this true in your family? If so, do you feel that you were at the top of the heap, at the bottom, or (in a larger family) somewhere in the middle?

3. Was the issue of parental favoritism openly discussed in your home, either among all the family members or just among the children? Why or why not? Some siblings are able to talk quite freely about "who is Mom's favorite" or "which one is Daddy's pet." They may even be able to laugh about it together. In other families, the entire topic is a big, bad taboo that no one dares to mention—or that generates conversations filled with sarcasm, innuendo, and barely veiled hostility.

4. Do you think your siblings would agree with the ranking you gave in answer to question 2 above? If not, why not? Occasionally, when siblings get to talking about their childhoods, they discover that they perceived the family hierarchy in very different ways. The revelations can be startling.

My coauthor grew up convinced that his brother, Jacque, was their mother's favorite. As far as Karl could see, nothing he ever did at school or at home was good enough to satisfy Mom, while Jacque was constantly showered with praise. (It didn't help matters that Karl and Jacque were opposites in terms of personalities and interests: Karl was artistic, literary, and a loner, while Jacque was mechanically gifted, athletic, and sociable. Karl felt his mom found Jacque's style much more sympathetic.)

This feeling about his childhood always bothered Karl. So

when he and his brother began sharing childhood memories at a family reunion many years later, Karl was shocked to hear his brother say, "Everyone knew that you were Mom's favorite. She couldn't stop bragging about you!" It turned out that their mother had no difficulty talking about Karl's good qualities to others, but somehow the words of praise stuck in her throat whenever Karl was actually in the room.

The conversation helped Karl realize an important truth: his mother's failure to express love for him wasn't due to a lack of feeling, but rather a profound inability to communicate. Recognizing this didn't wipe away Karl's childhood hurt, but it helped him feel a bit of sympathy for a woman who obviously suffered some form of deep emotional conflict. It also lessened his lingering feelings of jealousy toward his brother.

5. How was the family pecking order expressed in behavior? In some families, one child (perhaps the oldest) is put in charge of the others, enforcing parental rules and making decisions almost like another adult. In other families, material benefits continually flow to one child in particular, and all the best gifts, treats, outings, and special lessons seem to end up in his or her lap. And in still other families, the feeling of favoritism is expressed verbally, with one child being subject to frequent (often very subtle) put-downs or criticisms while the other is lavished with expressions of admiration and fondness.

6. What do you believe were the reasons for the ranking of siblings in your childhood family? Parents may favor one or another child for many reasons, some of them quite odd. Age and gender certainly play a role, but so do factors like intelligence, special talents, personality traits, or appearance—some parents, consciously or unconsciously, prefer a child who reminds them of themselves or resembles a favored relative. Even the circumstances of a child's birth may have an influence. Have you ever known a mother who felt the need to mention constantly how difficult or painful it was to give birth to a particular child? If you were that child, hearing the story of those maternal agonies repeated over and over again at family gatherings probably made you feel terribly guilty, and gave you a strong feeling that you were at the bottom of the family pecking order, unfair and irrational as that might be.

Sometimes, simply understanding the reasons for parental favoritism can make the hurt easier to deal with. When you recognize that your parents, like all human beings, experienced emotions that were often illogical or unreasonable, you can free yourself from the notion that you somehow "deserved" to be treated in a particular way, good or bad, as you were growing up.

7. Have you been able to talk about the family pecking order with your siblings? Have you made peace with them about any lingering resentment or guilt? As Karl found, it can be helpful to talk about childhood rivalries with your siblings after you've grown up and (hopefully) begun to stand on your own feet emotionally. And it's not just the angry child at the bottom of the totem pole who may benefit from such open sharing. Sometimes the favored child grows up with a strong sense of guilt and unworthiness, suspecting that he or she never deserved the special treatment provided by Mom or Dad. Talking through the issues, confessing the bad feelings, and asking for understanding and forgiveness can go a long way toward fixing the problems and helping you achieve a new level of friendship with your brothers and sisters.

THE BOTTOM LINE

It is probably inevitable than anyone growing up with one or more siblings feels that, at times, there was a lack of equality or fairness in the family, even though two siblings may have opposite opinions over which one was the favorite! Thinking and talking about your childhood rivalries can help adult siblings get beyond the old resentments and develop a new and better relationship.

The Story of the Prodigal Child— Which Role Do *You* Play?

Personality differences among siblings are an enormous cause of stress around money. Among the seven children in my childhood family, no two of us had exactly the same attitudes toward or behaviors about money. One of the major money events of our lives was the annual purchase of a new wardrobe at the beginning of the school year in September. Because we had little money, this wardrobe was never extensive—perhaps a new jacket, two pairs of pants, and a couple of shirts for me and my brothers, and two dresses and a coat for each of my sisters. The items were selected at a local store in June, paid for month by month on a layaway plan, and brought home in the fall.

Each of us children had a distinctive way of handling this annual event. I loved nice clothes, just as I do to this day. I certainly would have enjoyed having the freedom to buy an extensive collection of clothes. But I was always a realist. I knew what my mother could afford, and I carefully tailored my expectations and desires to match what was possible. I thought a lot about the kind of jacket, trousers, and shirts I would like, and made sure that I got the right colors, and sizes, so that I could enjoy the feeling of being nicely dressed all through the coming year.

My youngest sister was different. She never got used to the idea that she couldn't have as many outfits as some of our schoolmates, and she constantly wheedled and whined in an effort to get something more. And even when my mother gave in and bought her something extra, she still complained about what she didn't get.

Her money personality hasn't changed much to this day. Whenever she gets her hands on some money, she spends it right away, as if she can't stand being deprived for a single moment longer. She finds it impossible to save money, and in fact she begrudges the fact that I am able to do so.

Then there was the third child in our family, a boy with very modest demands and a quiet, self-sufficient personality. The kind of clothes he wore didn't matter much to him; he was happy with whatever our mother would pick out. He is the same today. He works as a cook in a restaurant, and he lives comfortably and happily on his relatively modest income, having mastered the art of being content with exactly what he has.

These kinds of personality differences centered on money are a central theme of the story of the Prodigal Son, one of the best-known and most-loved parables from the Bible. It's a story that reflects folk wisdom about relationships just as much as religious truth. Here's the story, as told in the fifteenth chapter of the Gospel According to Luke:

> There was a man who had two sons; and the younger of them said to his father, "Father, give me the share of property that falls to me." And he divided his living between them.
>
> Not many days later, the younger son gathered all he had

and took his journey into a far country, and there he squandered his property in loose living. And when he had spent everything, a great famine arose in that country, and he began to be in want.

So he went and joined himself to one of the citizens of that country, who sent him into his fields to feed swine. And he would gladly have fed on the pods that the swine ate; and no one gave him anything.

But when he came to himself he said, "How many of my father's hired servants have bread enough and to spare, but I perish here with hunger! I will arise and go to my father, and I will say to him, 'Father, I have sinned against heaven and before you; I am no longer worthy to be called your son; treat me as one of your hired servants.' "

And he arose and came to his father. But while he was yet at a distance, his father saw him and had compassion, and ran and embraced him and kissed him. And the son said to him, "Father, I have sinned against heaven and before you; I am no longer worthy to be called your son."

But the father said to his servants, "Bring quickly the best robe, and put it on him; and put a ring on his hand, and shoes on his feet; and bring the fatted calf and kill it, and let us eat and make merry; for this my son was dead, and is alive again; he was lost, and is found." And they began to make merry.

Now his elder son was in the field; and as he came and drew near to the house, he heard music and dancing. And he called one of the servants and asked what this meant. And he said to him, "Your brother has come, and your father has killed the fatted calf, because he has received him safe and sound."

But he was angry and refused to go in. His father came out

> and entreated him, but he answered his father, "Lo, these many years I have served you, and I never disobeyed your command; yet you never gave me a kid, that I might make merry with my friends. But when this son of yours came, who has devoured your living with harlots, you killed for him the fatted calf!"
>
> And he said to him, "Son, you are always with me, and all that is mine is yours. It was fitting to make merry and be glad, for this your brother was dead, and is alive; he was lost, and is found."
>
> [Luke 15: 11–31, New Revised Standard Version]

In religious terms, this is a story about sinning and redemption. But it's also a powerful story about family relationships. Here's the key question: *Whom do you identify with in the story of the Prodigal Son?*

Most people feel they are one of the two brothers—either the prodigal son who wasted his father's inheritance, or the stay-at-home who was responsible and hardworking. And depending on which of the brothers you most identify with, you have a distinct psychological profile.

If you are the prodigal child, you probably feel you have enjoyed the adventurous side of life, but you may also suffer the guilt that comes from knowing that you have not behaved in a responsible or mature fashion. If you are the stay-at-home, you probably feel happy about what you have accomplished through your hard work, but you may also feel resentful over the fun you've missed in the process.

What role have *you* played in your life? What about your siblings? Which of you has been the prodigal child, and which one the stay-at-home? The answer to this question may help to explain some of the tensions and conflicts in your family.

THE BOTTOM LINE

Both prodigal children and stay-at-homes may carry a psychological burden—one of guilt, the other of resentment. This can have a powerful destructive effect on the relationship between siblings. It means that both types need to make an effort to shed that burden in order to repair their relationship and to get on with life.

Managing Income Differences Among Siblings

Everything we've discussed so far—the powerful impact of sibling rivalry, the existence of an unfair "pecking order" among children in many families, the resentments that arise between the prodigal child and the stay-at-home child—takes on an added poignancy when financial differences are thrown into the mix.

Sometimes siblings live similar lives, settling in the same town or neighborhood, pursuing similar careers, even marrying the same kinds of people. But other siblings end up taking life paths that are surprisingly divergent. When this happens, the resulting money differences can cause real stress in the family.

My own family offers a vivid example. In economic terms, I am definitely the "odd man out" among my siblings. Raised with a houseful of brothers and sisters in poor, rural Florida, I was the only member of my family to go north for an advanced education. While I ended up pursuing a white-collar, professional career as an educator, author, and television personality, my brothers and sisters have remained in the South and work at more humble, lower-paid occupations. My siblings and I have stayed in touch and we still care for one another, but we live in different worlds.

A question that often arises in such a family is: What do siblings owe one another? There's no ready answer to this question. The expectations and desires that affect how siblings share with, support, and help one another are shaped by family history, ethnic and cultural traditions, and personal beliefs.

In some very close-knit families, there's an assumption that good fortune enjoyed by one sibling should be shared with the others. If one child receives a windfall, he or she is likely to give significant gifts of money or presents to the siblings or their children. Thus, for example, if one family member becomes the proprietor of a successful business, he may be expected to find jobs for his brothers and sisters and their children. The wealthiest brother or sister may establish education funds for the nieces and nephews.

In most families, however, the bonds of affection don't necessarily include financial ties. Except for the usual holiday or birthday gift-giving, what's mine remains mine and what's yours remains yours. Which is the "right" way to go? There's no one answer. Both sets of folkways are understandable and defensible, and each has its advantages and disadvantages. What's most important is for family members to feel able to talk openly with one another about their needs, expectations, and wishes, and to try to resolve disagreements freely, so that hurts and disappointments don't fester and produce lifelong estrangements.

Being the most prosperous member of my family occasionally forces me to make tricky personal decisions. It's rare that any of my sisters or brothers asks me for financial help, and when they do, the situation feels just a little awkward. I think they feel a bit embarrassed about having to ask for help, and I feel a little embarrassed about being in a position to help. I imagine we both feel relieved when the check has been sent, the moment of awkwardness is past, and we can get back to being just-plain-brother-and-sister again.

A while ago, one of my nieces called me to ask about borrowing money to help pay her college tuition. It was the first time she'd ever called with such a request, and her embarrassment was very evident. When she first mentioned that she'd like to speak with me, I asked her to call me before nine a.m., since I'm almost always occupied during business hours. Instead, she called and left a message at two in the afternoon, as if she really didn't want to talk with me (which I'm sure was true). She also said, "I guess people must call you about borrowing money all the time," which is not true, but which I can understand as something she wanted to believe. Finally, she gave up the attempt altogether and asked her mother (my sister) to call on her behalf. Of course, we worked out a way for me to help, but I felt sorry for my poor niece and the awkwardness she felt.

When I told this story to a friend, he offered an interesting interpretation. "Your niece views you as a boss and herself as an underling. And since she assumes that a boss must be some kind of ogre, she is afraid of you." It's funny how economic differences can make family relationships so complicated.

Here are a few rules for siblings dealing with money differences that can help preserve harmony in the family.

1. If you lend money to a sibling (or another relative), do it without expecting to be repaid or to receive anything else in return. If you can't lend on this basis, then don't lend at all. Lending money within a family is emotionally dangerous. It can lead to discomfort, anxiety, and resentment on both sides, perhaps to the extent of destroying your relationship.

Suppose you lend money to your brother with the understanding that he will repay it "as soon as he is able." In subsequent months, nearly every encounter between the two of you will be awkward and uncomfortable. If Billy gives you a check to repay some of the money, you will probably wonder, "Can he really afford to repay me that much? I hope he doesn't feel resentful over having to do it. Maybe I should tell him to forget about it. But I really could use the money . . ."

Conversely (and more common), if Billy fails to give you a check (and especially if he says nothing about the debt), your thoughts will run along these lines: "What's happened to my money? Did Billy forget about the loan? Maybe he misunderstood and thought it was a gift. Should I say something about it? No, that'll make him feel bad. Still, he does owe it to me . . ." And if Billy shows up at a family gathering with a new car or photos from a cruise vacation, you'll find yourself seething inside: "He has the money to throw away on *that,* but not to pay me back?"

The only way to avoid these emotional entanglements, I've found, is to think of the money as an outright gift, even if you refer to it as a loan. That way, if the money is never returned, you won't feel upset because you never expected to see it again. And if it *is* returned, it will be a pleasant surprise!

2. On the other hand, if you borrow money from a sibling (or other relative), pay it back in full as quickly as possible. Does this second rule contradict the first rule? Not really. I'm offering advice about how to manage your relationship with your siblings so as to bring you the greatest peace of mind. You can't control your siblings, but you can control your own behavior. So regardless of what your brother or sister may have in mind when making you a loan, make it a point to return the money as soon as you can, even if that means passing up that vacation, that new car, or that new bedroom suite you'd love to buy. Believe me, the clear conscience you'll enjoy once you pay back your debt will give you greater happiness in the long run.

3. Try always to treat siblings as siblings, not as parents or children. Taking responsibility for the life of a brother or sister may be tempting, especially if you've achieved financial success that has eluded your sibling. But acting on this temptation is almost always a mistake. It usually hurts the sibling just as much as it hurts you, as the following True-Life Tale illustrates.

TRUE-LIFE TALE:
GIVING UP THE RESPONSIBILITY FOR A SIBLING'S LIFE

Joe Fallon and his brother, Mike, were always close, despite their very different personalities. Joe was the responsible one—in terms of the biblical parable, the stay-at-home brother. Married with two small children, Joe managed an auto repair shop and owned a nice, modest home in a suburb of Chicago.

Mike was the prodigal. He squandered resources, not in loose living (as in the biblical story) but in pursuit of half-baked get-rich-quick schemes. For a time, he played bass guitar in a band that he was sure would become "the next Nirvana"; then he opened a shop selling sexy lingerie for women; still later, he launched an Internet business featuring entertainment news, with the idea of selling advertising space on the website. But the band broke up, the lingerie shop went bankrupt, and no one visited the website. Every failure drove Mike deeper into debt. For a time he was even sleeping in his car because he could no longer afford rent for an apartment.

Unlike the brother in the biblical tale, Joe was not resentful of

Mike. Instead, he felt responsible for him. "I'm all he's got," Joe would say. "I can't have him sleeping on the street." Every couple of months, Joe would give Mike a check for a few hundred dollars, "Just to tide him over until his luck changes." Unfortunately, Mike's luck never changed (unless you count "getting worse" as change).

Perhaps the main victims here were Joe's wife and children, who were shortchanged financially because of Mike's draining of the family resources. Over time, Cynthia's resentment of Mike became a major source of friction in the family. At one point, she even convinced Joe to get a new job in a different town, sell their home, and move two hundred miles away—in large part to put physical distance between him and Mike. But the move didn't solve the problem. The brothers remained in touch by phone, and Joe kept writing checks.

Eventually, Cynthia put her foot down. "I know you love your brother," she told her husband, "but he's got to learn to stand on his own two feet—or at least stop leaning on us. Otherwise, our marriage may not survive." Cynthia's ultimatum gave Joe the spine he needed to get firm with Mike. Joe turned off the money spigot to his brother, and within a few months Mike got a steady job and began earning at least enough money to take care of himself.

4. Be aware of the psychological impact your siblings have on you—and keep it under control. I've spoken about how siblings can be the supreme emotional button-pushers in our lives. Because of the complicated network of memories and psychological connections we share with them, siblings can sometimes drag us backward into negative childhood behaviors and attitudes through their words and actions.

Don't let this happen to you! When necessary, break away from your family for a time so that you can have the freedom to change and grow. (And if you are the button-pusher in your family circle—and if you are, you probably know it, deep down inside—try to resist the temptation. It may be fun to tweak your brothers and sisters, but it can also be destructive.

TRUE-LIFE TALE: WHEN BREAKING UP IS GOOD TO DO

Stella Davis was the youngest of four daughters, all born within six years. They were a close-knit tribe, each with a distinct and clearly defined family role. Jenna, the eldest, was the leader, the organizer, the authority; she planned the girls' activities, settled their disputes, and represented the children in negotiations with their parents. Alice, the second oldest, was the troublemaker; she goaded her sisters in mischief-making, misbehavior, and practical jokes. Diane, the third child, was the creative soul; temperamental and artistic, she wrote the playlets the girls performed, designed their costumes, and painted the scenery.

Finally, Stella was "the baby." Pampered by her parents, Stella was given few chores to do and was rarely expected to take on any responsibilities. The other girls picked up on the cues from their parents and treated Stella in the same way. Stella's lack of responsibility extended to her handling of money. If all the girls were given a set sum to spend on an excursion, Stella would always squander hers first, and the other girls would always laugh it off, saying, "That's our Stella!" and treat her from their own pockets the rest of the day.

These childhood patterns persisted into the girls' adulthood. Unable to get used to the idea of playing a responsible role, Stella flitted from job to job and often found herself living with a boyfriend who supported her in idleness. And her sisters, who always remained her closest friends, never encouraged her to change. They were so comfortable with Stella's girlhood role that they couldn't see the danger it posed for her as an adult.

When Stella finally decided she had to change her ways, she found that she had to "break off" with her sisters for a time. Otherwise, their attitudes and assumptions about her would encourage her to revert to her old patterns of behavior. When Stella talked with her sisters about getting a new job or about saving for the future, they would mock and tease her—"Oh, Stella, you'll never pull that off!"—or else try to discourage her from changing—"Why do you want to bother with that?" At times they even sabotaged her attempts to change (probably without realizing they were doing so); for example, they would invite Stella on outings she couldn't afford, then insist on paying her way, thereby keeping her in a position of dependency.

It was as if Stella's sisters felt threatened by the prospect of having their "baby sister" change. And of course many people do find change threatening.

Only by severely limiting her contact with her sisters for a year was Stella able to break her bad old habits and develop a new, more mature relationship to money.

5. When siblings join divergent cultural or social groups, extreme sensitivity to differing assumptions about money may be required. As I've noted, folkways vary from one family to another, with cultural and social influences playing a part. My advice about minimizing money lending within the family would seem selfish and hard-hearted in some cultures, where it's understood that any family member who comes into money will share it with the others.

The documentary film *Daughter from Danang,* directed by Gail Dolgin and Vincente Franco and nominated for an Academy Award in 2002, illustrates poignantly how cultural differences about money can cause pain within families. The film tells the story of Heidi, the daughter of an American serviceman and a Vietnamese woman, who was given up for adoption as a small child and raised by a family in Tennessee. Years later, as a thoroughly Americanized young woman, she seeks out her Vietnamese family of origin and visits them in Danang.

At first the reunion produces pure happiness. But after a few days, the enormous economic gap between the poor Vietnamese family and their "rich" American daughter, combined with profound cultural differences, causes a painful clash. Heidi's Vietnamese brothers tell her they expect her to send regular monthly checks to help support their mother. To them, this is only natural; in Vietnamese culture, children automatically band together to care for their aging parents. But Heidi is shocked. She feels that the expressions of love from her siblings and her birth mother have been exposed as a façade for their expectations of money. Heidi returns to America feeling hurt and disillusioned.

The film holds out a glimmer of hope for a happier future reunion. Heidi's Vietnamese brothers realize that they were insensitive to the cultural differences between themselves and their sister, and Heidi comments that she is "leaving the door unlocked" for further communication with her estranged family. Perhaps one day these siblings will find a way to talk about their differing values, expectations, and wishes, and become true members of the same family.

THE BOTTOM LINE

There is no one right way to handle money differences among siblings. But it's important that you develop a set of shared understandings concerning the role money will play in your sibling relationships, talk about them with those involved, and then stick to them. Where expectations and boundaries are unclear, misunderstandings and hurt feelings are likely to arise.

Dealing with the Trauma of Inheritance

As I've already mentioned, an inheritance can be a distinctly mixed blessing, with tricky implications for the relationship between children and parents. It's also a common source of disagreement or conflict among siblings. Which child will receive what portion of the parents' estate when they die? Which child will be entrusted with managing the disposition of the estate and carrying out the parents' last wishes? What obligations do the children have to one another in regard to distributing the parents' wealth?

Practical questions like these become a source of conflict because money is so often a surrogate for other issues—issues such as love, respect, and honor. When children fight over their parents' estate, they may be reenacting ancient battles over which child was most loved or which child is the most deserving heir of the parental name and power. The fact that these issues arise at an emotionally charged time—the period of grief and self-assessment that inevitably occurs when a parent dies—only worsens the trauma.

Psychologist Emily Stein has seen the emotional damage that an inheritance can cause, even when conflicts between siblings are not involved. "An inheritance may make you feel undeserving, kicking up guilt or stress. In can also make you feel nervous about managing the money properly. The result can be that people become depressed or engage in gestures that are excessively grand and generous—spending too much money on gifts, for example, or on treats for the family."

To overcome the guilt and stress of becoming an heir, Stein recommends reflecting on your relationship with your parents. "When you understand *why* you were chosen to receive a particular inheritance, it often serves to minimize the sense of guilt or anxiety. You can then focus on spending, saving, investing, or giving the money in a way that will make you proud and would have pleased your parents, too."

Conflicts among siblings, however, are harder to manage. Because money equals love in many people's minds, when people argue about inheritance the battle is often a disguised battle for affection, including, perhaps, a posthumous struggle for the affection of the parents. Unfortunately, as Stein points out, those involved will tend to deny this. Suppose you say to your sister, "Let's face it, the reason we're fighting about the summer house [or Mom's favorite necklace, or the china cabinet] is because we're fighting over who Mom loved the best." Chances are good she will respond by saying you are being crazy, overly dramatic, or even insane. She will probably phone all the other family members to enlist them on "her side" of the issue. And the fight will resume, just as intense as before, but with the added unpleasantness of your having had your feelings rebuffed by the rest of your family.

The following rules can help you minimize these kinds of sibling conflicts over inheritance.

1. Never act or speak in haste. The death of a parent is a painful time. You may be feeling more distraught than you fully realize. Don't make any quick decisions or promises. Instead, give yourself time to think through your choices, and avoid making rash statements about what you want, need, or expect from the estate or from your siblings.

2. Get professional advice. If your parents' estate is complicated, you may need the guidance of a lawyer, tax consultant, accountant, or financial adviser, particularly if you have been named the official executor of your parents' estate. Don't tackle a complex inheritance as a do-it-yourself project.

3. Be open with your siblings and any other heirs. Family conflicts over inheritance often arise because of a failure to communicate. Keep your brothers and sisters informed about decisions being considered. Share copies of financial documents, lists of possessions, and account records so no one can suspect that assets are being hidden or disposed of improperly.

4. When conflicts arise, express your own feelings rather than attribute bad motives to others. When people have strong feelings, Stein recommends communicating about family issues using "I statements" rather than "you statements"—that is, statements that focus on how I feel rather than on how others are behaving. Thus, "I feel hurt" is a more effective place to start than "You are being selfish."

5. Deal with your anger or anxiety rather than acting it out through arguments. It's crucial to understand how you feel, and it's often helpful to say it or to write it. But it's not necessarily helpful to confront the person with whom you are in conflict. Sometimes talking about the painful feelings with your spouse or partner, a best friend, a member of the clergy, or a counselor can be more productive than forcing a battle with a sibling, especially at a time when complicated financial legal matters may be at stake. Even simply keeping a journal in which you wrestle with your emotions can have a healing effect.

(Of course, family conflicts over inheritance can also be minimized through wise advance planning by parents. We'll offer advice about this later in the book, in chapter 9, "Money and the End of Life.")

Two pairs of siblings I know exemplify some of the worst and the best ways in which families can handle the inheritance trauma.

TRUE-LIFE TALE: WHEN EVEN STEVEN ISN'T FAIR

Henry and Philip Porter never really got along very well. Their differing personalities account for much of the problem. Henry, the older son, was hardworking, responsible, a follower of rules. He earned top grades in school, worked weekends and summers, saved his money, and launched a successful career as an accountant after college. As a result, he was always financially independent—a quality his parents seemingly took for granted.

By contrast, Philip was a black sheep. He just barely scraped by in school, cracked up the family car a couple of times, dropped out of college, and had trouble holding down a job. Whenever he ran short of cash, he would show up on his parents' doorstep—and they were always ready to help.

As a result, Philip ended up absorbing a significant amount of the family resources, while Henry got little or nothing. This was especially true after their father died. Their widowed mother, who'd always had a soft spot in her heart for her somewhat needy, helpless younger boy, periodically sent him checks to help cover his rent, car repairs, vacations, and other expenses. Meanwhile, Henry paid his own way, just as he always had.

The discrepancy caused a certain amount of friction between the two brothers, which came to a head when their mother died. In her will, she left her savings and the family house to be divided between Henry and Philip on a fifty-fifty basis. Paradoxically, this arrangement left both men dissatisfied, hurt, and angry. Henry reasoned, "This was Mom's opportunity to make up to me for the fact that I got so little from her over the years. But she didn't do it." Meanwhile, Philip thought, "Mom knew that Henry is the successful one, the one with plenty of money and no trouble supporting himself. Why did she leave him the same amount as me?"

Both men felt shortchanged. As a result, they had a serious quarrel soon after their mother's funeral. Today, five years later, they haven't spoken to each other.

When resentments over finances are allowed to fester for years, a time of crisis can bring out the worst in people and perhaps cause a serious rift in the family. You and your siblings need to find ways to deal with disagreements before they reach this point.

By contrast, the Ross sisters have been able to overcome their differences and make the most of their sibling ties in a way that has benefited them both.

TRUE-LIFE TALE: SISTERLY SHARING

Like Henry and Philip, Debra and Sharon Ross achieved very different degrees of career success. Debra became a successful attorney on Wall Street, part of a powerful law firm that represents major corporate clients. Sharon drifted from one job to another, spending time as a window dresser, an office receptionist, a manicurist, and a research assistant. Sharon's income was only about a quarter of Debra's.

Fortunately, the sisters were mature and thoughtful enough to prevent this discrepancy from souring their relationship. When they met for lunch or dinner, they usually picked a restaurant that Sharon could afford, except for the occasional special day when Debra would say, "I just won a big case, let me treat you to a fancy meal," with no hint that she expected Sharon to reciprocate. They went on vacation together a couple of times, and again they managed their financial differences with tact, choosing a hotel that was within Sharon's price range.

When the Ross sisters' widowed mother died, she left the women a tidy inheritance, divided fifty-fifty, just as with the Porter men. When Sharon and Debra talked about the inheritance, they realized they'd both had a longtime dream of owning real estate. They decided that a fine way of maximizing the investment value of their inheritance was to pool their resources and buy houses together, splitting the income between them.

They did this, and the financial results were excellent. Still, their different economic circumstances posed a challenge. When they bought a house that needed substantial renovation, Debra was prepared to write a check to pay for the work, which Sharon couldn't afford to do. They solved the problem by having each sister contribute appropriately: Debra hired the plumbers and the electricians, and Sharon provided "sweat equity," working evenings and weekends on painting the interiors, replacing light fixtures, installing carpets, and planting a garden.

The Ross sisters were able to manage their financial differences better than the Porter brothers for two main reasons. First, they talked about the need to share resources in a way they could both be comfortable with, rather than allowing resentment and jealousy to build up. Second, they found creative ways of contributing resources of time and money in ways that were equivalent in value though not identical.

THE BOTTOM LINE

Financial clashes between brothers and sisters regarding a family inheritance needn't spoil the relationship, provided the siblings are willing to be tolerant, flexible, and open in how they manage those differences. Be aware of the underlying emotional conflicts that fuel disagreements about money, and talk each other through those conflicts rather than denying them or merely acting them out.

TAKE-AWAYS

1. **Accept the fact that it's unlikely that you and your siblings were treated exactly the same.** Hurt feelings related to sibling rivalry are an inevitable part of family life. Understanding their causes can help you to move beyond them as an adult.

2. **Handle money dealings with your siblings (such as loans or gifts) with great care.** Talk through your expectations to avoid misunderstandings and hurt feelings.

3. **Expect differences in personalities, attitudes, and circumstances to lead to clashes with your siblings.** Making peace with who you are can help you overcome feelings of resentment or jealousy directed toward a brother or sister.

4. **Avoid trying to carry the responsibility for the well-being of a sibling.** Your brother or sister needs to control his or her own destiny in order to grow into an independent adult.

5. **Beware the tendency of siblings to drag you back into negative childhood patterns of behavior.** Sometimes you need to break away from family expectations in order to grow and change.

6. **Minimize the trauma of inheritance through communication.** Speak openly and freely with your siblings about your expectations and about the emotional meanings that a parental bequest carries.

4

MONEY AND YOUR CAREER

TEST YOURSELF. Is the relationship between your career and money a positive one, or are you losing out? To find out, answer the questions below—and *be honest!*

Yes	No	
☐	☐	1. Do you know why you chose the job you now have?
☐	☐	2. Are the reasons you chose your current job still relevant and meaningful to you?
☐	☐	3. Does your work meet your financial needs, from paying the monthly bills to providing enough extra for the things you love in life?
☐	☐	4. Does your work meet your intellectual needs, providing you with a mental challenge and an opportunity to test and improve your skills?
☐	☐	5. Does your work meet your emotional needs, giving you a chance to do things that are meaningful and satisfying in a safe, comfortable environment?

Yes	No	
☐	☐	6. If you are considering a change in careers, have you investigated the kind of jobs that might be appropriate for you?
☐	☐	7. Have you used networking to identify people who may be able to help you learn about new career opportunities?
☐	☐	8. Are you currently involved in learning new skills to expand your career horizons?
☐	☐	9. Have you considered the option of self-employment—working for yourself?
☐	☐	10. Have you looked closely at your own personality to see whether the entrepreneurial option is right for you?
☐	☐	11. If you've ever dreamed of owning your own business, have you investigated the economic and practical challenges involved?
☐	☐	12. When you are bored or frustrated with work, have you experimented with ways to revitalize your interest in the job?

HOW DO YOU SCORE? Every "no" answer indicates an area on which you need to focus to get your financial relationships in order. For helpful advice and guidance, read on.

IT'S ABOUT MONEY—AND SO MUCH MORE

Good work is one of the basic elements of a satisfying life. One reason, of course, is money; after all, most of us couldn't make ends meet without the income from our work. But just as important are the psychological rewards from working. The pleasure of producing something every day; of contributing to a project or task, whether great or small; of giving something back to society from our talents and energies; of working with other people in a cooperative effort—all these forms of satisfaction are essential to mental health. No wonder Sigmund Freud, the father of modern psychology, said that "Love and work are the cornerstones of our humanness."

This explains why so many people who retire find themselves bored and depressed, even if they've spent a lifetime complaining about work! Many take new jobs rather than face the tedium of another round of golf or (worse still) endless television. Those who don't or can't sometimes die from sheer lack of stimulation.

So good work, like love, is essential to a happy life. But bad work, or the wrong work, can be a source of frustration and unhappiness. In the space of a chapter, I can't solve every problem you might encounter in dealing with work. But I can offer some good advice about tackling this challenge—one that is crucial for the health of all your other money relationships.

Why Did You Choose the Work You Do?

Are you perfectly happy with your work? If you are, congratulations. But if you're like most people, you probably wonder from time to time whether there isn't something better out there for you. If so, one way to start thinking about better options is to trace the path that led you to the work you currently do.

What made you choose (or fall into) your current occupation? For most people, the answer is likely to be some combination of the following seven factors. Read the list, and decide which factors were most important in choosing your present job and which were least important *at the time you made your job choice.* Rank them in order from 1 (most important) to 7 (least important).

- **Family expectations.** Many people feel they were "steered" by their parents or other relatives into a particular line of work. Maybe your parents pushed you toward the same career they followed, or toward some career they perceived as prestigious, important, or lucrative (physician, lawyer, executive . . .). Or maybe you gravitated toward a certain job simply because, from an early age, you were told repeatedly that you were suited to that work ("Look at Tommy with those toy bricks! He's sure to be a builder some day").
- **Social pressures.** Careers go in and out of fashion. In the 1970s, when crusading journalists became famous for exposing government scandals, young people by the thousands gravitated toward work in the news media. In the 1980s, computer programming and systems development were the rage. In the 1990s, everybody seemed to be pursuing an MBA degree. Maybe you chose a particular line of work, in part, because so many of your friends were headed that way.
- **Education.** Many people study a subject in school that leads naturally toward a career path. And they may wind up following that path despite the fact that their deepest inclinations, interests, and abilities lie elsewhere. (After all, the educational choices you made in your late teens or early twenties may have been ill-informed, or you may simply have changed in the years since then.)
- **Desire for income.** Money, of course, is an important motivating factor in almost every career choice. So when the

press, school counselors, and career "experts" periodically trumpet particular industries or lines of work as being "hot," "in demand," "sure to grow," and especially "the most lucrative," many young people with no fixed plans or strong desires drift toward them. (Of course, predictions about which careers will be most lucrative tend to be self-defeating, since anytime a flood of people enters an industry, competition for jobs is likely to depress salaries.)

- **Desire for security.** People who are not very ambitious may opt for careers they perceive as "secure"—that is, not competitive, slow-to-change, undemanding, and offering lifetime employment (though at a relatively modest salary). Many people view government work and jobs in staid industries like insurance and utilities in this light.
- **"Fire in the belly."** Some people choose careers because of a deep-seated personal interest, a passion that makes everything about the particular line of work seem interesting, important, and rewarding. And because human beings are so varied in their intellects and temperaments, it seems that almost every occupation holds this kind of attraction for someone. We all know people who are passionately devoted to careers in the arts: aspiring musicians, actors, dancers, writers, and painters. But there are other people who feel just as strongly about their jobs as accountants, pharmacists, schoolteachers, bus drivers, hotel managers, and carpenters. Thank heaven! Since, as the saying goes, it takes all kinds to make a world.
- **Sheer chance.** Finally, some people drift into jobs by sheer chance. A friend from school offers them a job; they spot a "Help Wanted" flyer posted in a store window; desperate for money, they respond to the first advertisement they find

in the newspaper. In many cases, jobs chosen on this basis last just a few months; occasionally, people end up sticking with them for life, just as one sometimes encounters happily married couples who met on a blind date.

What does your 1 to 7 ranking say about your work history? What combination of motives underlies your current career choice? None of the factors listed above is necessarily good or bad in itself; a job you chose, in part, because of parental guidance or social pressure may lead to a perfectly satisfying career. But as time passes, motivations that once seemed important may lose their significance, while other factors gain meaning. What is your current evaluation of the job decisions you made in the past? Did you choose your career for strong and compelling reasons, or largely by accident?

THE BOTTOM LINE

It's important to understand why you are where you are, and to decide whether the underlying reasons for your present career path seem adequate and sensible to you today. This understanding can help you prepare to base your next career decision on factors that truly reflect the things that matter most to you. And as experience and observation show, when you do work that reflects your deepest inclinations and interests, you are likely to be more successful in every sense, including financially.

Does Your Job Meet Your Needs?

There are many needs—physical, intellectual, emotional—that work can help to meet. Which of these needs are most important to you? Which are least important? Which are being met by your present occupation? Which are not? The answer to these questions can help you decide whether it's time to consider changing to a new career.

Start by reviewing the checklist below, titled "Your Working Needs Inventory," and quickly rating each need on the following scale:

1 = Very important
2 = Somewhat important
3 = Not very important

(I want you to rate them quickly so that the ratings reflect your instinctive, gut reaction, not the opinion or feeling you think you "ought" to have.)

Then, for each need, check the appropriate box in the right-hand columns ("Being met," "Not being met"). Again, work quickly, by instinct rather than deliberation.

YOUR WORKING NEEDS INVENTORY

	Being met	Not being met
1. Income to meet your basic living requirements (shelter, food, clothing). **Your rating for this need:** ______	☐	☐
2. Income to meet your broader desires (entertainment, travel, treats, and toys). **Your rating for this need:** ______	☐	☐
3. Income to provide security for today and tomorrow (insurance, health care, retirement saving). **Your rating for this need:** ______	☐	☐
4. A workplace that is safe and reasonably easy to reach. **Your rating for this need:** ______	☐	☐

(continued)

YOUR WORKING NEEDS INVENTORY (cont.)

	Being met	Not being met
5. Hours of work that you consider acceptable and reasonably convenient. **Your rating for this need:** ______	☐	☐
6. A working environment that is physically pleasant and attractive. **Your rating for this need:** ______	☐	☐
7. Colleagues that you like and are comfortable working with. **Your rating for this need:** ______	☐	☐
8. A feeling that you and your work are respected and appreciated. **Your rating for this need:** ______	☐	☐
9. Work that is productive and satisfying (rather than frustrating drudgery). **Your rating for this need:** ______	☐	☐
10. Work that engages and stimulates your mind, emotions, and creativity (at least part of the time). **Your rating for this need:** ______	☐	☐
11. Work with a comfortable balance between independence and teamwork. **Your rating for this need:** ______	☐	☐
12. Work that you consider useful, beneficial to society, and ethical. **Your rating for this need:** ______	☐	☐
13. A job and an employer of whom you can feel proud. **Your rating for this need:** ______	☐	☐
14. Good prospects for long-term security. **Your rating for this need:** ______	☐	☐
15. A reasonable opportunity for career advancement, promotions, and pay raises. **Your rating for this need:** ______	☐	☐
16. An opportunity to help or serve other people. **Your rating for this need:** ______	☐	☐
17. An opportunity to lead or manage other people. **Your rating for this need:** ______	☐	☐

Notice how long this list is. You may not have realized all the various kinds of physical and psychological satisfactions that work may (or may not) offer. Having worked your way through the checklist, you should have several needs ranked 1 ("Very important"), others ranked 2 ("Somewhat important"), and still others ranked 3 ("Not very important"). Which work needs are most important to you? Which are least important?

In addition, some needs will be checked off as "Being met," others as "Not being met." Which needs are in each category? How many fall into each column? Very few people are lucky enough to have jobs in which all, or nearly all, of their needs are being met. Here's a self-ranking system you may find helpful:

If your number of *unmet* needs is . . .	The fit between you and your current job is . . .
0–3	excellent
4–6	good
7–9	fair
10–17	poor

In particular, which of your "Very important" needs are "Not being met"? In considering a possible career change, those needs deserve special focus.

The answers to these questions can help you decide whether it's time to consider a change in occupation, and if so, what new directions you should consider.

THE BOTTOM LINE

While money is important, it represents only a portion of the meaning of work—and a smaller portion than most people as-

sume. Salary is important; you need enough income to support your needs and those of your family, and you want to be paid a fair wage that reflects your value to the employer. But if you are unsatisfied with your job, don't assume that salary is the reason; and don't assume that a new job with a pay raise will solve your problem. It may not.

Using Networking to Explore New Career Paths

Once you've determined the work needs that are most important to you, you may want to do some research to identify jobs that will suit you. There are many books available that discuss jobs in a variety of fields, and virtually every industry has at least one magazine or journal devoted to it. Visit your local library and ask a librarian to point you toward the career and work resources. One full day spent among the books and magazines is likely to generate three to five interesting ideas for the kind of work you should pursue.

An even better source of real-life information about what it's like to work in a particular field is a conversation with someone who does that kind of work. If you already have a friend or acquaintance in the field, wonderful; call and ask for twenty minutes of their time for an "informational interview," which will give you a chance to gather insights and advice as to whether or not this career is appropriate for you.

If you don't know anyone to call, that's all right. Chances are good that you can identify someone by *networking*. Here are the basic principles of networking:

List your personal connections. Make a list of the people you know who may have a contact in your target field. List friends, relatives, neighbors, former and present work colleagues, teachers and schoolmates, acquaintances from organizations or groups (religious or social) to which you belong, people you've met through hobbies, sports, or other pastimes—anyone at all whose name you know. Expect to spend at least an hour working on this list, as one name sparks the memory of another and then another. If you're typical, you should be able to list sixty to a hundred people, if not more.

Start calling. Devote a little time each day—half an hour, to begin with—to calling the people on your contact list. Explain why you're calling: "I'm thinking about making a career change, and I'm looking for friends who might know someone who works in computer programming [or magazine publishing, or marketing, or corporate communications, or animal grooming, or interior decorating—whatever field you're curious about]. I'm interested in a short conversation to get information and advice about the business. Can you suggest someone I might call?"

After a few phone calls, you will probably find that a friend of a friend—or the cousin of a colleague's neighbor—is just the person you are looking for.

If necessary, try "cold calling." If you can't locate a source through networking, try cold calling—that is, simply calling someone who works in the field, introducing yourself, and asking for a few minutes of their time.

It's important to identify the person you will call by name and title. For example, suppose you're interested in learning about working with disabled children. You might call a few schools in your neighborhood and ask for the name of the teacher or administrator who develops programs for children with special needs. Then call that person and ask for a few minutes to talk about the field.

Don't let your shyness stop you from calling. The idea of calling people you haven't met before to arrange informational interviews may make you nervous. That's natural. But you need to overcome that sense of shyness in order to take advantage of the opportunities that networking affords.

It may help for you to know that most people actually like to talk about their work. They are pleased and even flattered to be asked for advice and guidance. You'll be pleasantly surprised when you make your first call or two by the positive reactions you will probably get.

Prepare before the interview. When you conduct your interview, stick to a twenty-minute time limit. It helps to prepare a handful of questions beforehand. Possible questions include:

- How did you get started in your career?
- What's the best possible preparation for a career like yours?
- What do you like most about your work? What do you like least?
- What do you wish you'd known about your career before you embarked upon it?
- How has your business or industry changed since you began to work in it?

During the interview, take notes on a small pad (otherwise you're likely to forget what you learn). Always thank the interviewee, and send a brief thank-you note afterward as well. After a few such interviews, you will have a much better idea about the kind of work that is likely to meet your needs most fully.

THE BOTTOM LINE

To make your next career decision smarter and more satisfying than your last one, arm yourself with information. The best source is someone who is actually working in a field you are considering. Overcome your shyness and use networking to find people who can help you learn the good points and bad points of a job you may want to try.

Developing New Skills for a World of Change

If you find yourself eager to change your line of work—or if you feel forced into making a change because of shrinking opportunities—don't assume that you've done anything wrong in the past. In today's world (unlike the more stable, secure world our parents and grandparents knew), most people find themselves changing careers at least once in their lives. Career planning in the twenty-first century is not about tracing a smooth path, it's about being prepared to master the unexpected.

Here's a True-Life Tale that illustrates the new reality.

TRUE-LIFE TALE: SABOTAGING HIS OWN CAREER

My friend Ronald Hartman is smart, likable, and hardworking. Yet he hasn't managed to land a full-time job in the last five years. Instead, he has been living hand to mouth, surviving on his dwindling savings account and the meager income from occasional part-time jobs.

Ronald's career difficulties, ironically, can be traced back to the enormous success he formerly enjoyed as an investment manager. For eight years, during the "bull market" of the 1990s, he worked at one of the big financial firms in Chicago. The problem is that he never totally mastered the details of how investments worked: the art of picking stocks, for example, or the complex mathematics that underlies the price movements of bonds. With the markets soaring, most of the investments Ronald chose for his customers made money, despite his "focusing on the big picture" and letting others handle the details. Nor did he fully learn the art of marketing his talents effectively to customers: providing superior service, educating clients about investment strategy, or analyzing customer needs. Instead, he simply rode on the rising tide of the bull market, assuming that the good times would continue forever.

Of course, they didn't. When the financial markets crashed in 2000, Ronald's company fired half of its employees. It kept the people who had mastered the details and were skilled at marketing their services. Ronald was out on the street.

To this day, Ronald doesn't understand what went wrong. It's true that the last few years have been tough in his chosen industry. But Ronald ignores the ways in which he contributed to his own difficulties. Rather than devoting time to learning new skills or trying a new field of work, he waits to hear about job openings for investment managers, even though these opportunities are few and far between. In interviews, he drops names but he doesn't listen well. As a result, he never gets the job offer he truly believes he deserves. And between interviews, he spends his days dreaming enviously about his friends who are millionaires.

By contrast, another friend, Tom Lee, loves his job. He is now head of marketing for a closet design company. He also loved his last job, working in sales for a home furnishings retailer. Before that, he designed office spaces, and before that, he did publicity for a long-distance telephone company. He also had stints of free-lance work in between these full-time jobs. He enjoyed all these occupations.

What's the common thread connecting all these phases of Tom's career? Realizing that a job is not an entitlement program, Tom is a man who constantly reinvents himself, always taking on new challenges and learning new skills. He is willing to travel, to tackle new assignments, to stretch himself. As a result, Tom is always ready for the next challenge.

Many people seem to assume that a job should stay the same, that the skills that got you in the door ought to keep you employed for a lifetime. That's not how careers work any longer—if indeed they ever did. Every day, the business page of the newspaper reports dramatic changes that will affect millions of lives: the latest computer memory chip, an amazing medical breakthrough, a new bioengineered crop that will be more resistant to disease. You have to view your career the same way. Just as great companies are constantly seeking new technologies, new products, and new services that will make their old offerings obsolete, you need to be constantly seeking new skills that will make you smarter, faster, more flexible, more creative, and more successful than before.

How can you go about developing these new skills? Here are some techniques you may not have considered:

- **Evening or weekend classes.** Most communities have colleges, trade schools, and community centers that offer educational programs suitable for career development. If a class you are interested in will enhance skills that are valuable on your current job, your present employer may even be willing to pay all or part of the cost.

- **Industry seminars and workshops.** Many industries sponsor educational programs, sometimes through specialized schools or institutes devoted to the industry, sometimes in connection with the industry's annual convention or conference. Again, your present employer may help subsidize your attendance at such programs.
- **Self-instruction.** Your local library and bookshop probably have a wealth of books, magazines, journals, and audio, video, and computer programs that teach work-related skills. These can be used on your own schedule, as time permits.
- **Volunteer or part-time work.** If you are considering a career change, you can test and develop your aptitude for the new work by doing it on a volunteer or part-time basis. Many a successful full-time career has grown out of a weekend or evening occupation, which can serve as a practical bridge from one line of work to another.
- **Special projects at work.** You can expand your horizons by offering to tackle special projects at your current place of employment that are outside your normal scope. For example, suppose you work in retailing but are curious about a career in Internet marketing. You could offer to help create, update, or maintain a website for your current employer, in the process getting a taste for online promotion and sales as well as developing some of the basic skills needed for success in the field.

Notice that none of these techniques for expanding your work horizons involves finding an employer who will pay for a complete course of training. That's unlikely. Instead, the trick is to continue to earn in one job while you find ways to develop new skills simultaneously, thereby preparing yourself for the next career leap. That's the kind of flexibility that today's demanding job market requires.

THE BOTTOM LINE

Most people will hold six to ten different jobs during their lifetimes, and most will pursue two to four different careers. The old idea of one job or one career for life is no longer applicable in today's rapidly changing world. It's up to you to develop the flexibility and the array of skills needed to adjust to this world of continual change.

The Self-Employment Option

Many people dream of becoming self-employed—starting their own businesses or becoming freelancers, working independently. It's a dream you may find especially alluring on a day when your boss is in a foul mood, the customers are being unreasonable, and your coworkers are slacking off. But don't quit your job and rush into self-employment for negative reasons: to escape a job you feel you hate. You need to make the move for positive reasons: because you know you can create a more satisfying (and hopefully more lucrative) career as your own boss rather than working for a company.

Like any major life change, self-employment involves both positives and negatives (as well as a fair number of unexpected twists that no one is ever fully prepared for). Here are some of the trade-offs to anticipate.

WORKING FOR YOURSELF: THE GOOD, THE BAD, AND THE UGLY

The Good	The Bad	The Ugly
You'll be working for your own benefit; everything you accomplish, and the profits you earn, will flow directly to you.	You'll lack the name recognition of a large company; you may find that doors that were once open to you are now tightly shut.	You may find yourself answering the phone using a disguised voice in hopes of passing yourself off as one of your company's mythical "employees."
You'll have control over the kind and number of tasks you take on (as limited, however, by the needs of the marketplace and your financial requirements).	You'll have to market your products or services—perhaps aggressively—if you hope to generate sufficient cash flow to stay in business.	You may find yourself praying that the prospective clients you are wooing over coffee don't see the desperation in your eyes.
You won't be responsible for indifferent, slipshod, or unethical behavior by others in a large organization.	You won't have the resources of a large company behind you; you'll have to pay for legal, accounting, and other services yourself.	You may find yourself changing the toner cartridge in the photocopy machine at four a.m. so you can deliver that proposal "first thing tomorrow" as promised.
You may be able to schedule your work flexibly (depending on the needs of customers).	You'll bear complete personal responsibility for the quality and quantity of your work.	You may find yourself asking, "Weekends? What are these weekends you speak of?"
You can tailor the benefits you purchase precisely to your needs and preferences.	You won't receive paid benefits such as health insurance, a retirement plan, or vacation days unless you pay for them yourself.	You may find yourself spending your wedding anniversary at the beach—arguing with suppliers on your cell phone.
You'll enjoy the prestige and satisfaction of creating a business that reflects your personal abilities, interests, values, and accomplishments.	You won't have a built-in array of colleagues, advisers, and supervisors to help you with problems and challenges on the job.	You may find yourself practicing your latest sales pitch on your pet dachshund.

As you can see, self-employment is quite demanding. Both Karl and I are self-employed, and we find it by turns exhilarating, exasperating, exciting, and nerve-racking. There are moments when we yearn for the safe cocoon of a corporate environment. But those moments are increasingly rare. On balance, we enjoy the freelance life and never want to leave it.

Is the entrepreneurial life right for you? Here's a quick quiz that can help you decide.

THE ENTREPRENEURSHIP QUIZ

1. You have a project due next week. Which do you do?		
a. Map out a plan and get started.	**b.** Decide that you will start the project over the weekend.	**c.** Put it off until the last minute, and find yourself crying in the corner of the library.
2. A friend asks you to go skiing. You've never done anything like that before. Which do you do?		
a. Decide not to go. You'd probably come back in several pieces.	**b.** Agree to go, but decide never to venture off the bunny slopes.	**c.** Go along! You know you'll be great—you'll conquer the black diamond slopes in no time.
3. You're assigned to a team at work for an important project. What's your response?		
a. You groan, because you know you'll end up doing all the work.	**b.** You suggest that your team meet and divide up responsibilities.	**c.** You like to work by yourself, but know you'll have a good team.
4. You are elected president of a club. Once in command, you . . .		
a. Run the club with an iron fist, and acquire the nickname "Saddam."	**b.** Feel overwhelmed with work at first, but then you delegate some responsibilities and create a schedule.	**c.** Have lots of good ideas, but it seems as if the club is all talk and no action.

(continued)

THE ENTREPRENEURSHIP QUIZ (cont.)

5. You are sent to a leadership conference where you hear a presentation on individual leadership styles. Which do you do?		
a. Stick the handouts in your folder, and wonder what's for lunch.	**b.** Take notes, because you might be able to use the information some day.	**c.** Have a realization about your own leadership style, and decide to make some changes on the job.
6. You are looking at information about European business on the Internet and you wonder what the abbreviation DM means. Which do you do?		
a. Write it down on a piece of scrap paper. You'll look it up eventually.	**b.** Immediately type it into an online dictionary and discover that it means deutsche mark.	**c.** Don't need to look it up. It stands for direct marketing, right?
7. You have a job interview tomorrow. How do you feel about it?		
a. You are self-confident and prepared to make a good impression.	**b.** You have nightmares about all that can go wrong, but you pull yourself together in time.	**c.** You get really nervous and don't show up.
8. You are walking to work when you realize that you forgot to prepare a report that is due this morning. What do you do?		
a. Go online and copy a report from a website, hoping no one will recognize the source.	**b.** Quickly throw something together. Maybe your boss will find it acceptable.	**c.** Call in "sick" and hope you can turn in the report in a day or two.
9. You are taking a walk when a car slows down and the driver asks for directions. How do you react?		
a. You do your best to give directions, even though the fellow still looks confused.	**b.** You continue walking; you don't talk to strange people in cars.	**c.** You tell him where to go, and even jot the directions on a scrap of paper.

10. You are playing softball in a local city league. What's your attitude toward the games?		
a. You are determined to win at all costs.	**b.** You try to improve your own game as well as win as a team.	**c.** You don't really care who wins.

Here's how to score your answers:

1. a = 2 points, b = 1 point, c = 0 points. An entrepreneur is comfortable with setting and pursuing goals.
2. a = 0 points, b = 2 points, c = 1 point. An entrepreneur takes calculated risks, being neither overly timid nor overly aggressive.
3. a = 0 points, b = 2 points, c = 1 point. An entrepreneur is willing and able to work with a team.
4. a = 0 points, b = 2 points, c = 1 point. An entrepreneur is a leader who is able to delegate responsibilities and motivate others.
5. a = 0 points, b = 1 point, c = 2 points. An entrepreneur transfers knowledge into behavior.
6. a = 1 point, b = 2 points, c = 0 points. An entrepreneur practices learning as a lifelong skill.
7. a = 2 points, b = 1 point, c = 0 points. An entrepreneur has the self-confidence needed to interact effectively as a professional.
8. a = 0 points, b = 2 points, c = 1 point. An entrepreneur makes decisions informed by values.
9. a = 1 point, b = 0 point, c = 2 points. An entrepreneur is able to communicate effectively both in speaking and in writing.

10. a = 1 point, b = 2 points, c = 0 points. An entrepreneur has the spirit of healthy competition.

The minimum score on the Entrepreneurship Quiz is 0 and the highest score is 22. If you have a score of 15 or more, you could seriously consider the self-employment option.

TRUE-LIFE TALE: ENTREPRENEURIAL FANTASIES

I have a friend I'll call Anderson Stewart who is a masseur—and a good one. But this profession doesn't satisfy him. Anderson longs to own his own successful business. And he always has business ideas he thinks are brilliant. Most, however, are ideas that other people have already failed at. But Anderson doesn't give himself the opportunity to learn from the mistakes of others. He won't talk to strangers because he fears having his ideas stolen. So he pursues his hot ideas with no research or information and thereby sets himself up for failure.

Over the years, a lot of money has flowed through Anderson's hands in pursuit of his entrepreneurial dreams. He opened a doughnut shop on a street in Brooklyn, New York, with a seemingly good location near a subway stop. He worked in the doughnut shop in the morning and in a massage salon in the afternoon, but with the demands of his business he often missed appointments.

Anderson's doughnuts were very good, and he treated his customers well. But there was another doughnut shop only a block away that responded to Anderson's arrival by starting a price war. One Monday, they posted a big sign: "ALL DONUTS NOW 35 CENTS EACH." Anderson had to match their price in order to attract customers. Then they went to thirty cents, twenty-five cents, and finally to twenty cents.

By this time, Anderson was losing money on every doughnut he sold. So was the owner of the competing store—but he had deep pockets. Within a few weeks, Anderson ran out of money and had to close down his store. Eventually all his equipment and everything had to be sold at rock-bottom prices.

His next business idea was closer to home: he started his own massage center. Assuming that he would achieve quick success, he rented a vast space with room for up to six simultaneous treatments. He even hired massage therapists to work for him. But the ones he hired weren't very reliable. When they didn't show up, Anderson was stuck doing all the work himself, and customers sometimes had to wait hours for a scheduled massage. As you can imagine, not many came back for a second appointment. Pretty soon, this business failed, too.

Anderson has since tried other lines of business, from importing and retailing fancy candles and incense to men's clothing. Each has flopped. But Anderson refuses to learn any lessons. He always blames circumstances or "unfair" competitors.

Now Anderson is looking for someone else to sponsor him. But he can't manage his own money responsibly, so why should someone give him their money to manage? In a telling moment, he said, "Well, if I lose the money, it's just the bank's money." That's exactly the kind of attitude that will ensure that no bank ever offers Anderson the capital to start yet another business.

THE BOTTOM LINE

Succeeding in business is an information-intensive art. You need to be willing to learn from your mistakes, not blame them

on outside circumstances. And if you are planning to start your own business, follow these three rules: (1) decrease your sales expectations by 20 percent; (2) increase your expected costs by 30 percent; and (3) if you think you won't have to work hard, don't even try it!

Mixing Business with Love

It seems like a natural idea: sharing a business partnership with your partner in life and love. Sometimes it works beautifully. Husband-and-wife teams, or loving couples without benefit of wedlock, have created some very successful companies, particularly when the two partners have complementary skills and interests. But don't assume that a love partnership will automatically translate into a business partnership. As with most other money challenges, there's nothing automatic about it!

TRUE-LIFE TALE:
CASTLE IN THE AIR—SOLID FOUNDATION WANTED

Unmarried but deeply committed to each other, Louise Howard and David Brenner shared a business dream: to move to the country and open a bed-and-breakfast in a New England seaside town.

This was surely not a grandiose ambition. Running a bed-and-breakfast can be a lot of work, from early mornings preparing coffee and breakfast for a houseful of guests to late evenings when straggling vacationers knock on the door for after-hours admittance. But many couples enjoy the camaraderie of innkeeping, and it can provide a steady, if modest income.

When I discussed their plans with Louise and David, however, I became concerned. It was quickly apparent that they had not researched their business plan in sufficient detail. For example, when I asked, "How long do you think it will take for your new business to become profitable?" David responded, "Well, we're assuming that we will cover our overhead expenses and make a little extra starting from day one." This was terribly unrealistic.

What was worse, the two had also failed to talk fully and frankly with each other about their hopes and assumptions, both for the business and their relationship. When I spoke with each of them separately, I discovered that Louise hoped to start a family with David within a couple of years, something that David was unaware of. And she assumed that, once the first baby arrived, she would stop working, which would have a significant impact on the costs of running a labor-intensive business like a B&B.

I also found that the depth of Louise's commitment to the plan was far less than David's. "Oh, this idea of a bed-and-breakfast is really David's plan. I want him to be happy, so I'm going along with it. But if it fails in a year or so, I won't really mind." David, on the other hand, was passionate about the idea and committed to doing anything necessary to make it work. He had no idea that, when push came to shove, Louise might be ready to bail out much sooner than he.

I worked with Louise and David on the issue of communication. I coached them through several conversations in which they revealed, for the first time, the hidden agendas each of them had. They discovered, to mutual surprise and relief, that they were very willing to compromise and find ways of accommodating what both of them wanted. For example, they developed a plan that, if the B&B earned sufficient profits, they would hire a part-time maid and helper during their third year in business, which would make it possible for Louise to have a child.

I also walked the couple through the process of researching the prospects for their business more realistically. They mapped out the number of competing B&Bs, hotels, and resorts in the surrounding area they'd targeted, and tracked down statistics on the number of visitors who came to the area. They also launched an intensive savings program so they would have sufficient capital to support themselves for at least a year or two while the business was building.

By the time Louise and David pulled up stakes and moved to the country, they had developed a much more solid foundation for their dream. Today, they have been running their little establishment for about four years. It is profitable—not enormously so, but steadily. And they still hope to start a family within the next year or two. So far it looks as though their family business saga is headed for a happy ending.

THE BOTTOM LINE

Open communication between business partners is terribly crucial—and terribly difficult. You might imagine that such communication is easier when the partners are also life partners, lovers, or spouses. Just the opposite is true. When you go into business with a love partner (or even a close friend), the battle to manage your work in a businesslike fashion is especially important and challenging.

Falling in Love Again—with Your Work

Starting a new business or a new job is heady stuff. Every day you are meeting new people, learning new skills, conquering new challenges. It's a bit like a new romance, filled with mystery, discovery, and excitement.

Inevitably, the thrill of those early days gives way to a more settled state. And herein lies the demon. Contentment can foster boredom, slide into negligence, and settle into mindless routine. All too soon, your once-thrilling job can begin to feel like the same old thing, day after day.

When this happens, how can you go about making the job you're married to feel exciting once again? Here are seven practical ideas that can help you rekindle the sex appeal in your career. With appropriate modifications, you can use them whether you work in a corporate setting, in a small company, or in your own business, or working as a freelancer. You'll find that breaking out of the rut at work will also help you reach your financial goals, since a person who is excited about the job will work more energetically and achieve more.

Dress your business in a new look. As we grow older, all of us want to remain attractive, alluring, and fresh. We change our hairstyles, our clothes, our colognes. Somehow, these changes energize us, give us a new perspective on ourselves.

The same logic can be applied to your business to keep it looking fresh and vital. As a freelancer, every three to five years, I hire someone to redesign my business cards, my stationery, change the type of note cards I use, and refresh my business's logo. Making this change forces me to reflect on what my company has been in the past and project an image of what I want it to evolve to in the future.

In preparation for the change, I make a list of five to seven words that describe what my business is (both its strength and its weakness) and a second list describing what I want it to become in the next stage of its evolution. I give both lists to the designers before I interview them. Often the designers' questions during the interviews help me to make my ideas more concrete.

When you change the look of your business, you give yourself permission to change your outlook on your work and your career, and you create a new landscape in which to do it. You are also telling your clients that you don't plan to rest on your laurels but intend to continue to pursue new forms of excellence.

The transformation does not have to be a total makeover. But it does need to be enough to stimulate you to make the necessary changes. And if your clients notice (and comment on) your new fresh look, all the better! This just might give you that little extra kick to make your new business vision real, especially if you are feeling a bit hesitant.

If you're not self-employed, apply the same "business makeover" philosophy on a more limited scale. Rewrite your résumé, creating new descriptions of your strengths, weaknesses, talents, and achievements, as well as a fresh new "career objective" paragraph. Redecorate your office, updating the art on the walls, the books on the shelves, the knickknacks on your desk, and the screen saver on your computer. Pick out a couple of new outfits for work, deliberately chosen to give yourself an updated business image—fresher, more dynamic, more imaginative. You may find your colleagues and clients looking at you a little differently, and perhaps listening with greater interest and curiosity when you speak up during business meetings or at the watercooler.

Pretend each new task is a brand-new job. Assume that each new assignment or task you undertake is a new business relationship, as if it were the very first time you'd done business with a particular client. This change in attitude will prevent you from becoming complacent, reinforcing the point of view that all your accomplishments are really in the past. The result will be a bit of an "edge," a slight sense of anxiety mixed with excitement as you try each day to establish your business credibility all over again, as if for the very first time.

Bring in some new blood. Hire someone to help you expand your business or perhaps to handle the things you hate doing. A fresh perspective on life around the shop, factory, or office can bring you the jolt of change that you need. Someone who is as hungry for success as you once were can spur you to become even more successful.

Change your routine. Take on a project that is out of your league or unfamiliar to you—something that will force you to learn new skills. Conversely, you can give up (or severely limit) the amount of time you spend on old, familiar tasks. This is a way of giving yourself a space for new ideas, new energies, and new interests to emerge.

If you are bored or frustrated with your work, it probably isn't because the job you do is awful. It is usually a few specific things that bore you or make you anxious. How do you recognize them? Here are some questions that will help you detect the emotions associated with things you may want to give up.

- **Boredom:** Which tasks make you feel unbearably sleepy even before you start them?
- **Procrastination:** Which tasks do you always put off doing? Has the procrastination gotten worse over the years?
- **Detachment:** Which tasks are so mindless that you can plan a dinner party for eight simultaneously?

- **Physical discomfort:** Which tasks would you willingly, even eagerly, trade for a visit to the dentist?
- **Rage:** When shopping for business attire, do you find yourself toying with the idea of camouflage fabric?

Once you've identified the parts of your work that you find truly mind-numbing, put into action a plan that will limit how often you do them and perhaps eventually eliminate them altogether.

In my financial training business (based in New York), I gradually came to dislike teaching all-day classes and night classes, especially those that lasted till nine p.m. They were lucrative, but I found them exhausting; my feet, my voice, and my brain would be so drained by the end of an all-day class that I felt as if I were imploding. My dread grew to the point where anxiety about those late-night classes began to consume me around noon on the day of the class and grew worse as class time approached.

Finally, I knew I had to act. I decided to teach no more than two three-hour night classes every two weeks and to divide the responsibility of teaching full-day classes with a trusted colleague (usually my friend John from Chicago).

As you would expect, my income dropped. But my attitude toward work improved. With the psychological and physical burden of all-day classes lifted, my teaching is better, sometimes even inspired. My clients and students have noticed the difference and are happier with my work, which in turn has led to more work but on my own terms and an increase in my income—significantly above the level it had been before the changes.

Let yourself fantasize. Having created some space for new ideas by limiting or giving up something old, let your fantasies go wild. Need help devising creative approaches to your work? Try turning to a successful friend with business experience, although preferably not in your industry. He or she may bring a fresh perspective to your situation and help you view it more objectively.

Over the last eleven years, every time I was becoming bored with my business, a friend in a totally different field (fragrance, cosmetics, art, advertising, or skin care) has given me an idea that I would not have thought of on my own.

For the first few years, I marketed my training business through mailings to training directors followed by a phone call to talk about the services my company offers. After several years, I'm sure I sounded as if I was just going through the motions. And I was!

A friend, who was at that time working in the fragrance and skin-care business, suggested hiring a publicist to place articles written by me on specific topics in industry publications. "Potential clients will read what you write and see you as an expert in the field. Later, when your mailing piece comes across their desk, it won't be an introduction. Instead, it will be a reminder of their positive impression of you."

This approach was much more exciting for me than the old dialing-for-dollars routine. The change not only rejuvenated my interest in my business, but it eventually enabled me to increase my fees and build a nice list of publications that I use to solicit potential new clients.

Stimulate yourself. Your parents may have told you that self-stimulation can make you go blind. Not in business! Here it can help you find creative solutions to your boredom.

One easy way to keep yourself stimulated is to set two new goals for yourself each year. One goal should force you to be creative (to learn something new, for instance), while the other should force you to confront something you fear or do badly (to master public speaking, for instance). Pursuing two new goals each year will keep you examining your business and evaluating your skills.

Share your experiences at the fountain of youth. For many years, Karl Weber has taught every summer at the Denver Publishing Institute, a program for young people interested in publishing careers. He explains his work, and many of the students eagerly engage him in personal conversations, sharing their dreams and excitement with him. They ask for career advice, which he happily gives. He loves this time away from his work, saying, "My visit to Denver always reenergizes me and reminds me of why I got started in this business."

Teaching, mentoring, and volunteering in areas related to your work can lift the veil of boredom from your mind. It may even put you back in touch with the eager, hungry, and idealistic young person you once were—and who remains alive inside you, hidden but ready to reemerge.

THE BOTTOM LINE

Falling in love again with your work requires creativity on your part. When you find yourself taking your job for granted, force yourself out of the comfort zone in which you've allowed yourself to become stuck. Pursue changes that will keep your business fresh and interesting for yourself—and ultimately for your clients, customers, and colleagues. Your reward will be a renewed and expanded sense of satisfaction with your work and hopefully greater financial success

TAKE-AWAYS

1. **Understand the motivations behind your current job.** Do those motivations still make sense to you today? If not, it may be time to consider a career change.
2. **Examine the work you do. Is it meeting all, some, or almost none of your physical and psychological needs?** Remember, money isn't everything; in fact, for most people, it is not the most important factor in work satisfaction.
3. **Reinvent yourself as needed to adapt to changing times.** The person who allows his or her skills and interests to stagnate is likely headed for career trouble.
4. **Learn continually.** You'll do your work better and enjoy it more.
5. **Plan before you leap into the entrepreneurial life.** Working for yourself can be exciting and rewarding, but make sure you understand the challenges involved before you take the plunge.
6. **Research your business ideas before launching your start-up.** Most would-be entrepreneurs underestimate the money they'll need and overestimate the income they can expect to generate from opening day.
7. **Refresh yourself and your career from time to time.** Rethink the work you do and give it a creative new twist or spin.

5

MONEY AND YOUR PEERS

TEST YOURSELF. Do you have a healthy relationship with your peers and money, or are you confused about who your peers really are and how you should relate to them? To find out, answer the questions below—and *be honest!*

Yes	No	
☐	☐	1. Do you frequently compare your financial situation to that of other people, wondering, "What must I do to catch up with them?"
☐	☐	2. Do you ever spend money on products or activities you don't really need out of a desire to "fit in" with your friends or neighbors?
☐	☐	3. Do you ever buy things for your children because they claim, "Everyone I know has one"?
☐	☐	4. Are you part of a social or work group whose members are noticeably more affluent than you are?
☐	☐	5. Do you sometimes feel pressure to participate in expensive gift-giving or social events in order to remain part of the group?

Yes	No	
☐	☐	6. Have you ever been caught up in social competition that involved unnecessary spending on clothes, food, gifts, or other showy items?
☐	☐	7. Have you incurred credit card or other debt as a result of spending in order to "keep up with the Joneses"?
☐	☐	8. Have you found yourself envying the lifestyle of characters on TV shows or in movies and dreaming about ways to emulate them?
☐	☐	9. Do you use high-end lifestyle magazines as a source of ideas for when you go shopping?
☐	☐	10. Is the idea of having a friend consider you "cheap" or "stingy" unbearably painful?
☐	☐	11. Would you find it emotionally impossible to tell a friend, "Sorry, I can't do that with you because I can't afford it"?
☐	☐	12. Have you ever made an investment decision based on a tip, rumor, or "hot idea" passed along by a friend?
☐	☐	13. Are you tempted by the investment "secrets" you see advertised on TV, in magazines, or on the Internet?

HOW DO YOU SCORE? For this quiz, every "yes" answer indicates an area on which you need to focus to get your financial relationships in order. For helpful advice and guidance, read on.

KEEPING UP WITH THE JONESES . . . BUT WHO ARE THE JONESES?

Nobody lives in a vacuum. Your sense of well-being, prosperity, even happiness itself comes, in large part, from what you see around you. If the things you have and the lifestyle you enjoy match up with those of your neighbors, you probably feel satisfied. If you seem to be lagging behind, you probably feel dissatisfied—even if all your "needs" are being met.

Andrew Diaz grew up in New York City in the depths of the Great Depression. Orphaned at a young age, he and his brother lived with their aunt and uncle in a tenement apartment in Harlem. Andy grew up, served in World War II, attended college with government assistance, and became an accountant. Many years later, his daughter Mary-Jo got married to my coauthor, Karl. Whenever Andy spoke about his boyhood with his son-in-law, he always made the same observation: "We were very poor. Lucky for us, we never knew it, because everyone around us was just as poor!"

By contrast, kids growing up in affluent neighborhoods may be very rich (relatively speaking) and never know it, because everyone they know is equally rich. Whereas young Andy Diaz took it for granted that he had to work as a shoeshine boy to earn money to pay for a weekly trip to the movies, a young Richie Rich may consider it "normal" to invite half a dozen friends to watch the latest DVD in the family's home theater. It's all a matter of expectations.

It's human nature for us to compare ourselves with the people around us, to measure how successful and happy we are by referring to our peers. But who are our peers? It's a more difficult question to answer than you might think. In a recent poll, when Americans were asked to rank their income in comparison with their fellow countrymen, fully 19 percent said they were in the top 1 percent! Clearly many people are putting themselves in a different financial peer group than the one in which they really belong.

In truth, we all belong to many different reference groups—potential sets of peers from whom we might derive our sense of what is "normal," "natural," and "appropriate." These groups include:

- Your family
- Your closest friends
- Your neighbors
- People you meet at your children's school; at church, synagogue, or other religious organization; at the mall or in other social settings
- Your colleagues at work
- Your classmates from school or college
- Your children's friends and their families

For many people, each of these reference groups may be at a very different social and economic level. And even within these groups, there's a wide variation: "Your neighbors" may include the couple down the road who are struggling to afford the little house they bought last year, as well as the wealthy businessman around the corner who lives in the nicest house in the neighborhood. Which one is "your peer"?

It's an important question, because so many of the life decisions we make are influenced by the peer groups we place ourselves in. Consciously or not, we tend to pick clothes, cars, furniture, holidays, entertainment options, schools for our children, and even investments based in large part on our sense of what "our peers" would choose. Advertising on television and in magazines is largely designed to foster the sense that "our peers" are buying X product, and that therefore we should buy it, too (the so-called bandwagon effect).

Is this a good way of making money decisions? Usually not. In some cases, the "bandwagon" is an illusion; you may notice that one or two particularly influential or popular people have bought a certain car or chosen a certain investment and leap to the conclusion that "everyone" is going that route. (Advertisers and marketers want you to make this leap, of course.) In other cases, the most popular choice among your peers is simply inappropriate for you. Wanting to "fit in," or simply abdicating your freedom to choose out of complacency or mental conformism, may lead you into a choice that ends up hurting you in the long run.

Still, we're all subject to peer pressure. And following the crowd isn't always a bad idea. Sometimes there are advantages to being guided by what "everyone" is doing. For example, buying the most popular style of music player, electronic game device, or computer may be preferable to buying a different gadget that is technically superior but less widely used. Why? Because the sheer numbers of users will attract the largest number of music offerings, games, and software. Where new technology is concerned, following your peers may be the smart choice.

The trick is recognizing when and how peer pressure is affecting you, and making smart decisions in spite of that pressure.

THE BOTTOM LINE

Everyone experiences peer pressure. But as a guide to wise money decisions, the behavior of the crowd is inconsistent at best. Thinking seriously about who your peers are and how you relate to them is an important part of knowing what you really want out of life and how you can achieve it.

Different Peers for Different Purposes

There is a certain logic to choosing some of your alternative peer groups for particular purposes.

Real Estate: Look to Your Neighbors. Your closest neighbors are a logical peer group when it comes to how you might decorate and maintain your home in order to maximize its value. Real estate prices are based largely on the neighborhood in which a home is located. This truth is the source of the old adage about the three most important factors in choosing a house: "Location, location, location." It's also the source of the old (and still valid) rule of thumb that a prime real estate value is likely to be the *worst* house in the *best* neighborhood. After all, you can always fix up the house, but you can't fix up the whole neighborhood.

Therefore, where real estate is concerned, the choices your neighbors make are a reasonable comparison point for your own choices. It would hurt your home's resale value if you allowed it to become noticeably more run-down or less well-equipped than the other houses on the block. It would also be financially foolish to decorate, expand, or embellish your house to make it far more elaborate than the others in the neighborhood, since it's unlikely you'd be able to recoup the full value of those renovations when you sell. (People interested in buying a million-dollar home are likely to look in a neighborhood full of million-dollar homes, not in a neighborhood where most houses are worth half as much.)

Thus, when making decisions about spending money on your home, it's sensible to consider the homes nearby as a rough guide. Only a rough guide, however; in the final analysis, you alone must decide what is best for you.

In the Workplace: Spend to Suit Your Career. It may be appropriate to consider your coworkers as peers when it comes to decisions about how to dress on the job, how to entertain clients and colleagues, how to invest in your own training and career development, and other work-related choices. You might damage your chances for advancement if you dressed much worse than others in your industry—or much better. You wouldn't want your boss to think "What a slob!" whenever she looks at you, but neither would you want her to think, "There's someone who's more concerned with how she looks than with the quality of her work!"

If you are ambitious and eager to rise in your occupation, a good rule is to look at those who are a rung above you in the organization for guidance in regard to money choices. To the extent you can afford it, try to dress and behave like the person who has the job you want. We are all influenced, consciously or unconsciously, by people's looks, and when someone on the job *looks* like "the boss," they have a better chance of someday becoming "the boss," simply because people find it easier to picture him or her in that role.

Your Children's Peers: Who Is "Everybody"? If you have children, you may find yourself viewing the families of their friends as peers, simply because your kids will judge and be judged based on expectations formed in that group. Be careful, however. Children know the power of the plea "But *everybody* has one!" and will use it to bolster their demand for the newest toy, outfit, video game, sneakers, or even car—and they may not be above stretching the truth. Sometimes, when a kid says "*Everybody* has one!" a more accurate translation might be, "I know three people who have one!" or even "My best friend says he knows someone in another school who has one!"

So when the issue of peer pressure arises in a discussion about money with your kids, start by asking "Who *exactly* has one?" and don't settle for vague answers. And never let peer pressure trump other factors. If you think a certain product or activity is too expensive, too shoddy, too tasteless, too dangerous, or just plain inappropriate for your child, don't be afraid to say "no"—even if it's true that "everybody" has one. (We'll share more ideas about kids and money in chapter 7.)

There are times, then, when it's sensible to consider one or more peer groups as a single factor in making a financial decision. But do so consciously and thoughtfully. Don't piece together a comparison by looking at the fanciest car on your block, the swankiest house, the most upscale kids' school, and the most glamorous vacation, and then decide that you ought to have all those things "because that's how people around here live." Each of your neighbors may well have chosen one of those expensive items to enjoy—and you should probably do the same. And remember, the person with a fancy car and house may have mortgaged his future to pay for it, which is *not* the model you want to follow.

THE BOTTOM LINE

When you find yourself subject to peer pressure, don't rush into any decision. Consider the situation, decide whether peer pressure is relevant, determine who is the appropriate peer group to measure yourself against, and think about them realistically and logically. Remember that people generally try to present an appearance of success and affluence to the world, which may or may not be valid.

When You're at the Back of the Pack

There are times when we find ourselves running with a crowd that's just a bit more prosperous than we are used to—and perhaps more moneyed than we can afford. It can happen in many ways.

I experienced this when I went away to college. Here I was, a poor southern boy from a little town in the Florida panhandle, a backwater region of America, at a northern school surrounded by kids whose parents were doctors, lawyers, engineers, architects, and other sorts of college-educated professionals. They all had nicer clothes than I did and a lifetime of memories I couldn't match, including vacations abroad, summers at camp, and trips to concerts, plays, and museums I'd never experienced.

Even today, some of my friends who work for financial service organizations or who have become CEOs of big corporations can afford to fly privately, maintain wonderfully large country houses or boats, and think of $1,000 as I would $100. I do not try to compete or keep up with them.

Others find themselves running with a fast crowd by virtue of the work they do or the neighborhood they move to. I have an acquaintance named Will who took his family to live in an upscale suburb not long ago. He didn't realize just *how* upscale it was until he had a startling conversation with his eight-year-old son.

Will: "You know, Joey, we're very fortunate to have the good things we do."

Joey: "What do you mean? We don't have anything much. We don't even have our own plane!"

What hurt the most is that Joey seemed to feel that his dad was letting down the family rather badly by not providing a private jet!

Living among a group that is at a noticeably higher economic level than your own poses a number of tricky challenges. Psychologist Emily Stein observes, “It’s hard if you are surrounded by people with a lot more money than you. It’s not fun to be the poorest. So if you’re living among people who are not at the same economic level as you, expect feelings of discomfort and inequity that you’ll have to deal with.”

Stein offers an example from her own life: “I have a circle of friends that includes some people with a lot more disposable income than I have. For example, they might chip in $200 each to buy a birthday gift for someone. That used to bother me, and sometimes I let myself feel pressured into joining the crowd, even when I couldn’t really afford it. Now, after reflecting on the problem, I’ve gotten to the point of feeling comfortable enough with myself and my friends so that I don’t mind saying, ‘That’s a little too rich for my blood. Can you scale back your plans so I can participate?’ ”

Stein has seen this problem escalate among other people. “In some circles, frankly, you *have* to spend to be a part of the group. In some law firms, for example, people play golf. That’s an expensive sport. You have to have golf clubs, shoes, and outfits, and you have to join a club. And many young lawyers feel that unless they’re a part of that scene, they won’t be networking, they won’t get the clients, and they won’t be fully accepted and trusted by their colleagues. So one might consider the spending on golf to be a kind of career investment. But it can easily turn into irresponsible overspending and a burden of debt. And when that happens, people often blame their surroundings, when really *they* are responsible.”

Dr. Stein continues, “I worked with a couple of hardworking European immigrants to America who lived in a fancy community where they were among the poorest. In order to help their son feel a part of the crowd, the parents bought him more and more stuff they couldn't really afford. Eventually, they got deeply into debt, and the kid ended up stealing from relatives in order to keep up the spending—all because he desperately wanted to fit in. As a result, the family was full of intense conflict."

As Stein's examples illustrate, trying to keep up with a more affluent crowd can be very stressful. It's a delicate balancing act that must be carefully managed. Remember, if your new friends are good people who really value you as a person, they won't reject you because you can't afford the same things they have. If you are honest about the fact that you are unable to spend as much, you may be able to find ways to participate in the group activities without getting into financial trouble. For example, if your crowd takes turns paying for restaurant dinners, perhaps when it's your turn you can invite the group to your place for a home-cooked meal, which can be both cheaper and more fun than a night out.

TRUE-LIFE TALE: POOR LITTLE RICH MAN

Judging by surface appearances, my friend George diStephano would seem to have the perfect life. A successful American businessman in London, he has an elegant wife whose parties are a highlight of the social season, two children who are attending exclusive schools, and a life filled with glamorous activities, from summers on the Côte d'Azur to film openings in Hollywood. George's material possessions match his lifestyle. He owns three cars and two houses; his two-hundred-year-old summer place in Cornwall was featured on the cover of a decorating magazine.

Most people who know George envy him. But whenever the two of us have lunch in downtown London, George spends most of the meal complaining about the financial burden he is carrying. George has racked up over $350,000 in debt mortgaging his two houses to maintain the family's extravagant lifestyle. And although George knows that what he is doing is self-destructive, he seems helpless to change course. Every year, the debt keeps growing.

When I ask George—who is a highly intelligent person with excellent judgment in most areas of his life—why he can't escape from this fix, he blames the insidious power of peer pressure. "Once you begin living a certain way, it's almost impossible to stop. We really need to cut back drastically: cancel the opera subscriptions, reduce the travel, quit the country club, probably sell one of our homes. But if we did all that, I can't imagine what our friends would say. They'd probably figure my business was failing. We'd stop getting our usual invitations to dinner and to parties. I might even lose some of my clients. I don't think I could face the questions and the gossip."

So George just keeps spending and borrowing, hoping against hope that some miracle will occur to save him from the inevitable crack-up.

THE BOTTOM LINE

If you find yourself part of a more affluent crowd, beware! True happiness doesn't come from putting up a brilliant façade, but rather from being comfortable with who you really are. When you begin measuring yourself by others' expectations, you put yourself on a lifelong treadmill that becomes increasingly difficult to get off.

Our "Peers" on the Television: Images From the Media

A new danger in which many people get trapped is measuring themselves, often unconsciously, against a "peer group" drawn not from real life but from images in the media. Hollywood movies and television shows are especially insidious in the way they often present lavishly upscale fantasies as images of "normal life."

This problem has gotten much worse over the years. In the 1950s TV comedy *The Honeymooners,* Jackie Gleason played a bus driver living in a run-down New York apartment with his wife; the image of working-class life in urban America was very realistic. But by the 1990s, the twentysomething singles in *Friends* inhabited spacious, attractively decorated Manhattan apartments that not one young person in a hundred could really afford.

When the 1950s movie comedy *Father of the Bride* was remade in 1995, the "everyman" whose experiences in helping to plan his daughter's wedding, which formed the basis of the movie, was transformed into the owner of an athletic shoe company living in a million-dollar southern California home. What's more, the movie showed him being overawed by the even greater wealth of his new in-laws, who lived in an enormous mansion! Is this the typical story of a "father of the bride"? Not exactly.

Few people take these media images literally (although some people outside the United States mistakenly think they accurately depict the lives of average Americans). But it's easy to let them influence our expectations and assumptions about life, generally on an unconscious level. The electronic media have opened up new worlds of experience for us to see and aspire to, and that can be wonderful, but those aspirations must always be measured against reality. If you find the glamour of New York City, southern California, or south Florida as depicted by Hollywood enticing, that's fine—but don't max out your credit cards to pay for a trip and fantasy vacation there.

And don't expect to dress, eat, decorate your home, or adorn yourself the way your favorite TV or movie stars do. Whenever I see someone wearing sequins in the daytime or flashing an especially showy watch or bracelet, I always suspect they've watched a few too many episodes of *The OC* or some other nighttime soap opera.

The print media also contribute to this problem. Every newsstand is crowded with home decorating magazines that show houses the size of Italian palazzos, travel magazines describing luxury resorts half a world away, fashion magazines filled with pictures of handmade couture creations, car magazines featuring vehicles too flashy for James Bond to drive, and "lifestyle" magazines that depict life as an endless cycle of shopping, spas, sports, gala parties, and still more shopping. It's almost impossible to distinguish the advertising from the editorial content in these magazines, and the product and service recommendations offered by the writers invariably focus on items only the richest 1 percent could afford.

Even if you consciously recognize the gap between these fantasy images and the reality of your life, the incredibly upscale depictions in the magazines can easily skew your perceptions and behaviors. If you visit the mall after admiring a magazine layout showing sweaters that cost $1,500, you may feel that a $200 sweater is really rather reasonable; you may even feel proud of your frugality when you buy it. In fact, however, your income and lifestyle may dictate that a $60 or $80 sweater may be the more realistic choice—and one that will give you greatest happiness in the long run.

THE BOTTOM LINE

Limit the amount of time you spend living in the fantasy worlds of TV, movies, and "lifestyle" magazines. Focus instead on ways to have fun and improve your life in the real world where 99 percent of us live.

Daring to Be You

Sometimes it takes real courage to break away from the prison of other people's expectations and simply be yourself. The pressures your friends, family, and peers may exert on you can be very overt or quite subtle. Here are some suggestions about how to keep your pursuit of the Joneses from turning into a costly nightmare.

Set your own financial limits. When people move into a certain neighborhood or subdivision, they often begin to feel obligated to behave like their neighbors, which includes buying the same cars, clothes, vacations, second homes, lifestyle accessories, and so on. This habit is often harmless, but it's dangerous when it lures you into spending money you don't have—for example, if you feel obliged to keep spending after losing a job or suffering some other kind of setback. Make a conscious effort to break away from the pack. Develop a spending plan that makes sense for you, your income, and your life aspirations, and stick to it.

Decide what's truly important to you, and focus your spending that way. For example, it so happens that I'm not interested in cars. And my lifestyle doesn't require that I own one. Dividing my time between New York City and London, I can generally get around by subway, bus, or taxi, and parking a car in these cities is an expensive hassle. So most of my life I haven't owned a car—and when I did, it was an inexpensive, reliable used car (an Oldsmobile Cutlass Supreme, which I bought mainly as an homage to my favorite female singing group). I do run into the occasional raised eyebrow when I confess that I don't own a car or really want to own a car, and I *could* give in to peer pressure and spend a lot of money on a Lexus, Mini, or Prius. I'm sure that, on the rare occasions I drove the thing, people would be impressed. But why bother? By doing without a car I save a lot of money that I can invest or spend on the things I *do* care about, like the photographic art I enjoy hanging in my home. Look at your own life. Do you feel compelled to spend money on things you don't really care about, simply because of social expectations? Eliminate them, and use the money for purposes more suitable to your life and the way you can afford to live comfortably.

Create a budget that ensures you'll always be able to afford the essentials, as well as a few things you really treasure. I've learned how to keep my monthly expenses at a level that, if I were to suffer a serious setback—for example, if I were laid up and unable to work for six to eight months—I'd be able to afford to keep my apartment in New York. I'd surely have to cut back on many luxuries, from dining out to purchasing art, but the thing that matters to me, my comfortable home, would not be endangered. I try to manage my money in a way that reflects my priorities and not those of any peer group.

Be prepared to live with the disapproval of your peers. I've been called "cheap" because I wouldn't join a friend at an ultra-expensive restaurant for dinner. (It was no special occasion or celebration, just an ordinary meal. Why squander big bucks on an evening like that when a dinner costing one-third as much would be just as enjoyable—and much more so, when I factor in the anxiety I'd feel thinking about the waste?) On the other hand, I've been called "extravagant" by my friend Howard, who refuses to pay for dinner at even the cheapest of restaurants. (When I want to spend time with Howard, we take in a movie and share a big tub of popcorn—that's as lavish as Howard gets.) If I were highly sensitive, my friends' criticisms might hurt me. Instead, I've learned to develop a thick skin, which makes it much easier for me to be myself and feel comfortable doing so. Remember, you'll never please everyone, no matter what choices you make, and the only person you really need to satisfy is yourself. In the end, most people you care about will respect you more for having the courage to be yourself.

Don't get sucked into social competition. For many years I was part of a circle of friends who enjoyed giving dinners for one another. We took turns hosting these parties, which were informal and fun—at first. It all took a sour turn when one of the group became an avid cook and began to use the dinners as an opportunity to show off the fancy and expensive dishes she'd learned. One by one, the group's members were drawn into competing to make lavish and extravagant dishes—things like a veal osso bucco that took eight hours to prepare, accompanied by a $90 bottle of French wine. The fun drained out, replaced by a mild sense of dread and dismay. Eventually, the group broke up. If

I ever join a similar group, I'll suggest some simple ground rules: no dinners that cost more than $10 or $20 per person, for example. Chances are good that everyone will end up having a better time this way.

Use your imagination in place of money. My friend Adrienne is quite wealthy (she and her husband own a very successful business together). I couldn't possibly keep up with her when it comes to spending, so I don't try. When it's my turn to host a dinner, I pick an adventurous, off-the-beaten-track place, like a soul food restaurant in Harlem or a Jamaican place in Brooklyn. When I travel, I buy Adrienne a souvenir that is small, personal, and thoughtful, like a box of the candied ginger I know she loves. The time and attention I devote to these choices expresses my fondness for Adrienne far better than if I simply bought an expensive gift at an upscale store.

Relish the pleasures of simplicity. It can be downright fun to live a relatively simple life: having a few nice clothes rather than a closet full of flashy, soon-outdated stuff; spending a few days relaxing at the beach rather than taking a suite at a five-star hotel; inviting friends over for a plate of fresh pasta, salad, and some crusty Italian bread rather than spending a night throwing dollars away at a private club or hot dance bar.

You might fear that opting out of the spending race will cost you the respect of your peers. Just the opposite is likely to be the case. You may be surprised to find that you end up the envy of your friends, who are secretly frustrated by the burden their costly lifestyles impose on them.

Think about characters in fiction who best exemplify the quest for respectability through material possessions. They aren't heroes but rather pathetic, comical figures, like the silly Hyacinth Bucket in the hilarious British television comedy *Keeping Up Appearances.* Everyone in town dreads her invitations—and no wonder: Hyacinth is so obsessed with protecting her fancy china that she terrorizes her guests rather than let them relax with a cup of tea.

THE BOTTOM LINE

Whenever you catch yourself wondering whether you shouldn't spend a little more money on something just to impress the neighbors, remember Hyacinth Bucket. You don't really want her as your role model, do you?

The Dangers of Imitating the "Big Money"

There's another kind of money mistake based on imitating a poorly chosen peer group. It's the assumption that a few people who are "in the know" have secret keys to successful financial management. The idea is that an elite group—usually thought of as "old money," or the newly mega-rich—takes advantage of a rigged economic system to enjoy financial benefits that "ordinary" people can't hope to experience.

Having experienced both ends of the economic spectrum (and various points in between), I can tell you that this assumption is just not so. Educated, experienced people, including those with the biggest bank accounts, make mistakes with money—sometimes bad ones. These people may be relatively well-informed by comparison with less-affluent people, but that doesn't make them immune to the same problems everyone else can suffer. And trying to imitate their financial strategies based on the comments they drop on the golf course, at a cocktail party, in newspaper stories, or television interviews can be disastrous.

Garnered from informal conversations I've had over the years on the beaches of St. Tropez, art fairs in South Beach, and clubby restaurants in New York, here are some of the mistakes I've heard most often that are made by *smart* people—mistakes that "ordinary" folks like you and me should avoid, not emulate.

Investing based on tips. People sometimes try to ride on the coattails of their more affluent friends by buying investments based on tips: "I heard Jeremy say he'd bought stock in that new biotech company. He's very successful, you know—his family runs a bank, and his uncle owns an estate. Maybe I ought to put my money into the same company." But this is a dangerous strategy. Most of the investment "tips" one picks up through casual conversation are mere rumors, usually unfounded. Sometimes they are deliberately spread by company executives or investment brokers who are trying to push up the value of the stock in hopes of selling their own large holdings. In other cases, they reflect real news about the company that has long since been digested by the marketplace. For example, a company announces an exciting new product on Monday morning. Within an hour, everyone on Wall Street has heard the news, managers of large investment portfolios have snapped up millions of shares, and the price has risen from $30 to $40 as a result. By the time you or I hear the story, it's too late to take advantage of the price blip; we'll end up buying at the new, higher price, which is apt to deflate slowly in the coming days or weeks.

Jumping on an investment bandwagon. Peer pressure can also take the form of TV reports and newspaper or magazine articles that promote a particular investment idea. These can create a sense of unwarranted urgency ("Invest now before it's too late!"), which destroys the calm, deliberate atmosphere that's conducive to smart money decisions. In the late 1990s, for example, with stock prices doubling every two or three years, many people became euphoric about the stock market, especially about high-tech companies. As a result, they forgot about the basic principles of sound investing. Seeing dramatic increases in the share prices of high-tech companies with no profits and small revenues, they allowed themselves to be convinced by TV commentators and magazine writers who said, "In the new economy, old-fashioned things like earnings don't matter much!" Throwing caution to the wind, they invested everything in high tech. Result? When the high-tech stock market collapsed in 2000, many years' worth of savings were wiped out.

Not having enough cash or other liquid assets on hand. Another effect of peer pressure can be the feeling that any money you *don't have* invested is wasted. It is not. It's important to have some cash on hand, safely accumulated in a interest-paying savings account. Having a sufficient cash cushion helps you avoid having to sell off your investments quickly—perhaps at a loss—to raise cash in the event of sudden unemployment or a family emergency.

Getting caught up in the trading frenzy. Some well-to-do people like to spend their days doing nothing but managing their investments. Glued to their computers, they continually track the movements of individual stock prices as well as more complex investments, such as futures and options, and they often sell investments within a few days or even hours of their purchase, trying to realize rapid gains the way traders at big investment firms do. Perhaps you've been tempted to try to join the trading crowd. You may have been lured by one of the many "gurus" who offer books, seminars, TV courses, or computer programs that are supposed to provide the "secrets" of being an expert trader, enjoying independent wealth and working at home just a few hours a day. Resist the temptation! Every honest study shows the same thing: that the vast majority of investment traders *lose* money, thanks to the unpredictability of market movements and the high costs of trading itself (including brokerage commissions and other fees). Of course, the gurus' programs *have* created some millionaires—the gurus themselves, who make much more money by teaching others to trade than they ever make through their own trading.

Making investment choices based mainly on their tax impact. Some financial advisers who appear on TV or in personal finance devote enormous attention to avoiding taxes. To hear them speak, one might think that the only goal of investment strategy is to reduce one's tax burden. Yes, it's important to think about the tax consequences of any investment you make. But a foolish strategy doesn't become smart because of its tax impact. For example, many people refuse to sell off investments that have risen a lot. Why? Because they don't want to pay taxes on the gain. But paying taxes on realized gains is a lot more satisfying, and lucrative, than accumulating losses that you may not make back for years—as millions of people have discovered during the stock market doldrums of the past several years. If you have investments that have risen sharply, don't hesitate to sell them just because you want to avoid taxes.

THE BOTTOM LINE

Don't try to manage your money in imitation of what you think the "smart money" is doing. The really smart strategy is to develop a sound investment plan based on your own goals and knowledge, and stick to it, ignoring tips, rumors, and fads.

TAKE-AWAYS

1. **Think realistically about who your peers are—and are not.** Don't allow yourself to be trapped into trying to emulate people with greater resources than your own.
2. **Avoid being manipulated by media images of "the good life."** Advertisers benefit from consumers' constantly escalating expectations and desires, but you don't have to play that seduction.
3. **Decide what material things are truly important to *you.*** Eliminate the unimportant things from your spending plan.
4. **Relish the pleasures of simplicity.** Learn to enjoy activities that enrich your life without emptying your bank account.
5. **Resist fads, peer pressure, and the "bandwagon effect" when it comes to making investment decisions.** There's no "in group" whose financial strategies you ought to emulate; instead, make thoughtful choices that are right for you.

6

MONEY AND YOUR PARTNER

TEST YOURSELF. Do you have a healthy relationship with your romantic partner and money, or is it a potential source of trouble? To find out, answer the questions below—and *be honest!*

Yes	No	
☐	☐	1. Do you feel comfortable talking with your partner about money matters?
☐	☐	2. If you've gotten married recently—or are currently planning a wedding—have you been able to stick to a realistic budget for the big day?
☐	☐	3. Have you had an open conversation about money with your partner during the past four months?
☐	☐	4. Do you and your partner know the basic facts about each other's financial situations, including your income, expenses, savings, and debts?
☐	☐	5. Have you shared your greatest financial fears and dreams with your partner?

Yes	No	
☐	☐	6. Does your partner know about your strengths and weaknesses when it comes to handling money?
☐	☐	7. Have you and your partner discussed how traditional gender roles may have affected your attitudes toward money?
☐	☐	8. Have you and your partner worked out a satisfactory agreement as to "who does what" in regard to money?
☐	☐	9. Are you prepared to deal with your personal finances if your current romantic partnership should come to an end?
☐	☐	10. If you've recently experienced a change in your financial situation—such as parenthood, job loss, or sudden affluence—have you and your partner dealt with it openly and in a mutually supportive fashion?
☐	☐	11. If you have significant financial differences with your partner, have you worked out an acceptable way of living together despite those differences?
☐	☐	12. If you live alone, are you comfortable with this way of life (rather than feeling vaguely ill-at-ease or unacceptable in the eyes of society)?

HOW DO YOU SCORE? Every "no" answer indicates an area on which you need to focus to get your financial relationships in order. For helpful advice and guidance, read on.

BREAKING THE SILENCE ABOUT MONEY

I've seen a number of marriages and other love relationships break up in the midst of conflicts over money. I would hesitate to blame the breakup entirely on money matters, since only a psychiatrist—or a mind reader—can really diagnose the ultimate causes of a breakup. But it's clear that money ranks high on the list of issues that lead to rancor and bitterness among couples—right along with sex, children, in-laws, and too much sports on the television.

The sad thing about money conflicts between romantic partners is that many of them are completely unnecessary. In most cases, when couples are divided about money, it's not because they have disagreements they can't handle. Most often, they never get to the point of discovering whether or not their disagreements are serious, because they can't even find a way to *talk* about them. The resulting silence is more deadly to a relationship than any amount of squabbling. When partners are unwilling to confront or discuss their disagreements frankly, the disagreements turn into resentment and finally into a profound and seemingly irremediable hostility.

What causes this reluctance to talk about money openly? Psychologist Emily Stein offers a couple of theories: "It's partly a cultural thing. Among certain kinds of people, the idea of talking about money is considered improper or unbecoming. So couples avoid the subject so they won't appear uncivilized—in their own eyes, or in one another's."

In other cases, there are more profound reasons for the silence. "To some people," Stein suggests, "money equals love. So if you bring up questions about money, it may mean that your love or your lovability is being questioned. Suppose one partner brings up financial questions on the eve of a marriage. Her intended may wonder, 'Does she really love me, or is she only interested in me for my money?' If a woman's fiancé wants to discuss a prenuptial financial agreement, she may think, 'He doesn't love me or trust me.' "

Perhaps it's understandable that couples shy away from money talk in the early stages of a romance, when people are giddy with the excitement of new love. The trouble is that the passage of time makes it harder and harder to broach the subject.

Imagine a man and a woman who have been dating for a few months. During that time, the man has been paying for everything, from dinners out to theater tickets to bagels and coffee for the morning after. At first he says nothing; in fact, he may not even notice that he is always stuck with the bills. But as time passes, he *does* notice. And as more time passes, it begins to irritate him, particularly if he knows that she earns as much as he does, or nearly as much. Still, he says nothing; after all, the relationship is blossoming, and he doesn't want to be the one to spoil the mood.

You know as well as I do what will happen. Eventually, he will blow up and complain bitterly about his beloved's failure to contribute, perhaps using words that go way too far ("stingy," "greedy," and "leech" come to mind). A minor problem has turned into a major one. Our couple would have been much better off if the man had worked up the courage early on to say something like, "I'm happy to be treating, but it would really make me feel good if at some point you could make me dinner or contribute something to our evenings out." Chances are good that his lady would have gladly agreed.

In other cases, people remain silent about money conflicts or disagreements because they are waiting for a serious commitment to be made—after which they expect to "reform" their partner. This rarely works. People are what they are, and the mere fact of getting engaged, married, or otherwise committed doesn't generally alter their psychology, values, or behavior.

THE BOTTOM LINE

Don't let the first blush of romance trick you into putting your head in the sand about money conflicts with a partner. Better to fight about them *before* the commitment becomes serious than later.

Wedding Bells and the Price of Love

Nothing carries as much symbolic weight in the early years of a romance than a wedding. The solemn act of promising fidelity to one another in front of loved ones, society at large, and even God Himself (in the person of a priest, minister, rabbi, or what have you) represents an awesome emotional and spiritual commitment. No wonder every detail of the ceremony and the festivities that follow—from the band to the guest list to the ingredients in the wedding cake—is often subject to heated negotiations, involving not just the bride and groom but their parents, relations, friends, college classmates, and other assorted people in their lives.

The fact that weddings are often enormously costly only intensifies the emotional pressures. In the frenzied atmosphere that often results, each decision is seen as a portent of the future of the relationship. Is the diamond on the engagement ring half a carat too small? He'll never be a good provider! Does she insist on the most expensive champagne? She'll spend him into the poorhouse! It's a wonder more couples don't break up before the big day arrives.

As a result, for some couples, lifelong financial problems begin on the very first day of the marriage.

TRUE-LIFE TALE: A TALE OF TWO WEDDINGS

Vivien Li is a young woman I advised after the collapse of her marriage. She and Paul fell deeply in love, and they decided to have what some call a "dream wedding." This means a wedding that plays out in reality every romantic fantasy the couple has ever had. Unfortunately, too many couples think that making dreams come true should be a process with no link to reality, including financial reality. As if hoping to create a dream befitting a glamorous celebrity couple, they behave as if money is no consideration, spending all their savings, and then some, on an ultra-lavish extravaganza.

In Vivien and Paul's case, the fantasy centered on a lush tropical paradise. Accordingly, they made arrangements to be married at a resort on a South Pacific island. All the usual wedding expenses—food, music, flowers, wedding outfits—were greatly expanded by the costs of transporting the wedding party to the location and hosting them there for the weekend. (Vivien and Paul didn't pay for the travel expenses of their guests, but this made attending the wedding prohibitive for many friends who would have liked to come.)

The event was wonderful: a setting sun illuminated the lagoon in the background as they said their vows, with palms trees waving in a gentle Pacific breeze. But the excessive spending left them in serious debt.

Soon the bliss of their dream wedding had worn off, and Vivien and Paul returned to real life. Only now real life included arguing over how to pay off the wedding bills, and what everyday treats they had to eliminate in order to get out from under the credit card debt. Buying a house would have to be put off for a while; they'd have to stay in a too-small apartment. Within a year, Vivien had had a baby, making their living conditions even more uncomfortable. Wedding-day bliss had given way to a life of squabbling and tension.

For a contrast, let me tell you about a wonderful wedding I attended a couple of years ago.

Like Vivien and Paul, Lauren and Ben had a very clear picture of the kind of wedding they wanted. They fancied an outdoor gathering, surrounded by the beauties of nature, with all their best friends and beloved family members in attendance. They wanted wonderful music—Lauren is a talented pianist—and delicious, unusual foods.

But unlike Vivien and Paul, Lauren and Ben's dream was tempered by reality. Recent college graduates, they knew they wanted to save money for future plans, including Lauren's further education and buying a home. So with the help of both sets of parents, they established a wedding budget early in the process and stuck to it—well, close to it.

The result was one of the most joyous celebrations I've ever experienced. Lauren and Ben said their vows on a brilliantly sunny June day in the Japanese garden of a tiny art gallery in the suburbs of New York City. Eighty friends and family were in attendance. (Lauren explains, "We didn't want a wedding with lots of people we hardly knew. Instead, we wanted to be surrounded by people we really loved! And eighty guests was a manageable number financially.")

The ceremony was accompanied by classical music played by a string quartet; dancing during the reception was to the tunes played by a small but very energetic and talented swing band. Lauren was gorgeous in an elegant but simple (and not overpriced) gown by Vera Wang. The food included a blend of Asian and Western delicacies, served buffet style. Everyone got a chance to talk with the bride, the groom, and their families, and the evening was a whirlwind of laughter and gaiety.

At the end of the party, just before Lauren and Ben left for their honeymoon, Lauren took her parents aside and said, "Mom and Dad, thank you! Everything was perfect." Lauren's parents will never forget that moment.

What's the big difference between Lauren and Ben's wedding and Vivien and Paul's? Both were wonderful, happy events. But because Lauren and Ben planned their wedding within the bounds of financial reality, they could leave on their honeymoon with a sense of relaxation and joy rather than anxiety and guilt.

THE BOTTOM LINE

Don't let the blindness of romance (and the temptations proffered by wedding planners, hoteliers, catering halls, and dressmakers) transform your wedding from a joyous celebration into a nightmare of debt. Spending lots of money doesn't guarantee a wonderful event.

Uncovering Your Money Values

It's not necessary that both partners have exactly the same financial aspirations, goals, and dreams. But it's important (as a friend of mine once put it) that you have visions of the future that are *essentially complementary*—that is, they fit together and can both be pursued without too much conflict. The only way to determine whether this is so is to talk about it frequently and explore your areas of agreement and disagreement.

Sometimes problems arise because of differences in money values between partners that only become apparent after the relationship has been in existence for some time. I have a professional acquaintance who used my experience as a financial counselor as an excuse to talk about his personal economic concerns. (This happens frequently, just as physicians are often buttonholed at parties by people who want to talk about their backaches or stomach ailments.) In a joking tone, Harry told me, "My wife and I could use the help of someone like you. I'm not so bad when it comes to spending, but my wife is another story. I can't remember the last day I came home and found that she didn't have something new to show me."

A subtle bit of exasperation and resentment crept into Harry's tone. "I sometimes wonder whether I'm working every day just so my wife can go out shopping. And I wonder when she has time to do anything else—if she does!" Then he quickly added, as though feeling nervous about having leaked some of his secret and suppressed thoughts, "But if she's happy, I'm happy." And he changed the subject.

This couple has all the earmarks of a troubled relationship. It's clear that Harry and his wife have different views about the purpose of money and different ideas about how to use it. What's worse, it's also clear that they have *never discussed* these differences. If they continue to drift in this fashion, trouble lies ahead—and not just financial trouble, but broader marital trouble as well.

To avoid this situation, I advise couples to begin having a conversation about money three or four times a year. One way to start that's nonthreatening and even fun is to share your fantasies about money. "What would you like to do if we won a million-dollar sweepstakes prize? How much of it would you save? What kind of vacation would you want to take? What kind of treat would you buy for yourself? Would you change jobs, or take a leave of absence from your current job?" As you share your dreams, differences and similarities will quickly become apparent.

To help you get started in exploring your deep-seated attitudes about money, here's a twenty-question quiz that you and your partner can take together. Set aside two hours in a pleasant setting; for example, over a picnic in the park, perhaps accompanied by a bottle of your favorite wine. Go through the questions together, answering each one truthfully. You may be surprised at some of the things you'll learn about your partner—and yourself.

REVEALING YOUR MONEY SELF—A QUIZ FOR COUPLES

1. How much are you worth? (That is, what are your total assets—savings, investments, property—less your debts?)
2. How much is your income? (Include salary, investment income, alimony or child support, and other sources of income.)
3. Do you save? If so, how much? Do you save regularly or in a haphazard, on-again, off-again fashion?
4. Have you ever been in financial trouble? If so, how bad was it and how did you get out of it?
5. What is your greatest financial fear? What is the worry that sometimes keeps you awake at night?
6. What is your financial dream? What would you love to do with your life if money were available in unlimited supply?
7. How much money would you need to have to feel set for life?
8. What dreams and aspirations do you have for your career? How important is it for you to earn a high salary? If you had to guess, what is the largest amount you will ever earn in a year?
9. Do you expect to go on working until retirement age? If you plan to quit before then, or take time off for family or other purposes, when do you think you'll stop working?

10. Do you imagine that you'll change careers at some point? If so, when? How will the change affect your income?
11. Are you saving for some special goal: a home, a fancy car, a spectacular vacation, to start a business or return to school? If so, when do you expect to reach your goal?
12. How do you handle routine money matters—bills, banking, saving? Are you usually well organized, or do you tend to be careless?
13. Have you begun to invest in stocks, bonds, mutual funds, or other financial instruments? How knowledgeable are you about investing? Do you have an investment plan that you are comfortable with?
14. Are there financial obligations that are important to you? For example, do you contribute to the support of a parent or another family member, or do you give regular donations to a religious organization (such as your church) or to a charity?
15. What is your greatest money weakness? (For example, is there some kind of spending that you have trouble controlling, no matter how hard you try?)
16. What is your greatest money strength? (For example, are you frugal when you shop, careful about paying bills on time, or unusually hardworking on the job?)
17. Describe the happiest moment in your life (so far) related to money.
18. Describe the most disappointing or painful moment in your life (so far) related to money.
19. Who is the person in the world that you admire most in terms of how he or she handles money—earning it, saving it, spending it, investing it, or using it? Why?
20. Do you have a will? What would you like to have happen to your money and other property when you die?

THE BOTTOM LINE

Any two people who are considering a serious emotional commitment to one another owe it to themselves to explore their money attitudes together. Start the conversation with the quiz above. Use it as a basis for talking about common grounds and areas for compromise, as well as how you can work together to try to make some of your shared dreams come true.

Old Ways Die Hard

Differences in money attitudes between partners often grow out of expectations and assumptions that are culturally based. Even in the twenty-first century, many people are still deeply influenced by traditional gender roles. When interviewing people for my television programs, I am shocked by the number of women under thirty who don't think they should have to participate in earning or managing the family's money. In fact, I find that men are more willing to share responsibility than the women.

Psychologist Emily Stein concurs. "Among my patients and other acquaintances, I sense a recent reversion to the values of earlier times. I grew up in the feminist 1970s, when women were proud to pay for their own dinners. Not that I always did! But those days are over. Some young women I meet can't even imagine a life in which men aren't arranging nice things and paying for them. It's almost as if the feminist movement never happened."

There are some good reasons for the persistence of traditional gender roles. Although the rules of the workplace have become more equal in the last three decades, in most industries it is still hard for women to earn as much as men. Thus, some male/female couples who want to live well find that the most practical choice is to have the man be the primary breadwinner. And of course biology assigns the task of childbearing to females, which tends to depress further the career potential of women.

Emily Stein also sees many cases in which couples, consciously or unconsciously, expect to emulate the old-fashioned relationships they saw around them as they were growing up. Sometimes this leads to a clash between expectations and realities. "People still want to live like their parents," she notes. "I worked with a couple in which the man didn't understand why he had to help his wife with grocery shopping and other household chores—at a time when she was taking care of four children and was pregnant with a fifth. When I challenged him on this, he replied, 'But my dad never did any cooking or cleaning!' "

Traditional gender expectations can also lead to other kinds of conflicts. "I counsel several couples where the wife earns more than the husband," Dr. Stein comments. "In some cases, this leads to real tension in the marriage. It's not that the husband is angry; instead, I sense that the wife is often unhappy about being the chief breadwinner. This isn't expressed openly, however. The complaints more often take the form of 'My husband is boring' or 'He's a wuss.' When we probe a little further, the financial issue comes to the surface."

When a love relationship is affected by tension concerning money, sexual intimacy often suffers. I think about my friend Marcus, whose sex life stopped dead after he was laid off. He and his wife, seemingly overnight, grew distant from each other. He isn't the only one to suffer in this way.

As Emily Stein observes, unhappiness about money can affect sexual functioning in several ways. "If a wife is unhappy about her husband as breadwinner, she may withhold herself sexually, often without realizing what she's doing or why. She may think she's "not in the mood" or that she has a physical problem. By the same token, a husband who feels as if he's "a loser" because he is out of work may find it hard to perform sexually due to the loss of self-confidence. As a therapist, I will try to get such a man to see that romance is separate from work. Even if he is struggling with one, he can be successful with the other—so long as he is willing to take some risks in his relationship, and can call on his partner to be supportive."

Of course, there's nothing inherently wrong with traditional gender roles, if both partners accept them. But when people have expectations that fail to fit reality, that's a recipe for trouble, especially when those expectations haven't been fully discussed. For example, in a couple with traditional expectations about the male role as breadwinner, when the husband is laid off, suffers an injury or illness, or simply fails to get ahead in his career, conflicts are apt to arise.

Emily Stein advises, "The key psychological point is that money often equates to self-esteem and power. In any relationship, it's bad for one person to feel completely powerless. If one partner has more money than the other, responsibilities should be divided accordingly, so that neither one feels helpless or taken advantage of. It all has to be discussed and worked out, perhaps by dividing your assets into three categories: your money, my money, and our money. But the specific arrangements needed must vary. What's right for one couple may not be right for their neighbors."

THE BOTTOM LINE

Are you "the old-fashioned type" partnered with a modern, "liberated" man or woman—or vice versa? Differences between these two sets of attitudes can lead to money conflicts if they

are not openly aired. Honest discussion is the only basis for discovering a solution that will satisfy both partners.

Hands On, Hands Off

Many people complain about a spouse who doesn't want to participate in managing the money. Sometimes the hands-off partner is a man who formerly lived at home with Mom taking care of him. Such a person may simply be immature or irresponsible. With counseling, therapy, or the passage of time, he may change to a degree, but it's unlikely he'll lose his immaturity trait completely.

In other cases, the hands-off partner may be the primary breadwinner who has abdicated control because of an unspoken assumption, "Since I earn the money [or the bulk of it], it's up to my wife to manage it." Often, however, the money management delegated to the wife includes only saving and paying bills, not investing or other forms of long-term financial planning.

In this kind of family, where the man is looking for relief from stress, the wife often ends up doing most of the money chores, acting almost as a kind of personal bookkeeper to her husband. Many women playing this role resent the burden of having to make all the financial decisions. Furthermore, it's not an ideal arrangement for making wise choices. The isolated spouse has no one to trade ideas with, and until recently women tended not to share this kind of problem with one another. Thankfully, today there are more financial professionals, including many talented females, who can offer help.

Sometimes, of course, the shoe is on the other foot: it is the man who handles the finances exclusively, and the financial role of the woman is confined merely to spending it. In this kind of family there is often an underlying expectation that the wife wants to be taken care of, especially after children begin to arrive. I sense (and have heard with my own ears!) that, for some women, managing money and raising children don't go together. For these women, money is "filthy lucre" to be kept apart from the precious innocents. So the idea of a mother managing finances somehow seems to be a contradiction in terms. (Having been raised in a single-parent household, I find this point of view quite flummoxing.)

In my experience, women like these require some cajoling to break out of the prison of their own assumptions. But when they do embrace money, they often embrace it with a cool rationale and become eager to learn more about saving, investments, and financial management.

Some wives also believe that their husbands don't want to share financial responsibility with them. This is sometimes true, but not always. In fact, I've met many husbands who would like to share the responsibility of money management with a spouse who is a full partner, sharing in the key decisions about how to spend, save, and invest money. Again, communication is crucial. If you simply assume that your partner doesn't want to have you involved, you may be making a mistake that could lead to real unhappiness and a needless gulf between you.

When I meet a couple where one partner is seeking help for this kind of problem, I urge them to start by considering the underlying expectations that lead to this division of labor. The two partners may need to delve into their individual psychological and emotional histories. Were they raised to believe that money is "a man's thing," or that only women could be trusted to handle money responsibly? They may be carrying around a burden of guilt, anxiety, doubt, fear, or shame in regard to money that is dictating the terms of their relationship. The sooner these negative feelings can be recognized and minimized, the better.

Then I suggest ways to ease the reluctant spouse into playing a greater role in the family finances. One good way is for the hands-off spouse to undertake a single recurring task—for example, paying the mortgage bill on time every month. If this works well, a second task can be added, then a third, so that the hands-off spouse can gradually become more involved.

Another approach is to have the hands-off spouse tackle a onetime project. For example, a wife who handles all the finances might say to her husband, "Over the past couple of years, I've saved a few thousand dollars for us. This money is in the bank, earning a relatively low interest rate. If we are willing to take a conservative risk, what investment can we make so that this money grows a little faster?" Her spouse's job would be to research the investment opportunities and make a recommendation for the two partners to decide on jointly.

TRUE-LIFE TALE:
BE CAREFUL WHAT YOU ASK FOR . . . YOU JUST MIGHT GET IT

When one partner in a relationship takes total control of financial decisions, it can be a warning sign. But some couples make the opposite mistake. They think every financial responsibility must be shared on a fifty-fifty basis, and therefore they force themselves into relating in ways that are unnatural and inappropriate for them.

I once advised a couple I'll call Barbara and Tom Hennessy. Barbara was completely dissatisfied with Tom's lack of understanding about, and interest in, money. She was knowledgeable about their money and managed it effectively, and she was frustrated that he didn't share her knowledge and sense of responsibility.

For his part, Tom was content with letting Barbara run the finances. She gave him a weekly allowance, handled the bank accounts, and made investment choices.

In our discussions, Barbara made it clear how she felt about Tom's "inadequacy." In fact, she used the counseling sessions as an opportunity to ridicule Tom's lack of financial knowledge. Tom was humiliated. Two weeks later they broke up. He then managed his own finances and did it fine.

THE BOTTOM LINE

Financial responsibilities needn't always be shared equally by life partners. The relevant questions are: Who does what best? Who enjoys doing what? Who has the time and energy needed? And is the burden-sharing fair? Money issues can be a source of tension in a relationship, or a mirror of other, unrelated problems in the relationship.

Work for the Best, Prepare for the Worst

Another major mistake many couples make is to assume that the rosy circumstances of their early relationship will always persist. When I urge people to imagine a worst-case scenario and plan their finances as if it will happen, they sometimes accuse me of being a pessimist or a negative thinker. But I think of it this way: if you imagine the worst, and the best happens instead, you'll be thrilled with your good fortune. But if you refuse to imagine that anything bad will ever happen to you, then if it does, you'll be utterly unprepared, and the dire consequences will be vastly intensified.

TRUE-LIFE TALE:
LOSING A SPOUSE . . . AND A MONEY MANAGER

Nancy Parks's husband left her just two years after their wedding. Unprepared emotionally, intellectually, and financially, Nancy quickly spiraled into a whirlpool of denial. She continued to spend money as if Howard's income was still available. She didn't call up the mortgage company and the credit card company to explain her changed circumstances and work out a realistic new schedule for repaying her debts. Instead, she simply hid the bills in a corner drawer in her kitchen and tried to wish them out of existence.

Nancy's model for female financial management was her own mother, who'd always seemed uninvolved. Nancy never heard her parents talk about money, and she saw no signs that her mother did anything with money other than spend what her husband earned. Only years after Nancy's own disillusionment and descent into out-of-control debt did she broach the subject with her mother—and what she learned startled her. Nancy's mother told her, "All through the years when you were growing up, I was constantly saving money from my part of the family allowance, just in case there was a rainy day. Your father knew nothing about it. But if he had known, I don't think he would have minded. It was understood that the money was there for me to use as I saw fit. And I knew it was wise to save some."

THE BOTTOM LINE

Being in love doesn't mean abdicating the responsibility for taking care of yourself. Is it possible today's love affair may end someday? Of course—and to ignore that possibility reflects either a willful denial of reality or a shocking lack of imagination.

You owe it to yourself to handle your finances as if you may need to manage on your own one day, because the chances are good it may happen.

Financial *Folie à Deux*

If you have a free evening some time, rent the movie *Days of Wine and Roses.* Lee Remick plays a party girl, while Jack Lemmon plays an alcoholic. After they meet and fall in love, they gradually become out-of-control drinkers, encouraging each other in what the French call a *folie à deux* ("madness for two").

Translated into financial terms, this image describes a couple that share a serious failing in regard to money and support one another in it. Take two people who are both overspenders, for example. Perhaps the worst thing two such people can do is to fall in love and become a financial duo. The problems that each person would create on his or her own are multiplied severalfold in such a relationship. The two spendthrifts will make excuses for one another's spending and thereby intensify the hold of their joint addiction. They will make plans for solving their financial problems that are really just evasions, such as switching repeatedly from one credit card to another in a vain effort to control their spending.

Breaking out of this kind of relationship can be very difficult. Not only do you love Mr. X or Ms. Y, but your attachment is heightened by the fact that he or she supports you in your guilty addiction. You may even find yourself using him or her as a justification for your own misdeeds: "Oh, I know I can't really afford this car, but I had to buy it to keep David [or Katherine] happy."

THE BOTTOM LINE

If you find yourself falling for a person who mirrors and encourages your worst financial failings, don't give in to the temptation to go blissfully insane together. The ultimate results will be devastating to you both. The best thing you can do, and the hardest, is to say, "You and I are not good for each other." You can be friends or even lovers, but don't entangle your finances together.

Stress in Times of Change

When partners fail to speak about their money expectations, the problem often surfaces at a time of drastic change in the relationship.

Baby makes three . . . or four. Suppose, for example, a female partner gets pregnant, quits work, and stays home for a time to care for the new baby. By the time the child is one year, or two years, or five years old, Mommy's partner may be expecting her to return to work. But she may not be planning to go back to work at all. What's worse, she may assume that it's understood. And as more and more time passes, neither party is able to figure out how to broach a subject they should have discussed openly long before—in fact, before they ever conceived a child in the first place.

The time when a woman is about to have a child and is consequently losing a significant part of her financial and psychological independence requires extraordinary sensitivity on the part of the man and honesty on the woman's part. This is one time when responsibilities cannot be shared on a fifty-fifty basis; instead, most couples find themselves forced to move to a seventy-thirty or even an eighty-twenty basis. Both parents need to expect and accept this.

I have two friends in London (call them Richard and Andrea) whom I admire greatly, not least because of the mature way in which they have dealt with financial issues. Richard runs his own business, and Andrea had launched her own fledgling company just a few months before she became pregnant unexpectedly. Once the surprise wore off, Richard and Andrea were delighted with the prospect of becoming parents, but of course the pregnancy forced them to alter their lifestyle plans. In particular, Andrea decided to put the growth of her business on hold. They worked out the compromises beautifully, discussing and sharing ideas about their businesses and their financial needs quite openly.

Recognizing how dependent on him Andrea now was, Richard managed the situation with unusual tact. Rather than forcing Andrea to ask him for money, he asked her, "How much money do I need to put into your account so you feel comfortable without feeling dependent on me?" For her part, Andrea got into the habit of asking questions like, "I really want to buy this, but I don't think we can afford it—what do you think?"

Thanks to their mutual consideration and openness, Richard and Andrea are now closer than ever before, which is how it should be when a new family is being started.

Good-bye job, hello trouble. Childbirth isn't the only kind of stress that can cause money disagreements to surface. A major career change can trigger similar conflicts.

When my friend Alan was fired from his job, he and his wife, Angela, agreed that he would take a little time off "to consider his options." Angela would continue to work at her job as a television executive, supporting them both. A few months went by. Then a year. Then two years. Alan was frankly becoming very comfortable staying home, walking the dogs, watching TV, and "considering his options." But Angela was on the verge of exploding with resentment.

This dysfunctional relationship could easily have ended in divorce. Thankfully, Angela finally managed to screw up the courage to confront her husband, and after the two of them sorted through their feelings about the situation, Alan agreed to go for career counseling and job placement help. Today both are working again, and the relationship is on an even keel. But it should never have got to the point of a near explosion in the first place. Once again, the lesson is: speak up sooner rather than later.

We're in the money! Even fortunate changes, such as sudden affluence, can produce enormous emotional stresses that test the strength of a relationship.

TRUE-LIFE TALE: THE WOES OF AFFLUENCE

I've known Patrick and Cynthia Rowley for many years. They were a very happy couple during the early years of their marriage, when they were earning an average income (about $80,000 between them). I used to enjoy dinner parties at the Rowley's condominium, where the conversation sparkled with lively exchanges about politics, business, the arts, and many other topics.

In the mid-1990s, the Rowleys' finances took a sudden leap forward. Patrick got an important job at a financial services company, the stock market took off, and he started earning a lot of money. His end-of-the-year bonus was impressive. Cynthia's job as a sales manager for a pharmaceutical firm also became more lucrative, thanks to three promotions in rapid succession. Within two years, the Rowleys' income more than tripled.

All this may sound like unalloyed good news. But even positive changes can bring severe stress to a relationship. After about a year at the new, higher income level, Cynthia decided that Patrick was earning and would continue to earn so much money that she didn't need to work. Although he was skeptical and nervous about this move, Patrick agreed and she happily quit her job, which she had never really loved but was very good at.

I visited the Rowleys six months later. The change in the Rowleys' relationship was stark. Having dropped out of the world of work, Cynthia's sphere of interests had become markedly more narrow. She seemed to have stopped reading newspapers and paying attention to events in the outside world. Over dinner, she chatted on about movies she'd seen, the new things she had bought for the house, and the contents of the latest fashion magazines. Meanwhile, Patrick was oddly silent, unhappy because he had never wanted to marry a woman whose interests were so different from his own. For her part, she'd completely stopped paying attention to his interests.

I had lunch with Patrick a week or two later. "What's happened to Cynthia?" I asked him.

"I don't know," he responded sadly. "She's like a Stepford wife. All she seems to think about is her looks and her shopping."

A year later, the Rowleys were separated; a year after that, they were divorced. Sadly, it seems that Cynthia still doesn't know what hit her. She thinks Patrick was having an affair, which is not true. Now she is living off the money from her divorce settlement, dating a succession of men, and becoming increasing blowsy—a little too loud, a little too showy, a little too snobby.

Must a drastic change in your lifestyle as a couple always result in disaster? Of course not. It all depends on how you handle it.

THE BOTTOM LINE

Whenever your financial status changes dramatically—for good or ill—expect emotional stresses to result. Talk about the implications for your lives and make decisions about the shape and direction of your new life openly and jointly. Don't let change drive a wedge between you and your partner; instead, make it a shared experience that lets you grow closer together.

Living with Money Conflicts

Some people are afraid to discuss money with their partner because they don't want to jeopardize the relationship. The underlying assumption is that a relationship in which there are financial differences is doomed. This isn't so. You may be able to live with such differences, and even with serious financial problems, so long as you recognize them and tackle them honestly.

The first step is recognizing and accepting the differences in your attitudes toward money. Avoid the temptation to assume that your own way of handling money is "right" or "sensible" and that your partner's is simply "wrong" or "foolish." There are many styles of money management, and while some are more effective than others, there's no law that everyone must conform to a single pattern.

Jack may be compulsively organized, keeping all his monthly bills sorted in stacks according to due date and updating his banking records via computer daily, while his lover, Jill, may be much more free and easy with her paperwork, simply tossing the mail in a drawer for sorting and managing once a month—and both may be perfectly solvent and happy. Jack and Jill can probably have a comfortable relationship so long as they recognize their differences, accept them, and work out a friendly system for coexistence. For example, they may divide their joint responsibilities in a fair way and then let each partner manage those tasks according to his or her own method.

Sometimes conflicts arise because one partner can't or won't earn the kind of money the other partner expects or considers necessary. If one partner feels the need for a lot more income, then it is probably that partner's responsibility to go out and earn that money rather than complaining. Again, open communication about expectations and desires is the key—preferably before the relationship becomes a serious commitment rather than afterward.

If you are involved with someone who is engaged in seriously self-destructive financial behavior—uncontrolled spending, for example—you have a more serious problem. Joint counseling may help. There may be things you can do to avoid encouraging or facilitating your partner's misbehavior. But in most cases nagging (or "reminding") your partner in hopes that he or she will change dramatically is unlikely to work. You may have to recognize that some of your partner's characteristic behaviors are cyclical and will continue to recur despite your best efforts to encourage change.

If your partner is locked into bad financial habits, you face a serious choice. If you love the person and are willing to deal with the consequences of the problem, you may be able to work out a way of staying together. For example, you might agree to maintain separate checking accounts (so that the irresponsible partner can't access the other's money). You might have to put your partner on a restricted allowance so that the financial damage he or she can do is minimal. Living with this kind of arrangement requires maturity and commitment on the part of both partners.

Traditional male-and-female couples aren't the only ones who face these kinds of problems. My friend Gerry is a gay man who fights constantly about money with his partner of five years. He dreams of remaking him into his fantasy of what a partner should be. Stanley tries to make the changes Gerry wants, but he just can't do it. Stanley views Gerry as "the problem" in the relationship, but the real problem is Gerry's unwillingness to face reality.

If you are the more responsible partner in such a relationship, you may find yourself feeling resentful about having to be the "grown-up" in the family. This feeling is understandable, but it's destructive. You may be able to overcome it by reminding yourself that you are managing the money in this way for your own benefit and to protect yourself, and not as a favor to your partner. If you find that you are unable to escape the anger, there's the risk that you may become bitter, and that your bad feeling about the flaws of your partner will turn into a poisonous grudge. In some cases, it may be best to end such a relationship. This is the kind of fundamental decision that only the partners themselves can make.

THE BOTTOM LINE

You and your partner may be able to maintain your relationship despite serious differences over money. But you must *recognize* those differences, *acknowledge* them, and be willing to *talk about* and *work through* them openly. Then you'll each

be in a position to decide whether the inevitable disagreements are minor enough to tolerate or major enough to justify splitting up.

And What About the Loners?

When you are a loner, as I have a strong tendency to be, you really need to know your money personality clearly and honestly. Because the only voice you are likely to hear when thinking about money matters may be your own, it is all too easy to lose a sense of balance and become, well, *odd* about money, as certain flaws or unfortunate tendencies become exaggerated.

Over the years, I have been lucky enough to have a few long-term, trusted friends (including my former college roommate, a retired cosmetics marketing executive, and the owner of a business management firm) who are the people I talk to and listen to when I have to make critical financial decisions or when I need an objective, truthful opinion of my own actions.

When I sometimes tell people about financial conversations I've had with these friends, they invariably express their worry that I may be trusting someone too much with information about my finances. I remind them that I have known each of these people for decades. They have repeatedly shown that, more often than not, they have my best interest at heart. Usually each of them sees the situation from a slightly different point of view, which is good. I then get to use their experiences, wisdom, and insights to help me make a better decision about my financial future.

So loners needn't be isolated when making key money decisions. A loner can turn to several different types of partnerships that can help him or her to manage and use money wisely. I like to joke that these partnerships are like a committed relationship but without the sexual obligation. Instead, it's all about the money.

THE BOTTOM LINE

If there's anything we've learned from our generation's movement toward greater openness and acceptance of human diversity, it's that we need to understand and accept people as they really are rather than trying to squeeze them into a mold designed by society. That even applies to those of us who prefer not to march through life two by two.

TAKE-AWAYS

1. **Dare to break the silence about money that cripples so many relationships.** It's better to bring conflicts about financial matters to the surface early in a romance rather than later, when the problems may have become almost insurmountable.
2. **Learn to live with your partner's different attitudes and behaviors regarding money.** If you simply can't, then find the courage to break away rather than sink into anger and bitterness.
3. **Anticipate the psychological and emotional stresses that come in times of change.** Chances are good that they will bring financial challenges that need to be confronted openly.
4. **Talk about your financial needs, dreams, and desires.** Only partners who reveal these aspects of themselves can find ways to pursue those goals together.

5. **Share financial responsibilities with your partner as much as you can.** It can be a lonely feeling to have to make all the money decisions by yourself.

6. **Prepare for the possibility that your relationship may someday come to an end, via death, divorce, or separation.** This may not seem romantic, but it is realistic.

7

MONEY AND YOUR CHILDREN

TEST YOURSELF. Do you have a healthy relationship with your children and money, or is it a potential source of trouble? To find out, answer the questions below—and *be honest!*

Yes	No	
☐	☐	1. Do you feel, deep inside, that it's inappropriate to talk about money with your children?
☐	☐	2. Do you sometimes feel anxious or uncomfortable when discussing unpleasant financial matters with your children?
☐	☐	3. Do you worry that you lack the skills or knowledge needed to teach your children about dealing effectively with money?
☐	☐	4. Are you concerned that your children may be learning some negative lessons about money from the example you set for them?
☐	☐	5. Are you confused about what your child is capable of understanding or practicing when it comes to money matters?

Yes	No	
☐	☐	6. Do you wonder whether the amount of money you spend on your children is appropriate?
☐	☐	7. Do you worry that you may be spoiling your children by buying too many things for them?
☐	☐	8. Have you ever found yourself overindulging your children out of guilt or to make up for disappointments in their lives?
☐	☐	9. Are you concerned that your teenage or young adult children may be overly dependent on you?
☐	☐	10. Have you ever struggled to find the right ways to deal with your children's financial expectations during times of difficulty?
☐	☐	11. Do you give your children clear spending limits or savings goals?
☐	☐	12. Have you and your partner shared expectations for dealing with your children and money?
☐	☐	13. Have you ever caught yourself trying to "buy" your children's love, or using money to keep them close to you?

HOW DO YOU SCORE? For this quiz, every "yes" answer indicates an area on which you need to focus to get your financial relationships in order. For helpful advice and guidance, read on.

YOUR CHILDREN AND THE FINANCIAL FACTS OF LIFE

Getting Past the Excuses

Have you talked with your children about the facts of life? No, not *those* facts of life. They've already learned those by watching

MTV. I'm talking about a topic that is even more taboo in most families: money.

Parents offer many excuses to explain why they avoid talking about money with their children. Which of these reflect things you've said or thought?

"They'll have plenty of time to worry about money when they're grown up. Why spoil their innocence now?"

The implication is that knowledge of money is a form of corruption, like learning about sex. Underlying this attitude is a stereotype of childhood as a time of utter innocence and lack of responsibility. Parents who believe in this stereotype try to swaddle and cushion their children, especially when one of the dreaded D words—disappointment, divorce, death—intrudes into family life.

We don't do our children any favors by trying to shield them from reality. I agree that there's no need to slam the harsh facts of life in children's faces. But there will come a time when our kids need a realistic view of the world and an understanding of what they can and cannot expect, as well as what's expected of them. Rather than hoping they'll develop this realism on their own, it's kinder to help them learn about the world gradually. In that way, they can be well prepared to cope with life when the time comes—unlike the kids I know who graduate from college without ever having been taught how to shop for food, balance a checkbook, or live on a fixed amount of money.

In any case, your kids are probably not as innocent about money as you may believe. Most kids are very aware of the importance of money. They know how you spend money on yourself and on them; they see the amount of time you spend earning, managing, and spending money; they catch snatches of financial news on TV; and they hear the anxiety in your voice when you fret about the monthly bills, the retirement account, or the college savings fund.

Chances are good that your children already think about money; they definitely fantasize about it, and some perhaps worry about it. Teaching them the financial facts of life will simply give them tools to master both the fantasies and the worries.

"My kids love to dream about how wonderful their future will be. I hate to throw cold water on those dreams."

I understand this point of view. It may seem cruel to discourage a six-year-old from fantasizing about a future life as a pro football player, prima ballerina, or star violinist by teaching him or her too early about the practical necessities of earning a living in a competitive world.

It's challenging for parents to strike the right balance between realism and aspiration. When children are very small, it's appropriate to let them dream without worrying too much about economic truths. But when the six-year-old becomes thirteen or fourteen, and the actual planning for higher education and careers is beginning, it's time to start counseling your child about the realities of work life. These conversations will be a lot easier if your child has already learned some of the basics about money and how it works.

"I just hate to say 'no' to my kids."

Virtually every family faces some financial limits. But some parents refuse to share this truth with their children. These timid souls end up buying their kids the sneakers that cost $250, getting them cell phones at age eight, and hiring a troupe of clowns for the birthday party, all because they can't bear to say "no." The truth is that "no" is not such a bad thing to say to a child. After all, they will hear the word sometime in their lives; why not experience it as a child and learn that it's not the end of the world?

If you refuse to accept this lesson, you'll end up like some friends of mine. Because the words "No, you can't have that" almost never come from their mouths, their children expect to have everything they want. When the family went on a weekend trip, their ten-year-old daughter brought along no fewer than twenty dolls (just a fraction of her collection). These parents are raising their kids to think of Mom and Dad as their personal money tree. Worse yet, when these children grow up, they will expect other adults to behave the same way. They are in for a rude shock.

"Why teach our kids about money? They can learn that stuff in school."

Many parents assume that their children will learn about money in school—in a math class, for example, or maybe in an economics course. This is not true. Some of the practical skills may be taught in school: how to balance your checking account, how to set up a budget, how to understand interest rates, and so on. But the real challenges of handling money—how to make it, save it, and use it responsibly—can only be mastered at home. And the personal values that inform wise personal money management must be transmitted from parents to children.

"The truth? I can't teach my kids about money, because I don't know enough about it myself!"

Some parents avoid talking about money with their kids because they feel inadequate about their own money skills. Men in particular may be afraid of seeming weak when it comes to handling money—a source of shame in our society, where men are unfairly expected to be masters of all practical skills.

Don't let your own lack of financial knowledge stop you from talking with your kids about money. You certainly know more about money than your six- to ten-year-old. And there are plenty of good self-help books that explain financial topics in simple terms. If your child asks a question you can't answer ("What does APR mean?"), you can simply say, "I'm not sure, let's look it up and learn together."

THE BOTTOM LINE

Get past the excuses! Start talking with your kids about money. If necessary, learn about finances together. You'll both benefit from the experience. Uncertain where to start? The rest of this chapter will help you.

What You Do Speaks Louder Than What You Say

In a way, it's unnecessary for me to urge you to teach your kids about money. The truth is *you're already teaching your children lessons about money, whether you know it or not.*

Even a parent who completely refuses to speak with her kids about money is teaching them a financial lesson: she is teaching them to be anxious, afraid, superstitious, and even ashamed about money. (That's the kind of lesson my mother taught me when I was a child. It took me many years of hard work in adulthood to develop better attitudes.)

The moral? The most powerful money lessons you teach your children will grow out of your own money behaviors. So the more you can get your personal house in order regarding money, the better job you'll do of raising children with good money attitudes.

You don't need a lot of money to give your kids healthy attitudes toward money. I've found that the parents who raise the most money-smart kids are those who obey certain simple rules. These effective parents:

- **Set clear limits on their children's behavior.** That includes financial limits: "The most you can spend for this is X." "No, you can't buy Y." "Yes, you can have Z, but we can't buy it today—wait until your birthday."
- **Link money with personal responsibility.** In some families, a child's allowance is based on household chores completed; in others, on acceptable school grades. The common thread is that the child must fulfill some responsibility to be entitled to an allowance.
- **Talk about the value of money.** Parents need not share every financial secret; your children don't have to know your income, for example, if you choose not to disclose it. But smart parents talk with their kids about earning, spending, saving, and investing money, so that the youngsters begin to understand at an early age that money brings responsibility.
- **Put spending in its proper perspective.** Wise parents don't treat shopping as a form of recreation; they don't give gifts or buy treats as a symbol of or substitute for love. Nor do they provide financial rewards for good behavior that should be expected—like being polite at dinner or in the supermarket. Instead, they teach children that money is used to buy things we need and that enrich our lives, but that spending money is never the be-all and end-all of life.

- **Treat money and material possessions with respect.** Parents teach by example the wisdom of owning a few good things, not necessarily expensive but well chosen and well cared for. They avoid wasting money on things they don't really need or want, and when possible they clean, repair, or fix old things rather than buy new ones.
- **Know how to have fun without spending money.** I still remember going out into the woods as a child with my brothers and sisters in the winter to hunt for sassafras trees. When we found one, we'd cut a little piece of root to take home and make sassafras tea. Experiences like this taught me the joy of simple things, a pleasure I still relish in the form of strolls around New York and London, visits to art galleries and museums, and afternoons with friends chatting about our lives, or spending time listening to a new recording by a favorite artist.

Notice the common thread that connects all these parental qualities: they reflect healthy attitudes toward money on the part of Mom and Dad.

THE BOTTOM LINE

Remember, you are the adult in the parent-child relationship. The example you set is crucial. Teaching your kids about money starts with getting your own money values straight.

What to Teach and When

Parents who have accepted their responsibility to teach their children about money may still hesitate to begin the process because of doubts about how much their children can grasp. I spoke with my friend Roger Bakeman, a noted psychologist of human development, who offered a helpful perspective on this question.

"Too many parents," Roger cautions, "demand behaviors from their children that aren't developmentally appropriate. That's why it's important to understand what psychology has learned about the capabilities of kids at various ages."

In this field, the key thinker is Jean Piaget (1896–1980). His theoretical framework regarding child development is persuasive and has been borne out, at least in broad outline, by thousands of studies in different cultures.

According to Piaget, the typical child goes through four major stages in his or her cognitive development—that is, in the development of greater understanding of the world. These four stages are the sensorimotor stage (which occurs in infancy), the preoperational stage (toddlerhood), the concrete operational stage (elementary school age), and the formal operational stage (adolescence). When it comes to understanding money, the crucial changes occur with the advent of the last two stages, and we'll focus on these two changes in the next few pages.

The arrival of the concrete operational stage (usually between the ages of five and eight) involves learning how to think in logical, quantitative ways. The classic example involves the so-called concept of conservation. Imagine sitting down with a small child and lining up five marbles in a row on a table in front of you. Now, suppose you say, "I'm going to rearrange these marbles so there is more space between them." And you then do so, all in plain sight of the child. If you then ask the child, "Are there *more* marbles now?" the preoperational child (a four-year-old, say) is likely to say "Yes," because the row of marbles is longer. By contrast, the child who is capable of concrete operational thinking (an eight-year-old) will understand that the number of marbles has not changed.

If you have a child of your own, try this experiment; the results will surprise you. A similar demonstration can be done using a ball of clay; the preoperational child is apt to think that a handful of clay rolled out into a long "snake" has more clay than the same amount squeezed into a ball.

Because the preoperational child's notion of quantity isn't very accurate, it's unrealistic to expect him to think clearly about quantities of money. Most four-year-olds can't really understand such basic ideas as the fact that a dollar is equal to a hundred pennies, or that if you save a little money every week, you'll have more money a month from now. That's why, if you offer a toddler a choice of two coins—one a smaller dime and the other a larger nickel—the toddler will pick the nickel every time.

For this reason, most societies begin training children in math around the age of five or six; that's when most kids begin to be able to handle it. There's really not much point in trying to teach math concepts any sooner than this.

Based on Piaget's insights, how should we expect a five- to seven-year-old to handle money? It's hard for such a child to understand and deal with consequences that aren't immediate. Delaying gratification is learned gradually and begins with a few very simple, concrete ideas. So your five-year-old may be able to understand the idea of saving part of her money today to buy a chocolate bar in a day or two. But she probably can't imagine saving money for three months to buy a more expensive item.

Most people enter the formal operational stage at puberty (around age twelve or thirteen). When it comes to money, the major change at this time is the development of the ability to understand and appreciate abstractions and what-if thinking.

An eight- or nine-year-old can't usually deal with speculative questions, such as "What if there were no such thing as reading or writing?" or "What if race didn't run in families?" (Imagine if a black or Asian child could be born at random to white parents, or vice versa. How would our attitudes toward race change?) By contrast, most twelve- and thirteen-year-olds have developed an ability to speculate and reason about such questions.

They also develop curiosity about what-if questions concerning money: "What if everyone in the world had the same amount of money?" "What if no one had to work for a living?" or, closer to home, "What if you saved half of your allowance every week for the next year?" or "What if you saved the money your aunt just gave you in a savings account that paid four percent annual interest?"

Like other abilities, this ability to speculate often gets overemployed when first developed. Perhaps this is why adolescents are often fascinated by science fiction and fantasy.

This shift makes it realistic to begin discussing career plans, saving, and even the basics of investing with children around age twelve. Some middle-class families think it's cute to get their eight-year-old children to buy a few shares of stock with money they get as a gift from their grandparents or other relatives. That's harmless, but it's unrealistic to expect a child below the age of puberty to have any real grasp of such abstract notions as "common stock," "dividend yield," or "fundamental analysis." By contrast, most thirteen-year-olds can understand sophisticated investment concepts, and those who are interested often manage their own portfolios with great success.

Of course, within the usual norm there is a range of variation that is greater than generally understood. Parents studying baby books sometimes react as if what is presented as typical is morally expected—as if a child who deviates from the norm is somehow flawed. The problem is exacerbated by the natural desire of most parents to want their kids to be "above average." And studies show that 80 percent of parents believe their kids are exactly that. (This is sometimes called "the Lake Wobegone Effect," named after humorist Garrison Keillor's mythical small town, "where all the women are strong, all the men are good-looking, and all the children are above average.")

THE BOTTOM LINE

Don't push your child to accomplish things beyond his developmental stage. If your kid is simply not ready to learn a particular lesson, no amount of scolding, punishment, bribery, or cajoling will make much difference.

Talking with Your Kids About Money Problems

Understanding Piaget's developmental milestones can help you decide how to talk with your kids about money. For example, suppose you or your partner have been laid off, causing financial stress to the family. It's clear that your children will be affected by this event. They may have to do without some treats or activities, and they'll certainly be aware of the anxiety you and your partner are feeling. Under the circumstances, it's only fair to share with the children what you can. But what aspects of the situation can your children absorb? It depends on their ages and psychological level.

With a four-year-old, explain what is happening in concrete terms. For example, if customary treats have to be eliminated, explain that "We won't be able to go to the movies right now. Mommy and Daddy don't have the money for that. We hope it will get better soon. But today we're going to stay home and watch TV together instead."

With an eight-year-old, you can explain more. But focus on

issues the child can personally understand and cope with. If there are things your child can do to help you manage, say so; this gives the child a good feeling of contributing and alleviates the sensation of helplessness that produces anxiety. So you might want to say to your eight-year-old, "Things are hard for Daddy right now. I need you to help by understanding when I have to say no. And this Christmas, we'll only be able to afford two presents. So think about what you'd *most* like to receive, and don't expect to get everything you want. Can you do that for me?"

By contrast, you probably don't want to say things like "I'm worried about paying the mortgage" or "If I don't find a job soon, we may have to move to a smaller place in another town." An eight-year-old doesn't really understand what a mortgage is, and can't speculate about the implications of a dramatic change in your lifestyle. Sharing these adult problems with your child is simply loading him up with concepts he can't fully grasp and can't help you with. It may make you feel better momentarily to talk about the issues, but it will leave your child with worries he probably can't handle.

With a twelve- or thirteen-year-old child, you can explain more of the details on a near-adult level. Handling this with tact may not be easy. When you face financial crisis, you are under stress, which makes it harder for you to keep your emotions and behavior in check, yet you need to be more sensitive than usual when dealing with the kids. Remember that your children will pick up on the emotional tone of the household, even if they don't understand the facts or the logic behind those feelings. Don't burden them too much with complex adult emotions.

For example, don't try to explain the office politics behind your firing, which is likely to evoke your own feelings of resentment, helplessness, and rage. Instead, stress the need for cooperation among the family members and what the kids can do to help: "If you help me make dinner, we can save money on going out."

To the extent possible, involve your children in decision-making at a level that's appropriate to their age. The four-year-old can help pick the TV show you'll watch together; the eight-year-old can help plan a family Christmas activity that doesn't cost much money; the twelve-year-old can take charge of baking homemade cookies and cakes to give as holiday gifts to your relatives. And when sacrifices are necessary, show that you are affected as much as the children: "Want to help Daddy change the oil in the car? I'm doing it myself to save money on a trip to the service station." In this way, you're taking a difficult situation and providing your children with positive, constructive ways of understanding it and dealing with it.

THE BOTTOM LINE

Almost all children are capable of understanding money matters to some extent. But tailor your conversations to your child's age. Talk with a four-year-old about the concrete, the here and the now, and about changes that affect him personally. Most eight-year-olds can understand ideas like saving and sharing. And most twelve-year-olds can grasp abstract concepts related to career planning and investment.

Scaffolds to Understanding

Another useful concept from developmental psychology is that of the "scaffold." This notion was originated by the Russian psychologist Lev Vygotsky (1896–1934), whose work only became well known in the 1950s. According to Vygotsky, children's maturation can become easier and more enjoyable if parents support them in their efforts. A way of supporting the child is with a "scaffold"—a system or structure that makes it easier for the child to learn and master a new concept or a new way of behaving.

For example, suppose you want to help your child learn about saving. This is a concept that most eight-year-olds are ready to grasp, but a scaffold can make it understood faster and easier. One scaffold you might try is to give your child two allowances, one for spending and one for saving. "Every week," you might say, "I'll give you a dollar to spend as you like, and another dollar to save. See? I'm putting the dollar to save in this piggybank in the kitchen. We'll add a dollar to the jar every week until you have enough money to buy something special, like that video game you asked me about." This scaffold supports the child's understanding of the concept of saving even as it gives the child autonomy to make certain choices, such as picking the special toy he is saving for.

Another important concept whose development can be aided with a scaffold is that of sharing. At a very basic level, sharing is a relatively easy concept for kids to master. It begins with the ability to empathize—to recognize and understand another person's feelings or emotions. Various researchers have found that most children are capable of empathy from an early age. For example, children as small as two or three will notice when a baby in the same room begins to cry, and will often begin to cry themselves, as if sharing the baby's discomfort. Thus, even a very small child can understand sharing on a simple level: "Let's cut this piece of cake into two so your sister can have some, too."

More complex notions of sharing that involve understanding a perspective or a set of values quite different from one's own take longer to master. One aspect of the shift to concrete operational thinking at age five to seven is the emergence of the ability to take another's point of view, seeing how the world looks to a different person. A scaffold can help encourage this understanding. For example, to strengthen your child's grasp of the importance of sharing what we have with people in need, you can help them create a budget for the child's allowance that includes a regular gift to charity: "Remember when we passed the soup kitchen the other day? We saw some poor people there who can't afford nice food for themselves. Suppose you put in your budget a gift to the soup kitchen every week? That would help those poor families have good meals like the ones we enjoy. Wouldn't that make you feel proud?"

THE BOTTOM LINE

Help your children develop their skills by creating simple scaffolds to encourage thoughtful, grown-up behavior about money.

Techniques to Help Young Children Develop Their Money Skills

Here are some specific suggestions that can help you with the job of educating your children about money.

- **Give your child an allowance.** Having a regular income, even if it's just a couple of dollars, is a great opportunity for your child to begin to learn about budgeting, setting priorities, spending, and saving. Make it a fixed amount, and consider an increase at regular, predetermined intervals (say, once a year). Resist pleas for extra money or endless "advances" against next week's allowance; a little discipline is necessary if these first lessons in money management are to be meaningful.

- **Take your child to open a savings account.** Between ages ten and twelve is a good time for you or your children's grandparents to take them to a bank to open their first savings account. Start the account off with a birthday check from a relative or other windfall, and perhaps supplement it with some matching funds from Mom and Dad. This should be an exciting experience for them—a rite of passage that symbolizes the "grown-up" way of life they are learning.
- **Make your child save for special purchases.** When your child wants a big gift like a stereo, an electronic game, or an iPod, require him or her to save (not borrow against) their allowance to contribute to it. The child needn't pay the full purchase price; perhaps you can agree on a fifty-fifty split. By watching the savings mount week by week until the great day when the item can be bought, your child will learn about deferred gratification—a valuable life lesson.
- **Don't use money as a substitute for love.** Some parents buy gifts for their kids to show them they love them, in particular, during times of family stress or unhappiness (a divorce, for example, or a period when Mom or Dad has to work long hours and is rarely home). This teaches a destructive lesson. Adults with bad money habits are almost always trying (in vain) to satisfy some emotional need. They usually learned this flawed approach to life as children.
- **Talk with your child about what money means to you.** Within the limits of your child's understanding, share some of the realities of money and life. Are you working

overtime to save money to buy a larger house? Explain that to your child, and she'll learn to connect extra effort with great rewards. Do you have to cut back on spending because your spouse has lost a job? Discuss what is happening with your child, and his understanding will help him manage his disappointment and anxiety better.

- **Be consistent.** Set up clear guidelines about how money is saved and spent, and stick to them. If you find yourself constantly saying, "Oh, well, just this once," or "Let's forget our rules—it's a special day," you are probably confusing rather than educating your children. And if you share the responsibility for child-rearing with a spouse or partner, try to agree on basic money principles and above all support one another in carrying them out.

THE BOTTOM LINE

Money is one of the most important aspects of ordinary daily life. The more you demonstrate wise ways of handling money to your children, the more comfortable and skilled they will be in handling it as adults.

MONEY, LOVE, AND LIMITS

Parenthood is perhaps the only opportunity most people have to experience what's called "unconditional love," a love that's based simply on the fact of the relationship itself. In most families, a child doesn't have to *do* anything to be loved—her mother loves her just because she is her mother. It's one of the glories of family life, and worthy of celebration.

Unfortunately, some parents behave as if "unconditional

love" means giving to their children in material ways without limitation. Many continue this pattern of overindulgence into the teenage years, and sometimes beyond. That may be unconditional, but it's not truly love, not in the sense of doing what is truly best for the children.

Spoiled Kids Sometimes Become Helpless Adults

I've seen the dire effects of overindulgence in many families. The bad results become most apparent when your children grow up and need to manage their lives and succeed on their own. If they've been indulged throughout their childhood, it's likely that their motivation to work hard and overcome the obstacles that adult life inevitably throws in their way will have been undermined, if not crushed. In a worse-case scenario, they will repeatedly turn to the parents to solve the most mundane problem that even a child could solve.

When I was traveling in Europe one summer with my friend Hal, his seventeen-year-old daughter called him one day on her cell phone. We were in Paris at the time, and Brigitte was touring Switzerland in a rented car. "I've got a flat tire, Daddy," she reported. "What should I do?" Hal spent an hour on the phone trying to help her, calling garages, car repair shops, the Swiss police, and so on. Worst of all, while he was working to solve Brigitte's problem, she was on the cell phone chatting with her friends.

Another time, I was talking business with a colleague when he got a call from his daughter complaining that her ATM card wasn't working. "Did you call the bank?" he asked her.

"Why should *I* have to call the bank?" she asked. With a sigh, Daddy called the bank for her.

As these stories illustrate, when kids don't learn to solve small problems for themselves, they have no resources for solving big problems. I shudder to think how these spoiled teenage girls will manage the more serious challenges of life—a lost job, an illness or accident, a divorce—when they are forty years old and their daddy isn't around to pick up the pieces for them. And make no mistake, I've seen young men who are every bit as helpless and pathetic as these girls, thanks to moms and dads who never learned how to say "no" and never taught them to take care of themselves.

By contrast, my friend Alice makes her young adult kids (aged seventeen to twenty) solve their own problems. She knows when she should and shouldn't step in. If one of her children loses his checkbook while away at college, she tells him, "You can solve that on your own." And she lets him do so. Does Alice worry about her kids when life throws them a tricky challenge? Of course she does—that's human nature. But she resists the temptation to take the easy solution: to step in and solve the problem herself. Instead, she bites her lip and stays away from the phone. Experience has taught her that her children can handle nearly every problem on their own. And each time they do, they are gaining knowledge, experience, and self-confidence that will serve them well for years to come.

THE BOTTOM LINE

If you haven't already learned to say "no" to your teenager, learn it now! The parent who steps in with a checkbook or phone call to solve every problem his child faces is simply preventing him or her from growing up.

How the Rich *Really* Do It

Among some middle-class people I know, the tendency to overindulge the kids is fostered by the delusion that rich people hand their kids everything on a silver platter—and if the rich do it, then why can't I?

Actually, my observations suggest that most rich people raise their kids realistically. Young heirs and heiresses often take entry-level jobs in a family business, for example; others prefer to try a different line of work, as if to prove to themselves that they can make it on their own.

A typical example is Jonathan Tisch, a New Yorker who happens to be a member of one of America's wealthiest families. The Tisches head Loews Corporation, a conglomerate that includes businesses ranging from insurance and oil pipelines to companies that make tobacco products and wristwatches. But Jon and his siblings have never lived in idleness. When Jon was a teenager, he worked the front desk and carried suitcases in one of the family-owned hotels. (He wore a name tag with just his first and middle names—"Jonathan Mark"—so no one knew he was a Tisch.) Later, when Jon graduated from college, he went to work as an assistant cameraman at a TV station in Boston. After a number of years in television, Jon decided to return to the family hotel company as a management trainee. Now, twenty years later, he helps run the business.

Jon's life is typical among the really wealthy people I know. There are exceptions, like the notorious Hilton sisters. They may become famous because they end up in the newspapers and magazines for attending over-the-top parties, carousing late into the night, wearing skimpy designer clothing, or engaging in salacious activities that are recorded and end up on the Internet. But these unfortunate cases are not the norm. The very rich, who know a thing or two about creating and keeping family wealth, understand that indulging kids is *not* a healthy thing to do.

THE BOTTOM LINE

Want to imitate the rich and famous? Those who hold on to their fortunes don't spoil their kids. Instead, they give them a chance to experience the fun and challenge of hard work. Try doing the same with your not-so-rich offspring.

Entitled In-Laws

In a well-to-do family, children may not be the only ones who develop an exaggerated sense of entitlement. Sometimes the infections spread to members of the extended family, producing conflicts that can be downright nasty.

TRUE-LIFE TALE: EMOTIONAL BLACKMAIL

Daniel Phelps is a child of successful parents. His father, a television producer, founded a production company that has grown over the past thirty years into a major player in the industry. As a result, the Phelps family has enjoyed a very comfortable lifestyle, including a large, handsome suburban home; a vacation house in Nantucket, Massachusetts; private schools for Daniel and his sisters; and other amenities of the good life.

Daniel didn't choose to join his father's business. Instead, after college, he launched a career as a marketing executive for a small pharmaceutical company, where he has had moderate success. At age twenty-seven, he married Olivia Kent, a pretty young woman of modest means. (She'd been working as an assistant in

Daniel's office when they met.) Daniel's parents generously paid for a handsome wedding and a two-week honeymoon in Bali, and within three years, the couple had started a family, with two energetic and charming small boys. The new grandparents loved the youngsters, spending lots of time with them, and for a while all seemed idyllic.

Daniel had been raised to expect to support himself on his own earnings, and he had every intention of doing so. But as time passed, the financial needs of Olivia and their sons seemed to grow and grow.

Olivia was quietly conscious of the fact that her marriage to Daniel represented a big step up in economic and social terms, and as time passed she seemed more and more determined to acquire and own those things that she felt were appropriate for her perceived financial status. In reality it was her in-laws' financial status that she was coveting and hoped to emulate. She began to overspend on clothes, home furnishings, vacations, and toys for the children. When they reached school age, she picked a prestigious—and expensive—school in their area for their two sons.

When Daniel protested that he couldn't afford these luxuries, Olivia urged him to ask his parents for help. "After all," she reasoned, "your parents go out for expensive dinners twice a month, and they take two grand vacations every year. They have the money. Why shouldn't we have the same kind of lifestyle as they do? We're all the same family, aren't we?"

Daniel felt uncomfortable, but he couldn't say no to Olivia. He somehow convinced his father to lend him a few thousand dollars, which he used to catch up on the bills he had allowed to accumulate.

The situation came to a head when Olivia decided the time had come for the family to move into a much larger home, in a better area, near a better private school. Without consulting Daniel, she toured several houses that were for sale and decided they would need $100,000 for a down payment on their "more appropriate" residence, which she expected her in-laws to provide.

Daniel was appalled and angry. He refused to ask his parents for the money.

So Olivia took matters into her own hands. During one of her afternoon visits with the grandchildren to see Audrey, Daniel's mother, she brought up the subject. Not only did she suggest that the $100,000 would make a suitable "gift" for the couple's upcoming wedding anniversary, but she brought up a subject she knew would make her mother-in-law feel emotionally vulnerable. "We've always gotten along so well in our family, haven't we, Audrey? The boys love you and you know I would never do anything to change that. I would never prevent you from spending time with our boys, no matter what happened in the future. I know how much you enjoy your time with them. No, I would never do such a thing."

The message was clear, and Audrey probably felt it more than she heard it. By protesting that she would *never* withhold the love of her children from their grandparents, Olivia subtly introduced the possibility that it could happen. No threat was made, just a seed of concern quietly planted.

Olivia's attempt at emotional blackmail has shattered the contentment and bonds of the Phelps family. Daniel's parents, understandably upset, brought up the issue with their son. An argument resulted, and although Daniel understood and could sympathize with his parents' position, he instinctively came to his wife's defense. As a result, their relationship has become strained. Daniel's parents haven't spoken to Olivia in almost six months, and have only limited contact with their son and grandchildren. The parents feel guilty for not wanting to part with their money, but they also feel that the money they have saved is theirs to do with as they wish. Olivia is bitter over the "stingy" treatment she feels she has received at the hands of her in-laws. And Daniel and the grandsons are caught in the middle.

It remains to be seen whether Olivia's marriage to Daniel can survive.

THE BOTTOM LINE

When your children are old enough to fall in love and start families of their own, their spouses or partners become members of your family as well—almost like adoptive children. In most cases, this is a source of happiness and pleasure. But when financial misunderstandings or excessive expectations enter the picture, painful conflicts can erupt. Just as you would with your own children, work to find ways to communicate clearly with your sons- and daughters-in-law about your family's economic realities, values, and plans, so that money matters don't end up causing needless rifts. And remember, sometimes it is beneficial to be discreet when sharing or disclosing financial information within the extended family.

Can't Buy Me Love

In many families, parents overindulge their children because of an unspoken (perhaps unconscious) desire to receive something in return. These parents maintain a kind of emotional spreadsheet that keeps track of how their kids repay them for what they've received.

What do these parents expect in return for the gifts they give their children? The same kind of limitless love, devotion, and attention they are giving.

TRUE-LIFE TALE: THE UNSPOKEN CONTRACT

My friend Paula gave her son virtually everything—great clothes, great trips, a fancy car, and all the spending money he wanted. At age seventeen, Tim just walked out the door. He got his own place to live and almost never called home. Today, several years later, Tim sees his mom like clockwork, just once a month—to ask for money.

Paula is bitter and unhappy over the way Tim turned out. In her mind, there was an unspoken contract: "I will do everything for you, and in return you will grow up to be a wonderful, loving child in my own image." Tim understood this expectation (at least subconsciously), and he rebelled against it. As soon as he was able to, he broke away from his mother and reduced their relationship to a minimum. But because he never learned how to take care of himself economically, he is still dependent on her, which deprives them both of the freedom they ought to be enjoying.

Some parents indulge their children because of an assumption that, in return, the children will take care of them in their old age. Sometimes this expectation is very explicit. Many men have said to me, "Alvin, you should have kids so you'll have someone to take care of you in old age." The idea seems to be that an eighty-five- or ninety-year-old parent should be able to live with his children and their families and be cared for by them. The related assumption is that placing an aged parent in a nursing home or other facility is a cruel thing to do.

These assumptions make little sense to me—even from the parent's point of view. I can't imagine wanting to be dependent on family members when I get very old. If I ever reach the point where I need to be fed, clothed, and bathed, I would much prefer to have it done by a nurse or attendant who is trained and paid to do such work. If a relative of mine were stuck with these tasks, it would only produce embarrassment and, in time, resentment on both sides.

I like the old saying "Every kettle should stand on its own bottom." To the extent possible, I believe that most people are happiest when they are physically and financially independent, and kids ought to be raised with that goal in mind.

THE BOTTOM LINE

Each of your children will love you in his or her own way; some will be more affectionate and attentive than others. Trying to buy your kids' love with material things simply doesn't work.

RAISING RESPONSIBLE CHILDREN

As I've suggested, one way of fostering your kids' sense of independence is by encouraging them to work part-time or during the summers while they are in school. Some parents seem to assume that working is a bad thing for kids. Just the opposite is true. Young people who lack practical work experience when they come out of university often have unrealistic life and career expectations that hurt them in the long run.

TRUE-LIFE TALE: NO ESCALATOR TO SUCCESS

Jennifer is a bright, attractive young woman who works as a receptionist at a company I sometimes visit; it's her first job out of college. When I originally met Jennifer, she was cheery and pleasant. But over the past year, her demeanor has drastically changed. Every time I see her, she seems to be gloomier and angrier.

One day I ventured to ask Jennifer, "What's making you so grouchy?"

She replied, "The truth is, Alvin, that I don't know why I went to college to work in this boring job! All I do is answer the phones and greet visitors all day. There's nothing creative or challenging about it."

I said, "I suppose you're right. Being a receptionist isn't the world's most fascinating occupation. But isn't it a stepping-stone to a better job?"

She replied indignantly, "That's just the problem: nobody's offering me a better job!"

Poor Jennifer. She seems to believe that her fine education entitles her to a high-powered job. She also assumes that career advancement is supposed to happen automatically, as if the stairway to success is an escalator, a glide to the top that requires no individual effort. Only someone who has spent little time on the job could have so unrealistic an image of the way the world works. In truth, success is about building your knowledge base and pushing ahead through your own efforts.

I know a couple who paid the rent and living expenses for their unemployed son for over two years. When I asked why, they responded, "Freddie has been unable to find a job worthy of his education, and we don't want him to struggle."

What's wrong with struggling? A little struggling is good for you. It might even help Freddie overcome the inflated sense of his own importance that his well-meaning parents have given him. Eventually he moved back home, still unemployed. Why not? His parents were already taking care of him.

I grew up in a family where it was understood: "At age eighteen, you're outta here! You may go off to college or you may get a job and a place of your own, but either way, you're history!"

When I mention this to people, some exclaim, "Oh, how cruel! Your mother must not have loved you."

Not so. Our mother loved us; in fact, she loved us enough to want us to learn to stand on our own two feet. As a result, I'm an independent person, and happy to be that way. Today I can reasonably predict which of my young friends are going to be strong, mature, independent adults, and which ones are not. The strong ones are those who know they can't have everything, who think before they ask, and who know that "no" means "no."

If your children have the opportunity to work outside the home, encourage them to do so. Monitor their hours of work, and don't allow them to spend so much time on the job that their schoolwork suffers. But five to ten hours of paid employment per week is a healthy experience for most teenagers, one that teaches important lessons about life.

If your kids don't work outside the home, then give them household chores to do. I'm referring here to tasks beyond the simple, basic jobs that children should do just because they are part of the family—setting the table, helping with dishes, making their own beds. When it comes to larger jobs that you might hire a local handyman or gardener to do—things like mowing the lawn, cleaning the windows, washing the car, or helping you clean your carpets—why not hire your children instead, paying them a reasonable amount for their services? Of course, you also need to demand a good level of work quality—and don't pay up until it's achieved.

THE BOTTOM LINE

Sigmund Freud said the two basic human needs are love and work. Freud was right. Let your kids experience the joys, difficulties, and satisfactions of work. They'll grow up to be better adults as a result.

When Frugality Is Excessive

I've warned about the dangers of overindulging your children. What about the opposite problem: being so frugal that you deprive your kids of material things they really need?

The vast majority of parents are fair when it comes to sharing with their children. They provide for their kids within the limits of their income. But there are a few who deprive their kids for psychological or emotional reasons of their own.

TRUE-LIFE TALE: AFRAID TO SPEND

My friend Becky Harling was a child in a family where material deprivation was the rule. Her father worked as an accountant in a government office. He also had significant investment income from a stock portfolio that he'd inherited from a well-to-do uncle.

Nonetheless, he and Becky's mother lived as if they were just one step above the poverty line. They lived in a dingy, run-down little house. They never went on vacations, never ate out, and rarely bought new clothes. And when Becky was old enough to go to college, they shook their heads. "We can't afford to send you," they told her. Becky went to work instead.

Why did the Harlings behave this way? It's hard to say. They'd grown up in near-poverty during the Great Depression. Perhaps this experience gave them a deep sense of insecurity that left them afraid to spend money, even for worthwhile things. Whatever the reason, the Harlings carried frugality much too far.

Years later, when Becky's parents died, she was amazed to discover that they'd left an estate of several hundred thousand dollars—all in trusts that were carefully designed to benefit Becky's three children.

Today, Becky has feelings about her parents that are profoundly mixed. On the one hand, she is grateful that her own children have been able to get fine educations thanks to the trusts created by her parents. On the other hand, she is sad that her mom and dad lived lives of deprivation themselves—and that she missed out on many of the good things her own children have enjoyed, including four years at college.

Stories like Becky's, I've found, are quite rare. More typical are people like the Gablers, who understand the proper limits of frugality.

TRUE-LIFE TALE: LIVING (WELL) WITHIN THEIR MEANS

Michael and Mona Gabler earn a good living as professionals, but they choose to live a simple, comfortable life. They apply that careful attitude toward money to their children. The kids wear

$75 sneakers, not $250 ones; they get a few new outfits at back-to-school time, not a whole new wardrobe; and when they want to buy something special, like a stereo, they are expected to shop for a bargain and contribute half of the cost from their allowances and their after-school jobs.

Michael once said to me, "As Mona and I see it, we earned the money. Our children didn't. So we have the right to decide how it gets spent." Some of our mutual friends are horrified, but I think the Gablers are perfectly right.

Like most children, the Gabler kids (who are now aged sixteen and eighteen) sometimes fight with their parents over things they can't have. Their simple, frugal lives have given them a keen sense of the value of money. Recently, the older son was admitted to a fine university and awarded a partial scholarship. He was rather stunned when his father congratulated him, then said, "Don't worry about the rest of the tuition expense. We can pay for it." He'd actually never realized that his parents were quite affluent.

In my judgment, being *slightly* deprived, like the Gabler kids, is not a serious problem. These Gabler boys are turning into hardworking and ambitious young men—not clawing for money but understanding the need to push themselves toward achievement in life. And they can live happily without the fancy trappings that many of their friends regard as necessities.

THE BOTTOM LINE

Every family must find its own way of balancing indulgence with frugality. Don't be stingy with your children. But overindulgence is a far worse problem—and a lot more common.

HELPING CHILDREN THROUGH TIMES OF TRAUMA

When your family goes through a time of change—negative or positive—it's even harder on your children than on you. You can be sure that when you are feeling highly stressed due to problems in your marriage, career challenges, illness, or other life changes, your kids are suffering, too. After all, they don't have the maturity, insight, and coping skills you've developed.

The last thing you want to do is make the youngest and most vulnerable members of your family pay the price for your troubles. But that is what happens in all too many families.

When Divorce Strikes

A wise person once said, "The best thing a father can do for his children is to love their mother." The reverse is true, too: the best thing a mother can do for her children is to love their father. The best possible foundation for a happy, healthy childhood is a home life under the protection and guidance of two parents who love each other and treat each other with respect and affection.

This doesn't mean that single parents are doomed to failure. We all know from personal observation that that's not so. Some single parents raise happier, healthier kids than many couples. But it is true that the quality of your committed relationship with the one you love inevitably will have a powerful impact on the lives of your children. In some cases, children suffer directly from being pawns in a battle for control or a competition for love between two unhappy, dissatisfied parents.

TRUE-LIFE TALE:
TURNING CHILDREN INTO PAWNS OF DIVORCE

Jane Prager married Richard Cooke, her high school sweetheart, and they had three kids together. Jane was raised in an old-fashioned household, and she maintained those values into adulthood. She believed "the man" should handle the family finances. So in eleven years of marriage, Jane never opened a bill or looked at a bank statement. She had no idea how much money her husband earned, how much he saved, or whether he was investing in their future. Her role in money management was limited to spending it, which she did with few controls or limits, buying clothes, toys, and other treats for herself and her children.

Jane's avoidance of responsibility for the family finances seemed especially ironic in view of the fact that she had a career as a bank examiner and therefore was quite financially sophisticated in her professional life. But she drew a sharp line between business and family, sticking to the traditional view of the female role as she had inherited it from her mother.

Jane's sheltered existence ended with a crash when Richard experienced a midlife crisis and walked out on her and their kids. Suddenly Jane had to figure out her personal financial situation. In search of advice, she turned to her mother and was startled to learn that her own assumptions about the "traditional" womanly role were quite wrong.

Jane's mother explained that, all through Jane's childhood, she had been fully aware of the family finances and had actually helped make most of the major decisions about earning, saving, spending, and investing money. "We never talked about these things at the dinner table, dear," Jane's mother told her, "but that doesn't mean I wasn't involved. It's important, you see."

But Jane was already developing bad financial habits. In fact, when I met her, six months after the breakup, she had gotten deeply into debt. As we discussed her spending habits, it became clear that Jane was spending money on her kids to make up for the divorce. Her kids were taking tennis and music lessons and buying clothes they didn't really need, and Jane said she didn't want to cut back on those because she felt that Richard owed her that. But she was simply assuming that Richard would pay for these things, which he actually had no intention of doing. She was about to lose everything because she hadn't come to grips with her own finances.

Jane had to learn both to control her own desires and to teach her kids to make choices. By indulging their every whim in an attempt to get back at her husband, Jane wasn't doing her children any favors. In fact, she was teaching them several terrible lessons: that material things are a substitute for love; that spending is a weapon to be used to hurt other people; that money is essentially beyond our control.

Is it too late for someone like Jane to change her life? No! One year after the breakup of her marriage, Jane had reformed her lifestyle and that of her children. She'd taught them to make choices: not "fast food for lunch" *and* "a toy from the store" *and* "a movie tonight," but *one* of those three treats. And as for her own habits, Jane still goes shopping for handbags (her favorite indulgence). But she only goes once a month, and she keeps her eagle eyes peeled for sales.

THE BOTTOM LINE

Divorce is profoundly traumatic for both spouses and children. Don't make matters worse by rebounding into destructive financial habits. Use the change in your life to take stock and set yourself on a positive course toward future security.

The Shock of Sudden Affluence

Problems arise in families when dramatic changes cause stress and anxiety. This applies to positive changes as well as negative ones. For some families, a sudden inflow of cash can become the cause of significant relationship problems.

TRUE-LIFE TALE:
OLDER KIDS AND THE CHALLENGE OF AFFLUENCE

Edward Santangelo, his wife Andrea, and their children found their lives turned upside down by an unexpected influx of wealth. They are still coping with its effects.

Five years earlier, Edward had started a sandwich shop on a busy main street in his hometown. His concept was a little unusual: drawing on two years he'd spent as a student in New Orleans, he concocted a menu with a variety of overstuffed sandwiches like those Louisianans call Po' Boys. The locals soon discovered the delicious taste of Edward's creations, and they flocked to his shop. He worked long hours, day and night, to keep up with the demand.

Then lightning struck. A restaurant franchising company scouting for new concepts stumbled across Edward's shop. After sampling his fare and observing the business for a month, they decided to try expanding the concept nationwide. The company negotiated a deal to purchase the franchising rights to Edward's business concept along with his menu and recipes—for a fee of over a million dollars (after taxes).

Edward, Andrea, and their three teenage sons were shocked and thrilled. They'd never imagined that Edward's hard work would pay off so handsomely. With $1 million in the bank, the family felt rich. And they began to live accordingly. They spent $400,000 on a new house and another $50,000 on a series of first-class vacations (Italy, Hawaii, the British Virgin Islands). Over the next three years, the money ran through their fingers quickly.

When I met Edward, his windfall was almost gone. He had about $150,000 in stock in an investment account and another $100,000 in the bank. Realizing that he needed to go back to work, he'd taken a job as a restaurant consultant. It involved a lot of travel and was not enormously lucrative, but at least it stabilized the family income.

The problem was the three boys—Thomas, Michael, and Henry—now sixteen, nineteen, and twenty years old, respectively. They've inherited their father's zest for life and his enjoyment of the good things money can buy, but not his entrepreneurial zeal or his determination to be successful.

None of the three has ever worked. All three live at home, enjoying the benefits of free food, clothes, and cleaning, and contributing little to the family. Henry, the oldest, frankly told me, "Oh, I suppose I'll get a job when the money here runs out. But not till then." When I asked the boys, "Can you imagine working as hard as your father did to build a successful business?" they simply smirked and shook their heads.

As this story illustrates, sudden wealth causes some families to sap their children of the personal incentive and motivation to work hard and achieve on their own. In such families, parental love may turn into unending financial support.

This is a surprisingly common problem. Statistics show that an increasing number of young people age twenty-one through thirty live with their parents. Admittedly, not all of these are spoiled kids of affluent parents. High rents and real estate prices encourage this pattern of dependency as well.

Still, I think it's unhealthy for young adults to feel they can live off their parents' largesse indefinitely. Even if you can afford to support your adult children, don't do it! For their own sake, as well as for yours, teach them the benefits of true independence by forcing them to support themselves.

THE BOTTOM LINE

Any kind of major life change—even a positive one, like a dramatic increase in your income—can produce dangerous stresses in your relationships. When confronted by such a change, take time to examine your life together in the light of your values. What matters most to you? What do you want to change—and what do you want to preserve? Take the time to make thoughtful decisions about your new lifestyle together, rather than allowing circumstances to push you toward a life you don't really want.

TAKE-AWAYS

1. **Teach your children about the realities of money.** Don't expect the job to be done by the school system, government, or the media; only you can show your child, by word and deed, how to handle money with responsibility and intelligence.

2. **Put money in its proper place in your own life.** Your children will absorb healthy attitudes toward money simply by observing your own behavior.

3. **Understand how kids change as they grow older.** Use this understanding to guide how you talk with them about financial matters.

4. **Build scaffolds.** Create simple systems that can help your kids develop essential skills for managing their money.

5. **Limit spending on and by your kids.** Children need to learn that life sets limits, and they need to develop their own skills for coping with them.

6. **Teach your children to be independent.** Overindulging your kids will not foster their love for you; instead, it will encourage them to become weak and helpless adults.

7. **Learn to cope with money traumas.** In times of stress, don't send your kids harmful messages about money.

8. **Team up with your partner.** Talk with your spouse about how you want to handle money issues, and support each other when dealing with the children.

8

MONEY AND YOUR RETIREMENT

TEST YOURSELF. Do you have a healthy relationship with your retirement and money, or is it a potential source of trouble? To find out, answer the questions below—and *be honest!*

Yes	No	
☐	☐	1. Do you know at what age you plan to stop working or reduce the amount of work you do?
☐	☐	2. Have you listed the kinds of life activities you want to enjoy in retirement (travel, hobbies, and so on) and estimated their costs?
☐	☐	3. Do you have plans concerning where and how you will live after retirement?
☐	☐	4. If you've considered moving from your current home when you retire, have you researched and calculated the costs involved?
☐	☐	5. Do you know approximately how much income you can expect after retirement from Social Security?

Yes	No	
☐	☐	6. Do you know approximately how much money you will receive from any private company pension(s) or retirement plan after you retire?
☐	☐	7. Have you begun a personal savings and/or investment program to help support you after you retire?
☐	☐	8. Do you have a specific goal in mind for the size of the retirement nest egg you need to accumulate?
☐	☐	9. Are you currently saving or investing enough money from your monthly income to achieve your retirement goal?
☐	☐	10. Have your retirement savings been put into investment vehicles with an appropriate amount of risk for your current age?
☐	☐	11. Are preservation of capital and long-term capital appreciation two of the investment objectives you stated when establishing your retirement account?
☐	☐	12. Do you monitor your retirement investments regularly and periodically rebalance or make adjustments in them as necessary?
☐	☐	13. Given your age and estimated retirement date, are you financially on track to achieve your retirement goal?

HOW DO YOU SCORE? Every "no" answer indicates an area on which you need to focus to get your financial relationships in order. For helpful advice and guidance, read on.

GETTING TO KNOW THE FUTURE YOU

I understand there are people who spend their working lives dreaming about retirement. Some literally count the days until their sixty-fifth birthdays, longing for the moment when they can finally escape the clutches of a despised boss or simply walk away from a job they find mind-numbingly boring.

I'm not in that category. Instead, I'm one of those people for whom the idea of having no work to do sounds dreadful. This is partly because I'm lucky enough to work for myself (no despised boss telling me what to do) in a field I find fascinating and worthwhile (teaching people about the workings of the investment markets and about personal finance). I *like* my work and I'm not eager to leave it behind.

But my attitude toward retirement also grows out of my feelings about myself. It's important to me to feel productive, to feel that I am accomplishing something and making a contribution to society every day. I need this to feel fully alive. And I confess, I like getting paid for my work. Earning money tells me that I am of some value to the rest of the world—that people appreciate what I have to offer and find it worthy of reward. That's a good feeling.

Still, as the years pass, I find myself thinking about retirement. I'm working as hard as ever, and I have no immediate plans to slow down. But I'm starting to change physically. I'm feeling a little less energetic on some days, with less stamina than I used to have. Evening lectures and all-day classes that I once sailed through are becoming more challenging. It's clear to me that I won't be able to work at the same high level of intensity forever. One day in the not-so-distant future, I will want to cut back on the amount of work I do. I'll probably retire in stages rather than all at once; I may even continue to work at least part-time until the day I die (or until they drag me away kicking and screaming from one of the classes I love teaching!). But retirement in some form has become visible in my future.

So when I think about retirement today, I am imagining how

I will feel and what I will need and want twenty or twenty-five years from now. In a sense, planning for retirement is like creating a relationship with a new me, a person who doesn't yet exist but who will exist in the future. The question is, who will that retired Alvin of age seventy be? Will he be struggling to get by, desperately piecing together pension payments, Social Security checks, shrinking book royalties, and investment income to pay his rent and his doctor's bills? Or will he be living a comfortable life, enjoying old age, able to travel, socialize, and pamper himself (just a little) without worrying about next month's bills?

The decisions I make today will determine the answer to this question. And the same, of course, is true about you, whether your retirement is ten, thirty, or fifty years in the future. You should not be lethargic or complacent about the financial aspects related to your retirement. Planning for retirement is not something you should put on autopilot and hope for a financially secure landing. Research shows that far too many Americans sign up for and then essentially ignore their retirement plans, whether in the form of pensions or company 401(k) plans, or else hope that someone will be able to help them figure out what's best when the time comes.

So how do you begin thinking about and being proactive now about that hard-to-imagine future you? The following set of questions, titled "Your Retirement Dreams," will help you. If you are in a marriage or another long-term relationship, answer the questions together with your partner. Otherwise, complete them yourself. It's a useful first step to making realistic plans for your life beyond work.

YOUR RETIREMENT DREAMS

1. Do you hope to quit your full-time employment one day? If so, when?
2. After you retire from your full-time employment, do you plan to continue working on a part-time basis or in some new career? If so, what do you estimate as your monthly retirement income? Be conservative. (For every question in this quiz, use current money values without considering the effects of inflation.)
3. Where would you like to live after you retire? Will you remain in your present home or move? If you plan to remain in your present home, when will the mortgage and any secondary home equity debt be paid off? How much money will be freed up each month once your mortgage is paid off?
4. If you are hoping to move after retirement, where would you like to live? Have you begun exploring the realities of such a move, such as housing costs, living expenses, taxes, the cost of travel (to visit family and friends), and so on? Can you realistically estimate the difference between the amount you are spending on housing now and the amount you will spend after retirement?
5. Do you dream about traveling after retirement? If so, where and how often would you like to travel? List your preferred destinations.
6. If travel is one of your retirement dreams, what form of travel do you picture—first class, with luxury accommodations; roughing it by camping out amid natural beauty; or something in between (like the group tours run by the Elderhostel program)? Have you begun exploring the costs involved in your preferred form of travel?
7. What kinds of activities would you like to enjoy during your retirement years? These may include sports, hobbies, visiting with family and friends, charitable or civic activities, artistic endeavors, and other activities. List them.
8. Are the activities you've listed ones that you are already engaged in? If not, have you researched the costs and other requirements for participating? Are you certain they will be enjoyable and rewarding for you?

(continued)

YOUR RETIREMENT DREAMS (cont.)

9. What is your current health status? Do you have any chronic health conditions that limit your activity or require regular medical attention?

10. Do you want to make regular gifts or financial contributions to your children, grandchildren, or other relatives after retirement? Does charitable giving to religious, social, arts, educational, or other organizations play a significant role in your life? If the answer to either of these questions is "yes," what are the annual amounts you would like to be able to give?

11. Have you estimated the amount of monthly income you will need to support the retirement lifestyle you are dreaming of? If so, what is that amount?

12. Have you checked into the amount of income you can expect to receive from Social Security? If so, what is that amount? Do you know at what age you want the payments to begin?

13. Are you eligible for a company pension or retirement pay provided by your current employer? If so, have you verified the kinds of payments you can expect from this pension? If so, what kind of monthly income is this pension likely to produce during your retirement years?

14. Are you eligible for any company pensions provided by past employers? If so, how much monthly income will these produce?

15. Have you begun saving in a personal retirement plan? If so, how much money have you accumulated? How much can you reasonably expect to save between now and when you retire? And how much monthly income will your savings produce after you retire?

16. What's the sum of the figures you calculated to answer questions 12 through 15? How does it compare with the answer to question 11? Are you on track to be able to live your retirement dreams, or is there a financial gap that needs to be filled?

The answers to these questions can tell a lot about the future you. Questions 1 through 10 will help you picture the kind of lifestyle you hope to enjoy after you retire. They can also help you recognize whether or not you've begun the necessary realistic thinking, planning, and research to understand what your dreams would *really* be like to live. If not, now is an excellent time to start!

Question 11 asks you to estimate what it will cost to live the retirement life you've imagined. If you can't gather all the information you need to calculate your future monthly expenses, you can use the widely accepted figure of three-quarters (75 percent) of your current, after-tax preretirement income as a rough estimate of the amount of money you are likely to need in retirement. So, if your current, after-tax monthly income is $7,000, you can estimate your required retirement income as 7,000 x 0.75 = 5,250, or $5,250 per month.

This is only an approximation, of course. While 75 percent is a widely accepted rule of thumb, you may decide you need more or less, depending on your circumstances. Any special plans for travel, expensive activities like subscriptions to the opera, or frequent outings with your kids, or regular charitable giving will increase the amount you need.

Questions 12 through 15 will help you estimate how much retirement income you can currently expect. Again, the calculations here may not be easy. The administrators of your company retirement plan or the financial firm to which you plan to transfer (or more common, roll over) your retirement funds can help you with questions 13 and 14. If you've also begun saving or investing for retirement on your own, then your banker, broker, or other financial adviser can help you with question 15.

Don't be overly optimistic in estimating either the amount you will save between now and retirement or the amount of growth your savings or investments will experience. If you've managed to put away around $3,000 each year for the past five years, for example, don't assume that you will suddenly start saving $10,000 each year—unless your salary goes up tremendously or you're prepared to make serious changes in your current lifestyle to make that possible.

Finally, question 16 asks you to compare your expected retirement income (based on current plans) with the amount you'll probably need to live the life of your dreams. I hope the result isn't too shocking. But don't be surprised if there's a gap between what you need and what you have on hand. Most people drastically underestimate the amount of money they will need for retirement. The challenge now is what to do about it.

As the philosopher Henry David Thoreau once put it, "Do not worry if you have built your castles in the air. That is where they should be. Now put the foundations under them."

THE BOTTOM LINE

Whether retirement is decades away or just around the corner, now is a good time to begin planning for it. The process starts with imagining what your life after work could be like, then taking stock of what will be required to make it into a reality. Be proactive in both your thinking and the actions you take with your money.

Getting Real About Your Dreams

An important purpose of the Retirement Dreams questionnaire is to force you to become very specific about what you'd like to do in your postwork life. Many people have vague hopes and desires for their golden years, which they've been too busy or perhaps too intimidated to transform into concrete, fact-based plans. They like to imagine themselves cruising the Caribbean in a sailboat, but they've never bothered to investigate the actual costs, risk, and challenges involved (they may not even have learned how to hoist a sail!). They fantasize about owning a home in a foreign country, having heard or read that "It's amazingly cheap to live in Portugal" (or Costa Rica, or Mexico . . .), but they've never actually researched the practical difficulties: acquiring the property, supervising renovations, getting visas, moving a houseful of furniture, even mastering a foreign language.

The questions I've asked are designed to uncover these gaps in your knowledge and help you (and your partner, if you have one) start exploring the realities that need to be considered if your dreams are to become reality.

TRUE-LIFE TALE: RETIREMENT DREAM . . . OR NIGHTMARE?

I once worked with a couple I'll call Charles and Julie Fowler. In their midfifties, the Fowlers were a fun and loving couple, having been married for thirty years and having raised two children to adult independence. But they were in very different places, psychologically and physically, when it came to planning retirement.

Julie was still immersed in the daily routine of employment, working hard as an administrator at a local insurance company. Charles, however, was already semi-retired, having cut back to twenty hours a week in his job as a taxi dispatcher. And when he wasn't on the job, Charles was hatching dreams of complete retirement . . . including an escape from their home in Brooklyn to a condo on a golf course in Boca Raton, Florida. He collected colorful brochures from real estate companies filled with photos of beautiful homes with sun-drenched patios being enjoyed by handsome and youthful white-haired couples. And he constantly peppered Julie with questions and suggestions: "This Internet site has a great apartment that fronts on the lake and backs on the golf course, and it costs just $350,000. What do you think? Shall we contact a broker and talk about buying it?"

Julie agreed that the idea of life under sunny southern skies was appealing. But she wasn't ready to sign on to Charles's dreams just yet. For one thing, she enjoyed her job. She'd worked at the insurance firm for ten years, liked the people there, and had fun getting away from the house every day. For another, she knew that she and Charles still needed her salary. They'd managed to accumulate in their company retirement plans about $400,000, which they had invested in a mixture of stock and bond mutual funds—not a bad start for a retirement fund, but far from what they'd need to support themselves for twenty years or more.

Finally, there was the personal and psychological side of the equation. Julie loved Charles dearly, but she knew that he wasn't the most practical man in the world. She managed the monthly bills and handled the family's checking and savings accounts, in part because they both recognized that she did a far better job than the dreamy and sometimes distracted Charles would have done. Although she hadn't done as much research into South Florida as Charles, she strongly suspected that some of his fantasies about retirement life were more than a bit unrealistic. Yet Charles was putting increasing pressure on Julie to chuck in her job and put their house in Brooklyn on the market.

It was at this point that the Fowlers turned to me for guidance.

"Slow down" was the first suggestion I made. "Starting a new life in a different city is one of life's big decisions, not something to do on a whim." I urged the Fowlers to take some time doing research into what life in South Florida would really be like for the two of them. I suggested that they visit the area for as long as possible—at least a couple of weeks—renting an apartment, if possible, rather than a hotel room, so they could get a more realistic sense as to what daily activities, which they took for granted in Brooklyn—getting around town, shopping, taking care of routine medical needs, and meeting other people—would be like.

I also urged them to think seriously about the real costs of a move to Boca Raton and other cities or towns nearby. What kind of town house or apartment could they really afford, once the costs of selling their Brooklyn home were accounted for? How much would it cost to pack and ship their furniture to Florida? How many times a year would they want to travel back to Brooklyn to visit their children and grandchildren, and how much would this cost? It's easy to overlook such realities when daydreaming about a move, but such costs and inconveniences can turn a pleasant fantasy into a real difficulty.

Finally, I suggested that they have a serious talk about how comfortable Julie, the family's "organizer" and "controller," would feel about moving to a new and unfamiliar town at the instigation of her husband. Would she suddenly feel as if she were no longer independent and thus too dependent on Charles, the happy-go-lucky and somewhat unreliable member of the marital team? And would she be happy, or at least content, to live like this?

When I last spoke with the Fowlers, they'd put the idea of moving to Boca on hold, at least temporarily. Julie and Charles had planned a couple of holiday visits to other cities in south

Florida, and they'd begun researching real estate and travel costs together. Whatever plans they ultimately make will have a better chance of proving successful now that husband and wife are working on them together with their eyes wide open and considering each person's emotional needs.

THE BOTTOM LINE

Don't fall into the trap of thinking that retirement is like a vacation that never ends. Whereas a vacation trip is a pleasant (and usually costly) escape from reality, retirement is about creating a new reality that you can afford to live with happily for years and even decades. Avoid choosing a retirement lifestyle on a whim, lured by tourism brochures and glossy photos. Instead, take the time to do research into the nuts and bolts of any change you are considering and be certain it is right for you.

Putting a Price Tag on Your Dreams

Once you've fleshed out your retirement dreams, the next step is to develop a savings program based on realistic projections of investment growth and your needs. The amount you will need in order to retire comfortably is probably greater than you may have assumed.

How do you calculate the amount you'll need to save? Here's a simple example.

Stuart and Eileen Collins are a married couple aged forty-five and fifty-one, respectively. They both work, Eileen as a midlevel corporate manager with an annual income of $65,000, Stuart as a pharmaceutical sales rep earning $55,000 per year. Eileen hopes either to stop working or drastically reduce her workload around the time she turns sixty-five, which is the same time they will finish paying off their home mortgage. Stuart may or may not continue working at that point (he'll be fifty-nine then). The Collinses' best estimate is that they will need about 75 percent of their current income after they retire—that is, about $90,000 (since $120,000 x 0.75 = $90,000).

The Collinses will want to be able to live entirely on their income rather than spending part of their savings each year. So now they need to consider the amount of income they can expect.

First, the Collinses need to visit the Social Security Administrations website—or call the office in their area—to find out what their monthly payments will be. The amount that's forecast based on their past earnings and a projected retirement date of sixty-five is about $29,000 annually for the two of them.

Second, they consult with a financial adviser who specializes in retirement planning to determine what they should do with the money accumulated in their companies' 401(k) plans. She recommends investing it conservatively in income-paying securities—that is, a portfolio of stocks and bonds that produce reliable dividend and interest payments over time. Their adviser calculates that the portfolio will generate an income of approximately $36,000 per year.

Thus, the total income from their 401(k) investments and Social Security will be approximately $65,000 per year, leaving a gap of $25,000 that the Collinses need to fill from savings. How large a nest egg will it take to produce that amount of income?

Here is where some economic guesswork is needed. Let's suppose that, on retirement, the Collinses can put their savings into an investment fund that grows by around 5 percent per year. (This is a reasonably conservative assumption.) To calculate the size of the nest egg needed to produce the $25,000 they need, the Collinses have to do a little math. Here's the formula:

- X is the size of the nest egg the Collinses will need
- 0.05 is the annual growth rate the Collinses are assuming for their money (0.05 is the same as 5 percent)
- $25,000 is the annual income they want
- X times 0.05 = $25,000
- To find the value of X, divide both sides of the equation by 0.05
- So X = $25,000 divided by 0.05
- Using a calculator to divide $25,000 by 0.05, the Collinses find that X = $500,000

So to produce the annual income they want, the Collinses need to save an additional $500,000 or increase their contributions to their 401(k) plan until the larger nest egg has been built.

You can calculate the size of the nest egg you'll need by following the same steps. In place of $25,000 in the formula, substitute the amount of annual income you need to generate for your retirement. You can use the same 5 percent growth assumption (0.05) or change it; for example, to make the formula even more conservative and cautious, you could assume 4 percent growth (0.04). Use a calculator to do the necessary division, and you'll come up with the amount, in dollars, that you need to save to generate the annual income you want.

THE BOTTOM LINE

The process of figuring out how much money you need to save in order to enjoy the retirement you want can be a bit daunting. Not because the math is complicated—as the example demon-

strates, it's actually fairly simple—but because it is scary to see the price tag of your dreams reduced to an unyielding, black-and-white number. Don't be afraid. Go ahead and do the calculation. Once you know the height of the mountain you need to climb, you can begin developing realistic plans for achieving the summit. One thing is sure: unless you know your destination, the odds of reaching it are very poor.

Creating Your Retirement Savings Program . . . and Sticking to It

If you're a bit startled by the size of the sum you calculated in the last section, you're not alone. Almost everyone is shocked by the amount of money needed to ensure a comfortable, happy retirement. I've been working to build my own investment nest egg for over nearly two decades now, and I still have occasional sleepless nights about it.

Based on my own calculations, I decided that I need to save a little more 25 percent (one-quarter) of my after-tax income toward retirement. Does this sound like a lot? Maybe it is, but when I talk to individuals and couples about their own financial plans, I find that many of them have reached a similar conclusion. It means that most people need either to cut back on their spending (so they can live on 75 percent, or three-quarters, of their income) or increase the amount of money they earn (by taking on a second job, for example) so they can save the correct sum each year.

Here is how I approach accumulating my retirement savings every year. (Remember that I am essentially self-employed. Take the approach that follows and adapt it, alter it, or use it as inspiration to develop your own proactive approach to accumulating the assets you need for your retirement.)

In late December, I calculate how much I need to earn after taxes to cover my basic expenses for the upcoming year—housing costs, food, insurance, clothing, and other necessities. I work very hard during the first half of the year with the goal of earning and saving that amount by June or July. I keep my discretionary spending to a minimum. Then, for the next three months or so (say, until October), I try to deposit every paycheck (or at least the majority of each one) into a special savings account, until I've accumulated the amount I need to save annually toward retirement. The income I generate after that point (during November and December) is all "gravy." I can use it for special treats (a nice vacation, a work by an artist I like, clothing) or, if there is nothing I really want, I invest the money in stocks or mutual funds that may be a little more risky than I would normally buy, hoping they will pay off handsomely. When late December arrives, I start the whole process again.

Other people have different systems for retirement saving. Some people simply take a percentage of every paycheck and put it into mutual funds. Some, who are very risk-averse, squirrel the money away in a money market or savings account where it earns interest until they decide whether and how they want to invest it. Others, especially people who are self-employed, earmark the income from one or two projects each year especially for retirement savings.

The important thing is to have a savings program and stick to it. If you don't, you may wind up like Margaret, a lady I have known for years.

TRUE-LIFE TALE:
LIVING FOR TODAY . . . NOT THINKING ABOUT TOMORROW

Margaret was divorced nearly twenty years ago. A professional woman with great talent, charm, and intellect, Margaret has always derived a sense of deep personal affirmation from her work. For example, she has taken on many creative assignments for nonprofit organizations like museums, schools, and charitable foundations—tasks that contributed enormously to society but which didn't always pay very well. These jobs were often the first to be eliminated when these organizations had financial problems or needed to save money. As a result, Margaret has moved from one job to another, viewing each as a self-affirming event and not paying enough attention to long-term personal goals, such as her retirement. When she did think about her retirement, she always believed that given her work experience and credentials, "one great paying job" would come along enabling her to "catch up" on what she needed in her retirement account so she could "slow down a bit."

Unfortunately, Margaret's quest for self-actualization has also led her to overspend, using the money she earned to reflect her sense of her creativity, intellect, and status. For example, during her peak earning years, she dressed wonderfully, wearing unusual, gorgeous, simple, and understated clothing—which also happened to be expensive. She also threw interesting parties for her remarkable circle of friends—artists, writers, scientists, professors—at which nice wines flowed freely. Margaret lived well . . . a bit too well for her income and for her future financial well-being. In fact, she only looked at her financial future out of the corners of her eyes—never directly.

Today, in her midseventies (she refers to herself as "a lady of a certain age"), Margaret lives from one Social Security check to the next in a state of fading elegance and halfhearted optimism. She's always anxious, although she masks it well. She would like to stop working, but she can't afford to. She spends her time helping a few budget-strapped nonprofit organizations edit and refine their grant proposals. And in her usual overgenerous (and unrealistic) manner, she charges them far less than the standard rate for such services. Margaret is struggling just to survive, with no obvious way out of her dilemma.

Margaret represents my own worst fears about retirement. Like her, I love to surround myself with nice things, and I enjoy taking on projects that may not be very lucrative but that are personally rewarding. At the same time, I know I can't necessarily work forever. I understand that I need the discipline of a retirement savings and investment plan to keep from ending up like Margaret, struggling to make ends meet in my seventies.

Most people find it difficult to stick to any savings or investment plan, especially one that is ambitious. Here are some specific tips that can help you do so:

- **Put saving first.** Set aside your targeted saving percentage as soon as you get your paycheck. In time, you'll become accustomed to living on the remainder, and you'll have the pleasure of watching your savings grow every month.
- **Establish automatic withdrawals.** Most banks are happy to arrange for automatic withdrawals from your checking account into a special savings account or a mutual fund. This will make your savings grow with no effort on your part.
- **Take advantage of tax-deferred savings or investment plans.** If your company offers a 401(k), make sure you sign

up to begin making contributions as soon as you can. Remember, you'll be saving before-tax dollars, so the impact on your after-tax income will be less than you think. And depending on your income level, you might also be able to contribute to an Individual Retirement Account (IRA) with either before-tax or after-tax dollars. Investigate all your options and take advantage of them.

- **Save your next pay raise.** Earmark all of your next pay increase for savings. After all, you've been living on your current income; after the increase, keep your lifestyle the same, and enjoy a painless boost in your savings rate.
- **Open a limited-access account.** This is a special type of savings account that permits just a few withdrawals every year. Keeping your retirement savings in a limited-access account reduces the temptation to raid the funds whenever you have a special or impulsive need or want.

THE BOTTOM LINE

Turning your retirement dreams into reality takes planning, hard work, and discipline. If you want your money to take care of you in old age, you have to take care of your money—starting today.

The Many Perfectly Awful Reasons *Not* to Save for Retirement

For many people, sticking to their retirement savings program is difficult. This is especially true in today's society, which is more focused on immediate gratification than ever before. This focus creates many handy excuses for not saving.

Here are some of the most common excuses people use to

justify—to themselves, to a partner, or to the world in general—their failure to save for their own futures. Do any of these sound familiar? If so, now is the time to change your thinking.

"I'm a long way from retirement. I can worry about it later."

If you find yourself using this excuse, the reason may be simple laziness or procrastination, two traits most people have to some extent. (It's always easier to put off till tomorrow the challenging chores you know you ought to tackle today.) On the other hand, when the subject is retirement, a more subtle motivation may be involved. It's hard for some young people to imagine themselves as being middle aged, let alone old. Looking at their parents or grandparents, they see people with lined faces, drooping bodies, and (perhaps) jaded personalities, completely different from the taut, toned, and (perhaps) idealistic qualities they recognize in themselves. The gulf between today's youth and tomorrow's old age seems almost impassable.

Well, take it from me, you *will* grow old (if you're lucky). And it will happen more quickly, easily, painlessly, and silently than you imagine. You are unlikely to feel any different the day of your thirtieth, fortieth, or (heaven help us!) fiftieth birthday than you do right now. With one exception: if you haven't done a thing to prepare for retirement, you'll feel very anxious!

"I'll be making more money in the future. I'll start saving then."

There's a modicum of truth to this excuse; most people do find that their salaries increase during their thirties and forties, potentially freeing up money for saving and investing. But relying on this as a reason to avoid saving today is unsound strategy, for several reasons. For one thing, your income may *not* increase in the future, or not to the extent you assume. People sometimes lose jobs, change careers (with consequent loss of seniority), suffer health problems, or simply experience stagnation at work. And an industry-wide recession (like that suffered in the high-tech industries from 2000 through 2002) or a nationwide business downturn (like the ones that have occurred periodically throughout history) can cause incomes to decline for years at a time, through no fault of the workers themselves.

Another problem with deferring saving until the future is that, in the years to come, your needs are likely to increase along with your salary. If you have children, they will be growing into teenagers, asking for more costly clothes and gadgets and ultimately needing college educations. You'll probably want a larger house, a nicer car, and more luxurious vacations. If you get promoted at work, you may need fancier clothes. All of this means that your increased income will not automatically translate into more spare money for savings.

Most important, there are huge benefits to starting a savings program today rather than tomorrow or next year. The sooner you put away a little money, the sooner it will begin to grow and take advantage of the miracle of compound interest—interest on interest. If you can start saving for your retirement while still in your twenties, even if the amounts you save are modest, you will put *time* to work on your behalf, with remarkable effects on the size of your nest egg.

"I'd like to save for tomorrow, but every penny goes for things I need today."

It's oh so easy to spend every dollar that we get our hands on, especially in our consumer-oriented society, with shops filled with enticing goods beckoning us seven days a week, websites promoting wonderful products available twenty-four hours a day, and television commercials depicting the allure of material culture on a nonstop basis. The only way to save in this environment is to begin redefining what you "need," eliminating some of the pleasant things that you currently spend money on, and putting aside a fixed portion of your income for saving *before* you begin spending. If you try this, you'll discover, after a period of adjustment, that the cigarettes, lunches out, magazines, cocktails, CDs, outings, shoes, lottery tickets, and other things that you once assumed you "needed" are really quite expendable—provided you are determined to live without them.

"Investing is just a racket. Not only do the financial firms charge high fees, but they'll probably lose my hard-earned money anyway. So why invest?"

Unfortunately, people have lost money due to dishonest brokers, companies run on a fraudulent basis (like Enron and Worldcom), and investment scam artists. But there are also millions of people who have benefited from investing because they use reputable and reliable financial firms to invest in conservative, dividend-paying stocks, interest-paying bonds, or income-producing mutual funds.

The key is to be clear about your investment objectives and monitor the performance of your accounts on a regular basis. For most people, preservation of capital in combination with long-term capital growth are the right objectives to choose for a retirement account. Make sure your broker understands these choices and offers investment recommendations that are appropriate.

Don't let yourself get caught up in the latest market craze, chasing high double-digit returns, as so many people did during the technology boom of the 1990s—to their regret. Don't put all your money into any one investment or one industry; instead, diversify your holdings, so that a loss in one area won't wipe out your entire portfolio. And remember the age-old advice that remains the best protection against investment scam artists: if a deal sounds too good to be true, it probably is.

"Why bother saving? I might be dead before I reach retirement age."

Ah, how cynical, fatalistic, and romantic this sounds—shades of Jim Morrison, Janis Joplin, Jimi Hendrix, and other hard-living nonconformists who died in their brilliant, beautiful youth! But with today's medical advances, it's unlikely to happen to you. Most people are living longer than ever, and retirements that used to last five to seven years are now lasting twenty to thirty years. Would you prefer to spend those years in a rooming house or single-room-occupancy hotel, eating toast, reusing the tea bag, and watching television, or would you rather enjoy a full, financially comfortable life? The choice is yours.

THE BOTTOM LINE

There are many excuses for not saving for retirement, and you're free to follow them if you like. But if you do, you will regret it.

The Benevolent Nanny and the Real Estate Windfall

There are two other misconceptions that discourage many people from starting or sticking to a retirement savings program: the myth of the Benevolent Nanny and the myth of the Real Estate Windfall.

One aspect of the retirement savings challenge is your relationship with the government and your employer. Many people, somewhere deep inside, regard one or both of these institutions as a kind of nanny that will save them in old age and free them from the responsibility of providing for their own future.

If you share this belief, it's time to shed it. Social, demographic, and economic changes of the past decade have made it virtually impossible for either the government or private industry to play the role of benevolent nanny for tomorrow's retirees. The key factors include:

- **The aging population.** Not so long ago, there were ten to fifteen people of working age to support each retired person in the United States, Britain, and other countries of the developed world. Today the ratio is closer to three to one, and soon it will be two to one. This means that government and private pension plans are accumulating less funds from current contributions even as the need for payouts to pensioners is increasing. Benefits cuts are the inevitable result.
- **Increased longevity.** With many more people living into their eighties and beyond, retirement funds and medical budgets must be stretched to cover more elderly people, including many who are infirm or disabled. This puts further pressure on both government and private business.
- **Increased standards of living.** Retirees of the twenty-first century expect much more out of life than their counterparts of the 1950s or even the 1980s. Standards of housing, food, medical care, transportation, and entertainment that were once acceptable would seem abysmal today.

For these and other reasons, neither government nor private industry can afford to support retirees in the style they want and deserve, even if public policy demanded it. The burden must be shared, which means you need to pick up the slack through savings of your own.

There's another myth I've been encountering with greater

and greater frequency. It grows out of the boom in real estate values of recent years. Because houses have grown in value so quickly, many people are assuming that they will be able to use the proceeds from a house sale to finance their retirements.

It is true that home ownership has contributed substantially to some people's comfortable retirements. And innovations like the reverse mortgage make it easier than ever for people to tap the equity in their homes, even without selling them. As a result, it has now become popular for people to think of home ownership as a kind of quick-and-easy, fail-safe retirement plan: all you have to do is buy a house, wait for it to quadruple in value, and then live happily ever after.

Ah, how I wish it were that easy! Unfortunately, even *with* the recent real estate boom (which is showing signs of cooling at the time of this writing), the idea of retiring "on the house" isn't always practical. Here are the realities that explode the myth of the real estate windfall:

- **Market fluctuations.** There are no guarantees that the value of your home will rise as quickly as you may assume. There have been extended periods of time, including recent years, during which real estate values fell or remained stagnant. The current growth may continue, or it may go bust. Don't bet all of your retirement on trends that are basically unpredictable.
- **Rollover costs.** You will still need somewhere to live after you retire. Therefore, some of the money you might make by selling your home will need to be rolled over into a new residence. Once you factor in the costs of buying and selling real estate, moving expenses, and other costs, the profits may be much less than you assume.

- **Trade-down realities.** Many people assume that they will be happy to "trade down" to a much smaller residence when they retire, enabling them to buy a relatively cheap home and pocket a large sum from the sale of their larger home. But when the time comes, you may not really want to trade down after all. You will probably have accumulated lots of furniture, appliances, clothes, gadgets, hobby gear, and other paraphernalia during your years in your current residence, and you may want space for a home office or studio, accommodations for visiting children and grandchildren, a garden, and so on. For many people, the windfall from trading down proves surprisingly small.

You may be able to realize some excess equity when you sell your home, and the money this frees up can be added to your retirement nest egg. But for the vast majority of people, it won't be enough to fund the entire package. Don't fall prey to the illusion that real estate values will eliminate the necessity of saving for your retirement—they won't.

THE BOTTOM LINE

Neither the government pension nanny nor the real estate windfall can take the place of a personal retirement program. Stop daydreaming; start saving and investing instead.

There Is No Automatic Pilot: Managing Your Investments Over Time

Having created and begun to put money into a retirement savings program, you need to monitor the growth of your accounts at regular intervals. It's not enough just to follow your plan unthinkingly, as if on automatic pilot. You need to keep track of and assess not only how your money is growing, but also whether changes in your investments or the economic environment require changes in your investment program.

TRUE-LIFE TALE:
MAKING ASSUMPTIONS VERSUS TAKING CONTROL

The contrasting stories of Tad and Eloise illustrate the difference between making assumptions about your retirement savings and taking control of them.

In his early sixties, my friend Tad was planning to retire. In some ways, Tad had been quite responsible about his retirement plan. He'd set up an automatic investment plan that put away some 15 percent of his income each month. When he got raises, he increased this percentage. But being very risk-averse and concerned with the safety of his money, Tad had specified that all of his money should be invested in the most conservative, virtually risk-free instruments, mainly mutual funds that invested in government bonds.

This turned out to be a miscalculation, which Tad compounded by assuming that his retirement program needed no further monitoring. Believing that his money was totally safe and growing fast enough, Tad rarely bothered to read the regular statements from his retirement plan administrator.

Thus, when Tad finally focused on his savings just a few years before his planned retirement date, he was shocked to find that his investment fund wasn't worth nearly what he thought it would be. Tad and his wife realized that they had to keep working for five more years. Tragically, he died of cancer only a year later.

By contrast, my friend Eloise illustrates how planning and

monitoring can make even a less-than-perfect plan work for you. Eloise's husband died while she was in her early forties and left her with almost no financial assets. Dismayed and chastened, Eloise determined to plan wisely for her own retirement. She calculated the amount of income she would need in order to live comfortably after she stopped working, set a price tag on the nest egg she would need, and began saving regularly to reach it.

Most important, she paid close attention to the growth of her investments. She channeled most of her savings into well-managed mutual funds (with consistent top-tier ratings from the respected Morningstar rating service). The rest she invested in shares of individual companies. As a result, the stock market boom of the 1990s provided Eloise with impressive growth and profits, a significant amount of which she captured by deciding to sell some of the investments in her tax-deferred retirement accounts

By 2000, when the stock market began to decline, Eloise had already begun moving some of her money into lower-risk investments, such as government and corporate bonds. As a result, when the tech bubble burst, the pain she suffered was minimal. Eloise also increased the percentage of her salary that went into savings after she reached age sixty, realizing that extra savings were needed if she was to reach her nest-egg target.

Although Eloise didn't start her savings program until middle life, it has served her well. She paid off the mortgage on her home at age sixty-five, making the last payment with her final paycheck on the day of her retirement. Today she is living a modest but comfortable lifestyle. "I may not be able to vacation in Hawaii next year," she says, "but Florida or New Mexico is still within reach." That's the result of planning and discipline.

As the stories of Tad and Eloise illustrate, retirement savings must be monitored and managed over time. But what does this mean? How do you know what to do with your investment money as you move toward retirement?

Investment strategy is an enormous subject in its own right, one we can't cover in detail in the next few pages. (There are many fine books and websites on the topic that you can use to educate yourself.) But you don't have to be an investment expert to manage your retirement funds effectively. The key is to adjust your investment plan over time, so that, as you get older (and closer to retirement age), the mix of investments changes to become less risky and therefore less subject to unexpected loss of value.

"Less risky?" you may say. "Why would I want my investments to have any risk at all? I want to sign up for a *no-risk* investment plan. Then I'll never have to worry about losing my money."

This sounds sensible at first. But sadly, the world doesn't work this way. For one thing, there is actually no such thing as an investment plan with *no* risk at all. Some forms of investments come close. For example, savings accounts insured by the Federal Deposit Insurance Corporation (FDIC) and U.S. government securities (Treasury bills, notes, bonds) are quite safe. The only way the latter group might fail would be if the U.S. government defaults on its interest payment, which it has never done. (If it did, it would probably produce a national panic . . . in which case the loss of value in your investments would be only one of many problems you'd face.)

However, even savings accounts and government-insured investments aren't totally risk-free. Here's why. Suppose you have a savings account with a guaranteed growth rate of 3 percent. This means that your $100.00 investment will grow to $103.00 next year, $106.09 the year after that, $109.27 the year after that, and so on. (The extra cents come from compound interest—interest earned by interest.)

But this doesn't take into account the effects of inflation. If the cost of the goods and services that you buy with your money increase by more than 3 percent per year—something that does happen periodically—the buying power of your money would actually decline in value rather than grow. So even guaranteed investments do carry some risk—in this example, inflation risk.

What's more, investment experts agree that some degree of risk is necessary if your investments are to grow. The question is: *How much risk should you accept?* The short answer is: *More risk when you are younger, less risk as you get older.*

Here's the explanation. Within limits, investments that carry more risk can also be expected to grow more quickly in the long term. The problem, of course, is that they also tend to be volatile—that is, to go up and down unpredictably in the short term.

Now, if you are saving for retirement, you don't need to have access to the money when you are young (in your twenties, thirties, and early forties). You can put it into somewhat risky investments, ones that go up and down in value, but, over time and on average, are likely to grow. This description applies particularly to stocks and to mutual funds that invest in growth stocks and mutual funds with capital appreciation as their investment objectives.

Later, when retirement is near (in your fifties and early sixties), you don't want to take chances with your money. After all, you'll soon need it to live on. So as time passes, you want to move your investments out of growth-oriented shares and into investments that may grow more slowly but have a more reliable dividend or interest payment history and be less volatile.

This description applies particularly to blue-chip stocks and to investment-grade corporate and municipal bonds.

Thus, a widely used rule of thumb for retirement investment is: When you are young, invest mainly in shares. As you get older, gradually shift from shares to bonds. In fact, a number of investors use the following formula to guide their investment strategy:

100% - Your age = Percentage you should invest in shares

According to this formula, when you are thirty years old, you should invest 70 percent of your savings in stocks (since 100 - 30 = 70). By the time you are forty, this should shift to 60 percent. And by the time you are sixty-five, just 35 percent of your money should be in shares, with the remainder in less-risky bonds or other fixed-income securities. Of course, if you are truly concerned about risk, you can move an even larger percentage into low-risk investments or a no-risk savings account at a bank or savings and loan.

I'm only skimming the surface of the complex topic of investment strategy. But the basic principle I've suggested is the crucial one: pay attention to the growth of your retirement funds as time passes, and adjust the nature of your investments as you get older.

Today, two important options are becoming increasingly available to people putting money aside for their retirement, but who feel uncertain about managing, periodically adjusting, or rebalancing their investment portfolios themselves. These options are *managed retirement accounts* and *life-cycle funds.*

With a managed retirement account, an individual financial adviser will actually manage your retirement account. The adviser automatically does all of the work for you: allocates your money among different asset classes (such as stocks and bonds), selects the specific funds in which the money is invested, and adjusts the investments in accordance with changing performance and economic conditions. In short, the adviser doesn't simply offer investment advice in accordance with your investment objectives and risk tolerance, he or she actually *carries out* the advice, making investment decisions on your behalf.

A life-cycle fund is a mutual fund that invests in a combination of stocks and bonds tailored to investors in a specific age group. As the investors in the fund age and move closer to retirement, the mix of securities changes to become less risky. A life-cycle fund is a one-stop, one-size-fits-all solution to managing a retirement account. All the money in the pool is treated the same; the financial circumstances of individual investors are not taken into consideration.

No matter which option you choose—self-management, a managed account, or a life-cycle fund—it's important to monitor and adjust your retirement plan as your financial situation changes, as the performance of your investments changes, and as you move closer to retirement. Don't let complacency undermine your retirement dreams.

THE BOTTOM LINE

It's not enough to put retirement funds into the bank or invest in a mutual fund and forget about them. You have to price out your retirement dreams properly, track your progress toward the goal you set to make sure you are on course, and make adjustments along the way as needed.

Hands Off Your Retirement Fund

Here is one last warning that I can't stress too highly. If you've been smart enough to build a nice retirement nest egg using a 401(k) investment program, resist the temptation to dip into that pool of money for immediate spending. It's almost always a bad idea—even when the purpose for which you want to withdraw the funds takes the form of an "investment."

TRUE-LIFE TALE: THE BIG RETIREMENT PLAN NO-NO

Walter and Lara have been married for twenty years. Lara works for a utility company and has long participated in the company-sponsored 401(k) pension plan, which matches her contributions dollar for dollar up to the first 6 percent of her salary.

Walter, meanwhile, worked as a manager in a heating-and-air-conditioning company. But three years ago, after endless conflicts with various bosses and customers, Walter decided to withdraw the money accumulated in his company retirement plan and use it to launch his own firm.

Unfortunately, Walter's new company quickly ran into problems. Jobs fell through, and some customers refused to pay Walter's bills because he was habitually late in completing projects. Walter soon found his new business strapped for cash, and he couldn't borrow money from a bank or any other source because of his poor credit rating.

In desperation, Walter persuaded Lara to withdraw a large portion of her 401(k) nest egg "to invest in my business." But the problems continued, and Walter eventually had to close the business and go back to work for someone else. All of the money invested in the business, including his wife's preretirement withdrawal from her 401(k) plan, was lost. To make matters worse, when Walter and Lara filed their tax return for the year, they were hit with a bigger-than-expected tax bill because the early withdrawal from Lara's 401(k) plan was subject to a penalty and taxes.

Withdrawing money from the 401(k) plan made a bad situation worse—and put Walter and Lara far behind schedule in saving for retirement.

THE BOTTOM LINE

Money accumulated in a tax-deferred retirement plan—a 401(k) plan, 403(b) plan, or IRA—should be sacrosanct. Early withdrawals are subject to significant penalties and taxation, and you will probably find yourself struggling for years just to catch up.

TAKE-AWAYS

1. **Take time to get to know the future you.** Think about your life in the future, after you've stopped working. What are your retirement dreams? Where will you live? What will you do with your time? And how much money will you need to make these dreams into reality?

2. **Put a price tag on your dreams.** Figure out how much income you may receive from government or private pensions. Then calculate the size of the nest egg you'll need to generate the income your retirement dreams will require.

3. **Create a personal retirement savings program.** Figure out how much money you'll need to accumulate between now and when you retire. Then start saving with that goal in mind, beginning with your very next paycheck.

4. **Abandon the excuses and myths that prevent you from saving.** Develop a realistic attitude toward the importance of retirement saving, and don't fall prey to the myths of the Benevolent Nanny or the Real Estate Windfall, which convince many people that saving is unnecessary.

5. **Monitor your retirement savings and make adjustments as needed.** Don't put your saving and investment plan on autopilot. Read your statements, increase your savings if necessary, and as retirement nears gradually shift to less-risky investments.

6. **Don't be tempted or persuaded to make an early withdrawal from your retirement plan.** Monies withdrawn early are subject to taxation at your normal income rate plus a substantial penalty. These costs are usually a significant portion of the amount withdrawn, thus making early withdrawal very unattractive.

9

MONEY AND THE END OF LIFE

TEST YOURSELF. Is there a healthy relationship between money and the end of your life, or is it a potential source of trouble? To find out, answer the questions below—and *be honest!*

Yes	No	
☐	☐	1. Have you written a will to set forth how your money and other assets should be handled upon your death?
☐	☐	2. If you have a will, has it been drafted by a lawyer for completeness and legal correctness?
☐	☐	3. If you have a will, do you review it regularly to make certain it is still up-to-date and appropriate?
☐	☐	4. Have you selected an appropriate person to serve as executor to carry out your wishes after you die?
☐	☐	5. Have you listed all your assets—not only money and investments but also real estate and personal property—and considered carefully how to dispose of them after you die?

Yes	No	
☐	☐	6. Have you made a list of your personal possessions and carefully planned who should receive each item after you die?
☐	☐	7. If you have children under age eighteen, have you decided (with your partner) who should care for them if you die?
☐	☐	8. If you have adult children, have you discussed with them what they should expect—and not expect—to receive after you die?
☐	☐	9. In planning your will, have you considered contingencies such as the possible death of your heir, your executor, or the guardian of your children?
☐	☐	10. Have you considered any possible requests you may have concerning funeral arrangements or other decisions to be made after your death?

HOW DO YOU SCORE? Every "no" answer indicates an area on which you need to focus to get your financial relationships in order. For helpful advice and guidance, read on.

DIE? WHO, ME?

For understandable reasons, most people hate to think about death and avoid the topic as much as possible. We hate the very word "death," and therefore have invented a long list of euphemisms: Uncle Fred "passed away," "made the transition," "breathed his last," "went to his reward," "met his Maker," "bought the farm," "went to greener pastures"—anything but "died." (Yes, I too choose to wimp out sometimes. Look at the title of this chapter. I felt "Money and Your Death" seemed just a little *too* stark!)

Even people who admit that they will die someday have difficulty coming to grips with the reality of what death means. (The writer William Saroyan put it this way: "I know that everyone has to die, but I always believed an exception would be made in my case.") As a result, people who are responsible about planning everything else in their lives, from vacation trips to home renovations, refuse to plan for the end of their lives, despite the fact that, as we'll explain, preparing for death is one of the most important things you can do.

The excuses that people use vary widely. Some are nihilists. They like to say, with a shrug, "What do I care what happens after I die? I'll be gone, that's all I know." A moment's thought should dispel this attitude. Of course it's true that you'll be gone, but the people you care about will remain behind (unless you can arrange a grand conflagration that will claim everyone you know at once, in the style of a tragic opera that leaves the stage littered with corpses). The future lives of those you love may be seriously affected by your passing, especially financially. If you don't plan to manage that impact, the results could be devastating. You surely don't want to be remembered forevermore as the selfish old fool who died and left friends and family with a giant mess to deal with!

Others are paralyzed by the fear of death. I know a man who's an awful hypochondriac—someone who is so afraid of illness that he is constantly taking his own temperature, medicating himself with over-the-counter drugs, and rushing to his doctor or the hospital at the least ache or twinge. I wasn't surprised when his wife told me recently that he hadn't bothered to write a will. It's only natural that a person who is obsessed with fending off death would choose to deny its inevitability.

Still others claim they have no need to plan for their final passing. "I won't need a will," they declare. "I'll spend it all and die with an empty bank account. All my kids will have to do is cart away my remains, clean out the apartment, and get on with their lives." Such people can often be seen tooling around sunny resort towns in a large car with a bumper sticker that reads "I'm spending my children's inheritance."

I'm all for older folks enjoying their money while they can rather than hoarding it for their children. But unfortunately it's not possible for us to time our own deaths quite as precisely as these people seem to think. Barbara Hutton, heiress to the Woolworth chain stores in the United States and a billionaire at one time, spent with abandon throughout her life and supposedly died with just $128 in her bank account. But this is not so easy to do. What if you guess wrong and outlive your money by a decade or more? The only really prudent course is, to have some money set aside in case you live to be eighty, ninety, or a hundred years old, and that means there will probably be something left over to be disposed of after you die.

These leftovers, however modest they may be, are known as your *estate.* Practically everyone leaves some kind of estate behind. Even the Indian leader Gandhi, who was famous for his vow of poverty and owned less than $25 worth of material goods at the time of his death, left behind a substantial estate. It consisted of his writings on political and spiritual topics, which still generate thousands of dollars' worth of publishing royalties every year.

THE BOTTOM LINE

It's only fair to your family and friends to leave some instructions about how your estate should be handled. If you don't, you are potentially creating trouble for the loved ones you leave behind. And this means that the topic of your death is not something you can avoid thinking about forever.

The Problems of Dying Intestate

Some people neglect planning for death because they don't realize how important such planning can be. Take my friend Karen, for example. She's a middle-aged, successful Seattle realtor with a husband, two teenaged children, and an average-size estate that includes a home, some retirement savings, and a few basic investments. But Karen has never written a will. "Why bother?" she says. "My finances are so simple. If I die, everything will go to my husband, Jonathan. Isn't that obvious?"

It may sound obvious, but Karen is wrong. When you die *intestate*—that is, without a valid last will—a complex set of state laws, known as the Intestacy Succession Rules (also called the Statutes of Descent) take effect and determines what will happen to your money, property, and other possessions. These rules may or may not distribute your estate the way you'd like or the way you think would be logical.

For example, when someone like Karen dies in the common situation of having a spouse and one or more children, the whole of her estate may *not* go to her spouse, but may be shared with other relatives according to a strict priority laid out in the Intestate Succession Rules. Jonathan, Karen's husband, may end up sharing the estate with their children, in-laws, or other relatives, depending on state laws. If Karen and Jonathan were "life partners" and not married, the situation is even worse for Jonathan. Under most state laws, a "life partner" is not a relative and therefore has no rights at all under the Intestate Succession Rules. And if the children are too young to manage their inheritance on their own, a trust is established under the oversight of a court, which must approve all spending on their behalf.

Sounds complicated, doesn't it? It is. Karen certainly doesn't want to create this kind of burden for Jonathan, but it's exactly what will happen if she dies without a will. And it doesn't take much imagination to picture the dire effects of legal entanglements that may result from relatives who feel ignored or cheated because they got nothing. And of course this will be happening at the worst possible time from an emotional perspective. Your spouse, life partner, children, and other friends and relatives will be deeply upset and saddened when you die (at least so we hope and assume). If you die unexpectedly—in a car accident, for example, or from the effects of a sudden illness—their sense of shock and dismay will be still greater. Now add to that the bewilderment of financial chaos—of having their lives turned upside down by lawyers, accountants, and state regulators—and of perhaps finding themselves cut off from the money they need to survive day to day.

You can get a sense of how thoughtless and inconsiderate it is to die intestate. No one wants to inflict this on the people they care about.

Nonetheless, it's estimated that a majority of Americans have not taken the time to create a legal will. It's terribly sad, and completely unnecessary.

THE BOTTOM LINE

You may not like thinking about your relationship with the end of your own life. But if you ignore this relationship and neglect to make plans about how your estate should be handled, all your other relationships and memories of you are likely to be undermined by the mess you leave behind.

Planning Your Legacy

Unlike most people, I've always had a reasonably comfortable relationship with my own death. We don't spend time together every day, but at least we're on speaking terms. Perhaps it's because I grew up in a poor farming area where birth, death, and other natural processes are daily facts of life to be treated in a frank and practical manner. As a result, I've never shied away from thinking about and planning for my ultimate end.

My grandmother, from whom I learned so much, set the best possible example in this regard. She planned for her death with loving care. When she knew that she was in her declining years (and began talking about them openly with me), she carefully began to dispose of or make succession arrangements for particular pieces of property in a thoughtful way. She even planned her own funeral. She bought the casket, the dress, the wig she would wear, even the plot in the cemetery in which she would be buried. She chose the choir and the music she wanted it to sing at her funeral service. She took care of everything except selecting her headstone and its inscription, which she asked me to do: "I know it will be nice if you choose it."

As a result, I remember her funeral as an event full of good music and a solemn burial, followed by nice food and touching conversations with relatives about "Miss Rosa." I had to do nothing but show up.

Thinking back about this time, my grandmother was amazingly level-headed, unsentimental, and determined about this. (I think this was a result of the blessing she felt for "having lived a lot longer than I thought I would.") She did not fear the end of this life. And she did not want memories of her to be sad, although the last years of her life were a slow decline. Our phone calls were always punctuated by laughter and her saying "Boy, you're so crazy," as I made some joke about the indignities accompanying her impending death.

Money was not the legacy my grandmother left me. Her legacy was something more intangible: a valuable lesson in how to prepare for death in a way that enriches the lives of those left behind. And having accumulated some assets during my lifetime, I know that creating a legal will is the best way for everyone to help shape their legacy upon death.

Does it seem morbid to think about such details and write them down in advance? I don't think so. A well-executed, thoughtful will is a gift to grieving relatives. It takes away some of the burden and fear of having to make critical decisions while in a state of shock and grief. The family can take comfort, as I did, in knowing that things are as "Grandma would have wanted." In our case, what Grandma wanted, and made possible, was for her many relatives and friends to remember and celebrate her long and good life. What a generous legacy from Grandma to those she left behind!

THE BOTTOM LINE

Take control of your death today—or at least of what you will leave behind when you die. Writing a will and leaving detailed instructions as to how your family and friends should handle your passing is a wonderful opportunity to shape the memories you leave behind.

How to Plan Your Will

If you are very young or have virtually no assets, you may not need a will. A student living at home with his or her parents, for example, or a single person with only a few hundred dollars in savings may be able to get by without one. Nearly everyone else ought to have a will. In particular, married couples and others in long-term relationships should give one another the protection that only a legal will can afford. Your state of health is irrelevant: you need a will because life—and death—are unpredictable.

In some states, it's possible to create a will without the help of a lawyer—possible, but not advisable. Chances are good that your estate is more complex than you realize, and a lawyer who knows the inheritance laws can walk you through a series of "what if" scenarios you might otherwise never consider. Furthermore, a lawyer knows how to draft legal language in a way that is likely to stand up in the face of a court challenge, which could be brought by a disgruntled family member.

I recommend that you start by spending an hour or two on your own or with your partner, sketching out the main provisions of your will. Then visit an attorney. He or she will help you flesh out the specific details of the document and put it into proper legal form.

The following questionnaire contains some key questions you should ask in planning your will. As you'll see, not all of them deal solely with the distribution of money or other assets. Answering all these questions in writing before you meet with a lawyer will save you time and minimize the chances of overlooking something important.

THE WILL-PLANNING QUESTIONNAIRE

The Question	How to Respond	Things to Consider
What will your estate include?	List everything you own, including bank and investment accounts, real estate, personal property, business interests, and any other assets.	Take time to be certain you haven't forgotten any items, including accounts you may not have thought about for years; pieces of real estate you may have inherited and ignored; securities for which you did not own a certificate or that were spinoffs of stocks you already owned, and personal possessions that may have become valuable with the passage of time. Also consider items that may have small economic value but are of sentimental importance to family or friends.
Who should be charged with carrying out your wishes after death?	Select and specify an "executor," an adult you trust to settle your debts, distribute your assets, and handle the paperwork involved in managing your estate. The executor may be one of the heirs named in the will or a close trusted friend.	Choose someone who is mature, responsible, and impartial (and therefore unlikely to be suspected of "favoritism" by any of your heirs). Some people select a trusted banker, accountant, lawyer, or investment adviser to serve as executor; in this case, a fee will be charged for the services provided. Before naming an executor, seek permission from the person you choose; serving as executor can be an onerous task that shouldn't be imposed on anyone who is unwilling. You should also name a contingent executor—a second choice who can serve if your first choice becomes unavailable.

The Question	How to Respond	Things to Consider
How should your children be cared for?	If you have children under the age of eighteen, you need to name a guardian who will care for them in case you die.	Don't assume that your nearest relation will automatically receive custody of your children; if you have a strong preference for Aunt Susan or Cousin Fred, say so in writing in your will. As with executorship, ask the person you'd like to name as guardian before doing so. And choose a contingent guardian who can step into the role if necessary.
How should your estate be distributed?	List your bequests, identifying who should receive each item in your estate, including both financial assets and other property. For bank and investment accounts, list the division of wealth in percentage terms ("50 percent to my sister Alice") rather than absolute amounts ("$40,000 to my sister Alice); that way, fluctuations in value won't distort your intentions.	If you have a number of personal items (such as jewelry, furniture, or mementos) that you want to distribute individually, consider writing a separate list that is referred to in the will (and stored in the same location). Try to specify the items clearly to avoid confusion: "The walnut cabinet with four drawers and three glass-fronted shelves in the dining room of my apartment in Boston," for example, rather than simply "China cabinet."
What final requests or preferences do you want to express?	Either in the will or in a separate document to be kept with the will, you may want to pass along any other requests to your heirs.	Consider including preferences about funeral arrangements (burial or cremation, type of religious service), the raising of your children ("I'd like them to complete their current studies at the Warwick School if possible"), the handling of business decisions, or other personal matters that are important to you.

I suggest you also consider leaving a final message to your family and friends. This can be a powerful healing gesture, especially in families where conflict or miscommunication have caused quarrels or fallings-out over the years (a description that I believe includes almost all families). You might want to express gratitude for acts of kindness or generosity, satisfaction with the life you've lived, and good wishes for the future happiness of those you've loved.

You'll want to draft your will with thought and care. For example, if you have two or more children, you may want to consider their individual money personalities and reflect those differences in the will. If you have a child who is very irresponsible, you may want to establish some controls over his or her access to money; for example, a trust account that isn't fully turned over to the child until the age of twenty-five or thirty. If you have several heirs with very different needs, you will probably want your will to address those needs; a disabled child or sibling, for instance, may need special provisions for long-term care.

Decisions about whether and how to treat your heirs differently can be emotionally and psychologically delicate. Suppose you have two children: Nicholas, who is single and childless, and Norman, who is married with three youngsters of his own. Should you divide an inheritance evenly between the two sons, or should you provide extra money to Norman to help him raise and educate his children? A good argument could be made for the fairness of either choice. What if one daughter (Julia) is a successful businessperson, while another (Maxine) is a dedicated but penniless artist? Should you leave extra money to Maxine, on the ground that she needs it more, or would you be "penalizing" the hard work of Julia by doing so?

These are decisions that only you can make (with the help of your life partner, if any). If your will includes these kinds of "close calls," consider explaining in the text (or in your separate farewell letter) the reasons for your decisions. You may also want to discuss your reasoning with your heirs in person, long before the will goes into effect, so that the ultimate reading of the document doesn't create any nasty surprises leading to disputes or recriminations. Remember that many people equate an inheritance with how much they were loved by the person leaving them the money or possessions. Explaining the real reasons for a bequest can prevent hurtful misunderstandings.

My friend Max has handled this issue with admirable clarity. A couple of years ago, he gave one of his three children $25,000 to help her make the down payment on her first house. When he did so, he told her, "In effect, I'm giving you part of your inheritance in advance, so you can buy a house now rather than later. Your brother and sister have different circumstances and don't need this kind of help. So when I die, you'll find that your share of any inheritance is $25,000 less than the amount your siblings will receive. Now you know why." The honesty and forthrightness with which Max has discussed this with his daughter should minimize the possibility of jealousy and blaming after his death.

When billionaire Laurence Tisch, the patriarch of the American Tisch family and cofounder of Loews Corporation, died in November 2003, he left primary control of the family business in the hands of his son James, despite the fact that there were many other young Tisches involved in the company. His choice reflected the fact that James had already assumed an important leadership role in the corporation and was highly respected, not only by his siblings and cousins but by the business community as a whole. Loews Corporation faces some difficult business challenges in the years to come, but a battle over control of the company won't be one of them.

Contrast this with the controversy surrounding the Pritzker estate in Chicago, where a poorly considered estate plan allowed the death of the patriarch to tear the family apart. When Jay Pritzker died in 2000, he left behind a $15 billion estate that included control of the Hyatt hotel chain. Unfortunately, the reasoning behind his division of assets was confused and unclear. Today, his niece and nephew are suing Robert Pritzker—their own father—over his handling of the trusts that were created for them, demanding $1 billion in damages and an additional $5 billion in punitive damages (to teach him a lesson, so to speak). The legacy Jay Pritzker built is being severely damaged in the process—to say nothing of the harmony and love that ought to exist within a family.

Your estate may not include a billion-dollar business, but family relationships have been broken over seemingly insignificant quarrels: "Who gets Grandma's dining table?" "I was promised that brooch!" "Where did that picture go?" These kinds of conflicts can be avoided or minimized by making your decisions thoughtfully in advance; describing them clearly; and sharing the reasoning behind them with those affected.

THE BOTTOM LINE

Whether your estate is large and complicated or small and simple, you need a will. Use the "Will Planning Questionnaire" to map out the basic decisions you need to make, and then consult a solicitor who can put the will into proper legal form.

Keeping Your Will Up to Date

One of the enormous benefits of having an experienced attorney help you with the drafting of your will is that he or she can help you anticipate the full range of circumstances in which your will may be applied. Curiously enough, I've found that most people have developed fixed ideas as to when they will die and which members of their family will die first. These ideas generally grow out of the peculiarities of their relationships; for example, a man who thinks of himself as "helpless" around the house without his wife may tend to assume that he will be the first to die, simply because he can't imagine living without her.

Of course, assumptions like these have little basis in reality, and mustn't be used (even unconsciously) as a basis for planning. Your will needs to include provisions based on the possibility that you will die first, that your spouse or partner will die first, and that you will die virtually simultaneously (for example, in an automobile accident or plane crash). You also need to plan for the possibility that one or more of your heirs may die before you or with you, as may the executor of your estate. (This is why naming a back-up executor in your will is so important.)

It would be nice if we could arrange to die under ideal circumstances—which I might define as a painless passing at the age of one hundred—still in possession of all our faculties, and surrounded by loving family and friends. Unfortunately, life doesn't often work like that. Death is often sudden and shocking for those left behind. A thoughtful will can help to cushion the blow.

Drafting a will is not a onetime event. You need to review and probably revise it every time your life circumstances change. Reconsider your will whenever you:

- Get married
- Get divorced
- Have (or lose) a child
- Buy (or sell) a home
- Start (or sell) a business
- Experience the death or incapacity of any major heir or executor named in your current will
- Experience any major change in your financial status

I'm a bit fickle myself; I change my will fairly frequently, on average about once every year or two. Since I'm unmarried and childless, friends play a role in my life rather like the role family plays for some other people. Therefore, I like to rethink my bequests whenever I make new friends, when the needs and interests of my old friends change, and when life events trigger changes in my relationships. For example, if I buy a great piece of art that I know a particular friend would like, I might decide to add a clause to my will that specifies that this artwork will go to that friend after I die.

When a will is poorly conceived or outdated, it can produce results that are far from those intended—sometimes to devastating effect.

TRUE-LIFE TALE: THE LAW OF UNINTENDED CONSEQUENCES

James Calhoun and Cynthia Browne were business partners, having founded together a company that sold fine cabinetry by mail and over the Internet–things like beautiful jewelry boxes, media cabinets, and occasional tables. They loved the business and enjoyed working together, and they had developed a deep personal bond during their six years of partnership.

Two years ago they got devastating news. Cynthia had developed a malignant brain tumor—a form of cancer that is almost always fatal and generally leads to death within months.

Suddenly the lives and business of James and Cynthia were thrown into chaos. Cynthia had to spend much of her time and energy dealing with medical issues, including travel to a distant city to take advantage of experimental treatments her doctors hoped might prolong her life. She and James were both emotionally devastated, of course; neither had the energy or the strength of will to focus on such mundane matters as the future of their business. And the deep friendship between the two complicated the problem. How do you raise the issue of money and business succession at a time like this without seeming crass or heartless? There never seemed to be a right time to bring up the topic. So James stayed uncomfortably silent and Cynthia was absorbed in her treatments and their unfortunate side effects.

When Cynthia died, her will was read. It turned out to be a document she had created eight years earlier—before the founding of the business—and never revised. In it, Cynthia left the whole of her estate to her favorite relative, her nephew Stewart, who was just eleven years old.

Of course, Cynthia's estate included her half of the business, which means that little Stewart (actually his guardian) and James were forced to become partners. Cynthia's house and everything inside it also became part of Stewart's inheritance, including vital documents and materials related to the business. James has had to spend years wrangling with lawyers and the courts to try to get control over the company he helped to found. As a result, he feels increasingly bitter and angry toward his onetime partner and close friend, Cynthia, whose carelessness (or thoughtlessness?) about her estate he feels shattered their business and part of his life.

THE BOTTOM LINE

As the story of Cynthia and James illustrates, the distribution of your assets after death can undermine rather than foster goodwill among your survivors. To avoid this, think through your wishes carefully and make them known and understood before you die. Revisit your will frequently, revising it whenever changes in life circumstances make that necessary. And if you own a business or property with a partner, make sure you talk about inheritance issues when you first set up the business or venture, not later when it may be difficult to bring up the subject.

When Children Are Waiting to Inherit

As I discussed in an earlier chapter, in some families, an inheritance disrupts relationships even before death occurs. This happens especially in families where there are tensions, hostilities, and unmet needs that people are unwilling or unable to talk about—and which consequently end up getting expressed through money.

I was startled several years ago when a young woman I met told me that she planned to go to her parents and ask to receive her inheritance now, while they were still alive. "After all," she reasoned, "if they do that, they can watch me enjoy it during their lifetimes. Isn't that better for them?"

It takes a lot to shock me, but this shocked me.

I've since realized that an amazing number of young people are quietly looking toward their parents' future passing as a financial windfall. They secretly tally the estimated values of the house, savings, and investments they believe their parents have, and think about all the security they will have and the good things they'll be able to buy for themselves when the inevitable occurs.

I can't begin to list all the reasons this attitude offends me. It's bad for the children because it destroys their motivation to be responsible, ambitious, and hardworking. Rather than saving for themselves, they look to their expected inheritance to save them from their wastefulness or poor planning. It's bad for the parents because it transforms what should be a loving parent-child relationship into a matter of dollars and cents. It even gives the children a reason to be what I call curiously neutral and calm when their parents get sick. Talk about disturbing!

At this point, it would be easy for me to launch into a denunciation of the heartlessness of Generations X and Y. I could probably even find some way to blame MTV, glitzy pop idols, nighttime soap operas, or the educational system. But the truth is that parents are almost always at least partly responsible for this. Sometimes they make a point of talking frequently about all the things the kids will get: "When I die, these pearls will be yours." This is generally a form of emotional manipulation, a way of bribing the children to treat their parents with respect and affection. (I'm reminded of the opening scene in Shakespeare's *King Lear,* where the foolish old king makes his daughters compete for their inheritances by declaring their love for their father. If you don't think this sort of thing ends up badly, read the famous insanity scenes from later in the play!)

Furthermore, offering specific inheritances ahead of time is a way of making promises that may prove to be hollow. No one can know for certain how large their estate will ultimately be; the behavior of investment markets is too unpredictable for that. And suppose you end up suffering from some costly long-term illness? It may be that your house will have to be sold to pay for your care.

If your children have been taught to think of it as *their* house, then they will resent it.

Here is my advice for parents of adult children: *draw a line in the sand defining what is yours.* If you want to give your children money, investments, or property to help them get started in life or to deal with unexpected problems (such as illness or a lost job), go ahead. But then make it clear to all concerned that what you keep is for *your* benefit—it's not an inheritance-in-waiting.

The message I would deliver to my children—my potential heirs, if I had any—would be something like: "As your parent, I did the best I could for you. I've fed you, clothed you, cared for you, and enabled you to have a good education, as much education as you needed and wanted. Now it's your time to go out into the world and build a life for yourself. My basic responsibilities to you are fulfilled. I intend to live the rest of my life to the fullest. If there is anything left over when I go, fine. But don't assume I'll be leaving any money behind. I may or I may not. In any case, my legacy to you is not embodied in my estate. My legacy to you is the love, guidance, nurturing, support, and discipline that I gave you over the years. I hope you'll make the best of it."

THE BOTTOM LINE

If you sense that your adult children are living in expectation of a significant inheritance from you, talk with them. Encourage them to plan and create independent lives, assuming that they will have to support themselves through their own efforts. With the air thus cleared, you can go about living your life—and spending your own money—as you see fit, rather than thinking of every dollar in your bank account as somehow "owed" to your children.

More Than Money

When a financial legacy is handled wisely, as simply one part of a broader inheritance that includes a strong sense of family values and a sense of responsibility to the larger society, its positive impact can resonate with future generations for many years.

I've spoken often of the wisdom I gleaned from my grandmother. She was a simple woman whose activities never strayed beyond the margins of her family, her hometown, the church where she worshipped, and her circle of friends. There was much she never understood about the broader world, and, as she grew older, there were many features of modern life that baffled her. When I went away to college back in the early 1970s, she generously bought me a set of Samsonite luggage and three sets of clothes. If she were alive today, I doubt she'd understand why a college student now needs to have a microwave oven or an iPod, too. Nonetheless, her homespun wisdom has stood the test of time. The values she taught me—independence, foresight, self-discipline, moderation, simplicity—are just as powerful today as they were two generations ago.

For whatever reason, I was the family member to whom Grandma always felt closest. Somehow her teachings simply took hold with me to a greater extent than with any of my brothers or sisters. As a result, Grandma had a strong sense of trust in me, and the financial arrangements she made toward the end of her life reflected this. She and I actually had a joint bank account, which meant that, after her passing, her relatively modest savings went directly to me, without even the intervention of a will. (Opening a joint account in this fashion is a simple, and usually effective way of making sure that your assets go where you want after you die, but it requires *absolute* trust in the person with whom you share the account, since he or she has access to the money at any time, before or after your passing.)

In the decade since my grandmother died, I've been very careful with the almost $20,000 she left behind, using it only for purposes I think she would have approved of. I kept part of the money in the bank and invested part of it in the stock market. During good years on Wall Street, those investments grew; during bad years, they shrank, and I replenished the account from my own earnings. When my niece needed help with college tuition, I wrote her a check using Grandma's money; a good education is an investment in the future, which Grandma would have believed in. When another sister needed money as a deposit to have the utilities turned on at her new house, I sent her a check using part of Grandma's money. On the other hand, when my youngest brother wanted money to buy a stereo, I turned him down. I know that's what Grandma would have done.

In many families, an inheritance is quickly squandered and forgotten. But my grandmother's bequest has actually grown over time—not just in financial terms, but in terms of her influence on me and my siblings. Because I think frequently about how Grandma would have liked to see her money used, her wisdom is continually nurturing me and enhancing the quality of my life. People sometimes complain about the stipulations in wills as being like a "dead hand" from the past controlling the future. In my grandmother's case, it's more like a living hand supporting the younger generation with love and guidance.

I hope that, when my own time comes, I'll be able to leave a legacy to family and friends that is as powerful and positive as the one my grandmother created.

THE BOTTOM LINE

Money is important because of its effect on how we live. When planning how your assets should be handled after you die, don't think only about the dollars and cents; think about the kind of life you'd like your loved ones to enjoy, and draw up your final wishes accordingly.

TAKE-AWAYS

1. **Face the reality that you will die someday, and plan and prepare for the event.** If you ignore or neglect this truth, the people you care about will suffer.

2. **Consult an attorney when you draft your will.** A lawyer can help you anticipate various circumstances and ensure that your will is drafted in accordance with legal principles.

3. **Include arrangements beyond financial ones in your will.** You should cover not only the disposition of your financial assets and belongings but also instructions about the care of your children, the handling of your business interests, and any other matters that your heirs will have to manage.

4. **Review your will whenever your life circumstances or relevant laws change.** Revise it as needed.

5. **In joint businesses or partnership, discuss the issue of death when the partnership is being established.**

Have upfront discussions with your friends or partners in the joint business venture about what will happen if either partner dies.

6. **Explain to your heirs the reasoning behind your bequests.** Don't encourage children to develop a sense of entitlement to your assets; remind them that your true legacy as a parent is not the money you leave behind but the love and wisdom you have given them throughout your lifetime.

AFTERWORD

MONEY AND THE MEANING OF IT ALL

Following a recent lunch during which a friend and I shared stories about money in our lives, he e-mailed me the following comment: "It's amazing how personal money talk tends to be equal parts funny and equal parts sad." His statement reflects perfectly the mix of feelings we have about money and the roles it plays in our lives.

While there are common themes from our individual money stories, in the end, your ability to manage money effectively comes down to what money means for you and how you deal with that meaning. Here are five of the most common meanings of money that I've observed.

Money as security. Some people see money as their shield against every danger, up to and sometimes including death. In their minds, having enough money is a way of keeping their little garden safe from the outside world's turmoil. "If I only had more money," such people are inclined to say, "my worries would be over."

Is this way of viewing money good or bad? It depends. When fearful people cling too tightly to money as a source of security, it can produce a sad spectacle. I once visited an elderly man in a nursing home (he was the uncle of a friend of mine). After a little chitchat, he suddenly asked me, "Guess who my friends are?" He pulled out a roll of cash and riffled them with an almost gleeful expression on his face. "*These* are my friends!" he cackled.

I can sympathize with the feeling. We've all had the experience of feeling disappointed or let down by (human) friends. But I certainly hope I'm never reduced to believing that money is the only thing in the world I can trust or believe in.

In a more positive way, the notion of money-as-security can motivate a person to be a careful saver, not being miserly but taking pleasure in knowing that a significant bank account means freedom from financial fear. When handled this way, money as security can be a benign image that leads to positive life results.

Money as the key to life's doors. I have a friend whose grandfather's favorite aphorism was "With grease you slide." Of course, by "grease" he meant money—money used to provide entrance into new worlds. This can be as simple as slipping a folded twenty-dollar bill into the hands of a maître d' to get a table at a hot, new restaurant; it can be as grandiose as when a newly minted millionaire or billionaire makes a large gift to an opera company or an art museum as a way of gaining entry into fashionable society.

Again, this meaning of money can have either a positive or a negative connotation. The dark side of money-as-key can be seen in societies where bribery is commonplace, and "democracy" and "equality" are only words. (Think of some of the developing countries of Latin America, or some segments of post-Soviet Russia.) In such societies, the wealthy enjoy every power and privilege, and the poor, no matter how smart and hardworking they may be, are doomed to live off the scraps. This kind of society is probably headed for a dangerous crack-up as resentments and jealousy grow to the boiling point.

But the image of money-as-key can have a good side as well. When people work hard and save to create a family nest egg and then use those resources to visit distant lands, enjoy new experiences, send their children to fine schools, or help those less fortunate than themselves, that money is serving as a well-deserved door-opener. If everything good were available on an equal basis to the poor and the middle class as well as to the rich, the world would be a fairer and more enlightened place. But as long as this goal remains elusive, it's only natural that people will want to pursue money as a way of gaining entry to the most desirable places in society and the world.

Money as status. For some people, the primary meaning of money is as a symbol of status. The more money they have, the more important and respectable they feel. Think again about Hyacinth Bucket, the amusingly dreadful social climber of *Keeping Up Appearances.* Although money is rarely discussed explicitly on that television program, it's clear that the things Hyacinth values most—from her Royal Doulton china to the fussy dishes she serves at her "famous candlelight suppers"—can only be enjoyed by those with the cash to purchase them.

Again, there can be both a negative and a positive side to this meaning of money. People who are desperate for status, probably due to some deep-rooted insecurity, may misuse money in its pursuit. They spend in advance of what they earn, living in anticipation of next year's salary hike, often buying showy objects they don't need. They divert funds from causes that are essential to long-term happiness—like saving for their children's educations or their own retirements—to mere *things* that bring short-term gains in status, like fancy cars, jewelry, or designer clothes. When the desire for status makes you spend money in ways that are unproductive and unsatisfying, then it becomes an evil.

Yet the pursuit of status by way of money can also be positive. For example, a person who gives money to charity partly for the satisfaction of being well thought of in the community—and perhaps having his name printed in the list of donors—is benefiting society by his generosity. And an entrepreneur who gets a thrill out of watching his company climb the ranks of the biggest and most profitable firms (because he knows it will improve his status at the local country club and generate envy from his fellow businesspeople) is also producing goods or services, creating jobs, and helping to build a stronger economy. Yes, there's something vain about pursuing money-as-status, but the pursuit needn't be harmful, provided it's conducted in an ethical manner.

Money as freedom. For some people, money mainly represents freedom. They know that the absence of money generally reduces the options a person has, in the worst case forcing him or her into virtual "wage slavery," working long hours at a job that is boring, painful, or difficult simply because of a desperate need for cash. By contrast, having money gives you the freedom to do the kind of work you like or even, if your bank account is really substantial, stop working altogether.

I've glimpsed the negative side of money-as-freedom when encountering rich people who boorishly assume that money exempts them from the ordinary rules of etiquette and decency. They assert their (often ill-informed) opinions as facts that everyone must acknowledge, abuse waiters and other service workers, and ignore people they consider unimportant, as if to say, "I have so much money that I don't have to recognize your humanity." Thankfully, most rich people I've met are not like this, but the few exceptions are quite unforgettable.

Of course, money-as-freedom also has a very positive side. In its most common form, it's the idea behind retirement: having worked hard and saved money to provide a decent nest egg, everyone should enjoy a few years of freedom in the later years of their lives to travel, enjoy their families, pursue a hobby, or just do nothing at all, answerable to no one (which is the very definition of freedom).

A more extreme form of the same idea is represented by the MacArthur Fellowships, generous grants of $500,000 given by a charitable foundation to some of the world's most brilliantly creative people so that they can enjoy several years of freedom to pursue whatever projects fascinate them. In recent years, MacArthur Fellows have included talented people of every sort, from a novelist and a human rights advocate to a robotics expert, a farmer, and a microbiologist. Freeing these individuals from financial constraints is likely to create long-term benefits for society as a whole through the new discoveries, inventions, social movements, and creative works they generate.

Money without meaning? Finally, there are people who claim they have no relationship with money, that money has no special meaning for them at all. They say things like, "Oh, I never think about money, it's just something I need to pay the bills," or "Money? What a boring topic. I don't care about it at all."

Frankly, I find this attitude both hard to understand and a little unbelievable. After all, money is essential to our lives and represents (for most of us) so great a commitment in terms of time and energy, that it's hard to see how money can be "meaningless" or "unimportant." I suspect those people who claim to consider money meaningless fall into one of two categories. They may be people who are fortunate enough to have a reasonable, reliable stream of money to meet their needs and who deal with it by habit, automatically and even unconsciously; or they may be people who are in fact deeply anxious about money, so much so that they are unable even to think about it without feeling overwhelmed and fearful. In either case, money isn't really "meaningless" for these people; it's just that they are unaware of its meaning for them (and therefore in danger, ultimately, of making painful money mistakes due to their willful blindness).

What about me? What meaning does money have for me?

My own attitude toward money is a bit of a hybrid. From my grandmother, I inherited the belief that you need money as protection against the vagaries of life (money-as-security). At the same time, I certainly like to enjoy life and the good times that money can buy (money-as-freedom). So money plays a dual role in my life: it lets me do what I want and also gives me the security I need emotionally. Perhaps this dual role is why I find myself thinking a lot about money in terms of *balance:* between spending and saving, generosity and frugality, risk and reward. This is the philosophy that guides my own money management as well as the advice I offer on my television programs and in books like this one.

A friend once said to me, "Alvin, you could have been a lot richer if you loved money more." I think he was right. My experiences and observations of life have shown me that getting money isn't the hardest thing to do, provided that's your primary goal in life. What's much harder is acquiring money while also learning to identify, appreciate, and enjoy the many other riches in life.

The truth is that I love what money can buy—nice things, eye-opening experiences, and free time to enjoy them both with family and friends—a lot more than I love money itself.

This is the true art of money management: to discover your own personal formula for harmonizing your connection with money and all the other connections in your life, giving money its due importance—but no more.

As you embark on your quest for this goal, remember the road to financial well-being is never straight up. There will continue to be parts that are funny, parts that are sad, and parts that are amazing. There is wisdom and self-insight in each of these parts. Reflect on them, learn from them, and make the changes in attitude and behavior that will help you find and maintain your own balanced relationship with your money through all the facets of your life.